The Great War and the Remaking of Palestine

The Great War and the Remaking of Palestine

Salim Tamari

UNIVERSITY OF CALIFORNIA PRESS

University of California Press, one of the most distinguished university presses in the United States, enriches lives around the world by advancing scholarship in the humanities, social sciences, and natural sciences. Its activities are supported by the UC Press Foundation and by philanthropic contributions from individuals and institutions. For more information, visit www.ucpress.edu.

University of California Press
Oakland, California

Five of the chapters in this book appeared in shorter forms in the *Jerusalem Quarterly*. They have been expanded and modified for this collection. "Shifting Ottoman Conceptions of Palestine", JQ47–48 (2011), "The War Photography of Khalil Raad" JQ52(2013), "Issa's Unorthodox Orthodoxy" JQ59 (2014), "Nabulsi Exceptionalism and the 1908 Ottoman Revolution" JQ60 (2014), "A Scientific Expedition to Gallipoli" JQ56/57 (2014).

Library of Congress Cataloging-in-Publication Data

Names: Tamārī, Salīm, author.
Title: The Great War and the remaking of Palestine / Salim Tamari.
Description: Oakland, California : University of California Press, [2017] | Includes bibliographical references and index. |
Identifiers: LCCN 2017028637 (print) | LCCN 2017030863 (ebook) | ISBN 9780520965102 (Ebook) | ISBN 9780520291256 (cloth : alk. paper) | ISBN 9780520291263 (pbk. : alk. paper)
Subjects: LCSH: Palestine—History—20th century.
Classification: LCC DS125 (ebook) | LCC DS125 .T29 2017 (print) | DDC 940.3/5694—dc23
LC record available at https://lccn.loc.gov/2017028637

Manufactured in the United States of America

25 24 23 22 21 20 19 18 17
10 9 8 7 6 5 4 3 2 1

CONTENTS

ILLUSTRATIONS

ACKNOWLEDGMENTS

I owe a great debt to a number of friends and colleagues who read earlier drafts of these essays over the last five years: Nazmi al-Jubeh, Rema Hammami, Khaldun Bshara, Talha Çiçek, Adel Manna, Rochelle Davis, Seteney Shami, Beshara Doumani, Rashid Khalidi, Lisa Taraki, Sari Hanafi, Suad Amiry, Samera Esmeir, Ayhan Aktar, Selim Deringil, Michael Dumper, Maria Mavroudi, Dana Sajdi, and Ilham Khuri-Makdisi.

I am particularly indebted to Alex Winder, Issam Nassar, Penny Johnson, and Carol Khoury, my colleagues at the *Jerusalem Quarterly* in Jerusalem and Ramallah, where early versions of some of these chapters appeared, for their careful reading and critical feedback. Alex Baramki, who disagreed with almost everything I wrote, was particularly helpful in making me rethink the nature of Ottoman rule in Syria and Palestine.

Rashid Khalidi and the late Raja al-Issa, of blessed memory, provided me with copies of the papers and memoirs of Issa al-Issa. I was very fortunate to receive the Jaffa notebook of Adele Azar from her grandson, Dr. Efteem Azar, who was also very generous in reading the chapter on Azar and giving me corrective advice. Edgar Zarifeh provided me with valuable biographic material on the life of Alexandra Kassab Zarifeh in Jaffa.

Research for chapters 2 and 3 was supported by a grant from the Friends of the Institute for Palestine Studies, in the spring of 2012. I would like to thank İrvin Schick, Edhem Eldem, Hasan Kayalı, and Sibel Zandi-Sayek for their comments on *Filistin Risalesi* and the material on Ottoman ethnography, and Muhammad Safadi for his expert translations from the Ottoman Turkish. My gratitude goes also to Alex Baramki for guiding me through the mazes of the Library of Congress; to the Cartography Department of Cambridge University and the Mapping Department in the Library of

Congress; and to Professor Ertuğrul Ökten and Bahcesehir University in Istanbul for providing me with facsimiles of Kâtip Çelebi's maps of Anatolia and Syria. Mona Nsouli, Jeanette Saroufim, Mirna Itani, and the staff of the Institute for Palestine Studies archives in Beirut were invaluable in providing me with research material on World War I from their collection. Debbie Usher, archivist at the Middle East Center of St. Antony's College, University of Oxford, kindly helped me acquire copies of Khalil Raad's photographs in the Alan Saunders collection.

The editors and staff of the University of California Press were invaluable in the preparation of the final draft for publication. I am particular thankful to Niels Hooper, Dore Brown, and Bradley Depew for their guidance and advice. Bonita Hurd's masterful editorial interventions and suggestions were crucial in improving the readability of the book. Finally, but not least, I am grateful to the two anonymous reviewers of the manuscript. Their criticism and advice not only helped me avoid some embarrassing pitfalls but also opened up alternative interpretations of the material.

ONE

Introduction

RAFIQ BEY'S PUBLIC SPECTACLES

ON THE EVE OF WORLD WAR I, Azmi Beyk Effendi, the governor of the province of Beirut, commissioned Muhammad Bahjat and Rafiq al-Tamimi, two young civil servants from Imperial College in Beirut (Maktab Sultani), to undertake a comprehensive survey of conditions in the province—which included at the time the districts of Beirut, Akka, Nablus, Tripoli, and Latakiyya. The governor felt that the official almanacs (*salnameh*) for the Syrian provinces were hastily written and inaccurate; moreover, they contained mostly statistical information and biographical entries for public figures. He instructed the authors to prepare "a scientific guide" to serve "civil servants and the educated public at large" concerning the civic and social conditions in Palestine and Syria.[1]

The survey, published in Ottoman Turkish and Arabic in Beirut in 1916 in two comprehensive volumes, took two years to produce, and it involved arduous field work in remote areas, including nomadic encampments, as well as visits to scores of villages and district centers.[2] It covered detailed ethnographic descriptions of habitat, customs, religious practices, and what the authors saw as "social problems" facing these communities. The overall frame of their analysis was to examine the modernization schemes of Ottoman reforms (Tanzimat) and the "impediments to the progress" in these communities. For a number of selected cities, such as Latakiyya, Tripoli, Akka, and Nablus, it included an investigation of the quotidian "social spirit" of urban life that addressed issues such as "temperament" (*mazaj*), social differentiation, leisure activities of the middle and working classes, dialects, and the intellectual milieu of the local elites.[3]

The authors, Bahjat Bey from Aleppo, and Rafiq Bey from Nablus, were accomplished scholars and dedicated civil servants. Although working in unison, they divided the work between them. Rafiq Bey undertook themes related to the archeology, geography, education, social ranks, and religious practices of the communities, while Bahjat focused on dialects, arts and crafts, and what they termed "public spectacles" (*mashahid 'ammah*) in reference to urban social conditions.[4] The bibliography attached to their compendium shows that the authors used the entire stock of geographic and historical literature on Syria and Palestine available then in Turkish, Arabic, French, English, and German. But the bulk of the study was based on their own direct investigation of local conditions through field visits, interviews, and verbatim records of narratives in the regional dialects. Their methodology is carefully indicated in the introduction to each section. Using a variety of means of transport—train, ship, and carriage—they undertook most of their visits on horseback, accompanied by local guides. In a chapter titled "Investigations and Local Follow-Up" the authors detail their mode of investigation. They would arrive at the locality and establish their residence in the local school, mosque, or government offices. There they would meet with the mukhtars, village elders, teachers, and local notables, who were interviewed in situ. The responses of these individuals were then extensively cited.[5] They also talked to elderly women, gendarmes, and balladeers (*zajjaleen*), often providing the reader with extensive samples from the songs and ballads of the region.[6]

Most of the work on the Palestinian districts (Akka, Nablus, Beisan, and the Jordan Valley) was written by Rafiq al-Tamimi, including an original treatise on the local customs and practices of the Samaritan community in Nablus, his native town.[7] Rafiq al-Tamimi (1881–1956) had extensive schooling in the Ottoman system before embarking on his commissioned study. He received his early education in Nablus and in Istanbul (at Murjan College, 1902, and Imperial College, 1905) and received a degree in literature from the Sorbonne—where he wrote a thesis on the governorship of Midhat Pasha.[8] Upon completion of his studies he was appointed as professor of history in Maktab Sultani (Imperial College) in Salonika, and in Kharboot (eastern Anatolia), and later as a lecturer in social studies at the Maktab Sultani in Beirut. When Cemal Pasha established Salahiyya College in Jerusalem during the war, Tamimi joined its faculty as a senior lecturer in history.[9]

Throughout his academic career, Tamimi was active politically in Ottoman and Arabist associations. During the constitutional revolution, he joined the Union and Progress Party (Young Turks, known as the CUP) in Damascus and later in Beirut. In 1909 he was one of the seven founders of al-Arabiyya al-Fatat (the Young Arab Movement), who included his Paris companions Rustum Haydar and Awni Abdulhadi. Al-Fatat became a leading force in the establishment of the first Syrian government under Prince Faisal.[10] It was during this period that the term *Southern Syria* became synonymous with *Palestine,* but the expression gained an added political significance after 1918—for example, in the creation of Aref and Dajani's newspaper, *Surya al-Janubiyya,* signaling the unity of Jerusalem with Damascus, in response to the British-Zionist schemes of separating Palestine from Syria. In other words, the term *Southern Syria,* which so far had been a geographic designation, was now explicitly used instead for Palestine as a reaction to the attempts by the British Mandate authorities to excise Palestine from Syria.[11]

It is most likely that Tamimi was also the main author of *Filistin Risalesi* (Treatise on Palestine), which was published during Tamimi's tenure at Salahiyya College. The treatise, published in 1915 (1331 according to the Ottoman calendar) in Turkish, was basically a manual for military officers on the topography and ethnography of Palestine during the Great War. Although published anonymously, the book contained the imprint of Tamimi's (and Bahjat's) style and content that we encounter in their book *Wilayat Beirut.* This includes the use of ethnographic material on local customs and traditions, as well as topographic descriptions of the Nablus and Akka districts. Taken together, the two books constitute an important benchmark in the literary discourse on the remaking of Palestine as an autonomous geographic entity within greater Syria and the Ottoman Arab provinces.

But where is Palestine located in this discourse, and what does the "remaking" of Palestine signify? During the eighteenth and nineteenth centuries, Filistin was a not a separate administrative unit within the Ottoman sultanate; but the term *Filistin* was designated for a region embedded in the provinces of Bilad al-Sham (Syria). It was frequently used to indicate the southern region of Syria, corresponding to the combined *sanjaqs* (districts) of Akka (Acre), Nablus, and Jerusalem. After the mid-nineteenth century it was a term increasingly used for the independent *mutasarriflik* (autonomous province) of Jerusalem, which extended from Jaffa north to the northern part of the Sinai Peninsula. The importance of Tamimi's work, in this regard, is that it provided unique ethnographic distinctions to each of those districts, with detailed and sharp field observations about the customs, mores, and cultural practices of southern Syria as a whole.

The eight essays of this book provide an analytical discussion of this remaking, focusing on the themes of imperial planning; the transformation of urban public space; local historiography; wartime mobilization; and the rise of regional, nationalist, and religious identities that sometimes reinforced and often challenged the ideology of Ottomanism (Osmenlilik).

In chapter 2, I discuss the evolution of Filistin as a region, as well as the various usages of the term *Filistin* in late Ottoman cartography and ethnography of Syria—culminating with the work of Tamimi and Bahjat, discussed here. Beginning with the sixteenth century, and possibly earlier, the term *Filistin* was systematically used to designate the southern Syrian districts—often referring to the region equivalent to the Holy Land in European and biblical travel literature. Both in travel and cartographic publications, the terms *Syria* and *Palestine* (Filistin) were used frequently, together and separately, to designate the Shami *sanjaqs*. In Ottoman and Egyptian Khedival mapping, the border separating Palestine *from* Syria was amorphous and overlapping, depending on the political context.

In chapter 3, I examine how new urban sensibilities grew out of the secularization of public space. It involved the transformation of ceremonials from traditional religious celebrations to popular carnivalesque avenues for leisure (most notably the Nebi Rubeen (Rubin) and Nebi Musa festivals, known as *mawasim*), now stripped of their religious motifs. A significant drive boosting these urban developments was the substantial investment in public infrastructure (road, rail, and telegraph line construction) dictated by German-Ottoman war planning. These schemes can be seen also as part of earlier Ottoman policies, beginning with the work of Midhat Pasha in the mid-nineteenth century, to integrate the Syrian urban centers within the Ottoman centralizing state.[12] This process was speeded up during the Jerusalem governorship of Ali Ekrem Bey (1905–1908), and Cemal Pasha's war administration of Syria and Palestine. Hasan Kayali's important work "Wartime Regional and Imperial Integration of Greater Syria during World War I" outlines the scope and limitations of these plans for the emergence of a new urban environment.[13]

The plans involved the development of urban planning, the schooling system, and the introduction of new cultural institutions, such as museums, to buttress the integration of Syria and Palestine within the Ottoman system. Substantial investments were made in Beersheba (Beer al-Sabi' in Arabic), Jaffa, Jerusalem, and Haifa to construct public buildings, monuments, public parks, museums, and schools of higher education—such as the Salahiyya College in Jerusalem and Damascus. The expertise of German archeologists (such as Karl Watzinger) and museumologists (such as Theodor Wiegand), urban planners-architects (Max Zurcher, and Karl Watzinger) was sought by the pashas Enver and Cemal to initiate and implement many of these plans.[14]

This widespread use of German and Austrian experts in modernization schemes often created tensions within the Ottoman establishment—which increasingly surfaced during the war years. Their work often overshadowed the contributions of Arab and Turkish educators like Halide Edip, and architects such as Raghib al-Nashashibi, Sa'id al-Nashashibi, and Pascal Effendi Sarophim, the municipal engineer who built the Jaffa Gate clock tower in Jerusalem. The Nashashibis, for example, contributed significantly to the early planning of Beersheba as a garrison city and to the extension of waterworks in Jerusalem. The Great War was a catalyst for many of these projects, especially in the area of rail and road building but also a cause of declining services in the public sector—as military needs diverted many projects and resources intended to the serve the civilian public.

In the aftermath of military defeats (Suez, Beersheba, Gaza, and Jaffa) many of these public projects were seen retrospectively as Turkification schemes, meant to enhance imperial grander. Nevertheless they contributed significantly to the remaking of Palestine as a distinct entity within Ottoman Syria. Five developments will illustrate this geographic distinction: First was the development of Jerusalem not only as the seat of an independent Ottoman *mutasarriflik* but as the major administrative center for the northern regions as well. Second was the extension of the Damascus-Medina-Hijazi railroad system to link Palestinian urban centers internally, bringing Haifa, Jenin, Jaffa, Ramleh, Jerusalem, and Beersheba into the grid. Third was the building of new, or the expansion of hitherto underused, public squares as arenas of political assembly. This happened in Haifa (Telegram Square); Jerusalem (the clock tower in Jaffa Gate); Jaffa (Saraya Plaza); and Beersheba (Cemal Pasha Public Square). Fourth, the creation of the Imperial Museum of Antiquities in Jerusalem (1901–1917), as a precursor of the Palestine Museum, introduced the notion that the heritage of the region as a whole (Canaanite, Israelite, Roman, Byzantine, and Islamic) was a continuous base for the cultural patrimony of the Holy Land as well as that of the sultanate.[15] And fifth was the creation of Jerusalem's Salahiyya College as an institution of higher learning for the intelligentsia of southern Syria (and later of other parts of the non-Ottoman Islamic world, including India and Indonesia).

But how were those changes experienced at the local level? In many ways the city of Nablus was the most "Ottoman" of urban centers in southern Syria, in the sense that its elite were highly integrated into the agrarian economy of the empire in their capacity as feudal potentates and, later—with capitalization of agriculture—in the *iltizam* system of tax farming (the periodic auctioning of tax-farming contracts usually taking place in six-to-ten-year cycles). They also exhibited a high level of continuity in maintaining tax-farming rights, which circulated among a recurrent elite—the Jarrars, the Tuqans, the Abdulhadis, and the Aghas. During this period we encounter several Nabulsis among the inner circle of Sultan Abdul Hamid. Nablus was also unique among Palestinian cities in having a bona fide mercantile "antifeudal" party. In chapter 4, I examine the period of the constitutional revolution as a prelude to the Great War, interpreted by two eminent local historians of the life of Nablus, Muhammad Izzat Darwazeh and Ihsan al-Nimr. Here we encounter two contrasting perspectives on how the city potentates, its middle classes, and its artisans reacted to the removal of Sultan Abdul Hamid from power.

What is striking in this "farcical moment" was the strength of support for the old regime by the city's merchants and artisans, and the general hostility toward the new freedoms promised by the Young Turks. Nimr attributes this hostility to the substantial autonomy enjoyed by the Nablus region during the earlier periods of Ottoman rule. The city was divided against itself during the Hamidian putsch against the Young Turks (1909), and a contingent of armed locals was sent to Istanbul to fight for the restoration of the old regime. During World War I, Nablus continued to exhibit support for the Ottoman war effort, and many Nablus soldiers chose to withdraw with the remnants of the Turkish army toward the north when the British and the Allied forces entered the city.

Christian Orthodoxy was a major force in the late nineteenth-century literary renaissance in the Arab East, as well as in the creation of a contentious radical intelligentsia in Palestine immediately before the Great War period. A significant ideational feature that was current among this intelligentsia was the belief that they represented the residual native progeny of the earlier cultures in the region, in particular Byzantine traditions, who had resisted Frankish invasions, Islamic hegemony, and Western missionary "civilizing missions." Jurgi Zeidan, Mikhail Nu'aimi, and Yusif al-Hakim are the towering Syrian and Lebanese magnets of this current. In Palestine the names Najib Nassar, Issa al-Issa, Khalil Sakakini, Khalil Beidas, Kulthum Odeh, Bandali al-Juzeh, and Adele Azar are those of but a few intellectuals who laid the foundation of a humanist, nationalist, feminist, and socialist intellectual movement in Palestine at the turn of the nineteenth century. All of them belonged to the Eastern (Rumi) Orthodox Church through communal membership. And virtually all of them were secular to various degrees, some fiercely, and hostile to the ecclesiastical establishment for what they considered to be "Hellenic hegemony" over native rights. In chapter 5,

I examine the meaning of this denominational affiliation in the conflict between two towering intellectuals of the war period. Yusif al-Hakim was a leading Syrian judge and public prosecutor in Jaffa and Jerusalem, and a significant force in the Arabization of the Antioch Orthodox Church. His nemesis during the years immediately before the war was Issa al-Issa—arguably the most important journalist in twentieth-century Palestine—who founded, published, and edited the *Filastin* daily paper (it was founded in 1911, suspended during the war, then published again until the 1950s). One of Hakim's tasks as a public prosecutor was to apply the Ottoman press laws against *talasun* (religious blasphemy) and *qadhf* (defamation of character), which Issa was often accused of.

Issa and Hakim were on opposite sides in the ideological battles of the Ottoman constitutional movement. Hakim was a firm advocate of constitutionalism and an active member of the CUP, the leading Young Turks movement. In his memoirs he came close to writing an apologia for the regime of Cemal Pasha.[16] Issa, on the other hand, while flirting with the early phases of Osmenlilik (Ottomanism), became a convinced advocate of decentralization and, later, secession from the sultanate. He was punished dearly by the regime, first through continued suspension of his paper, and later by imprisonment and exile to the Ankara region during the war. Issa was also a crusader for the Arabization of the Jerusalem church, unlike Hakim, who was on closer terms with the Greek hierarchy. What united both intellectuals was a rejection of the minority status of Arab Christians, and the implicit belief that Orthodoxy was a native doctrine with indigenous roots in Byzantine and Arab-Islamic culture. It is no accident that both Issa and Hakim at the end of the war became pillars of the Faisali movement and members of the first independent Arab government in Damascus in 1919—Issa as Prince Faisal's private secretary, and Hakim as a minister in charge of the Public Works (Nafi'a) portfolio.

Chapter 6 discusses Muhammad Kurd Ali's leadership of a large number of journalists, preachers, poets, and writers from Syria and Palestine who were mobilized in support of the war effort in the Dardanelles. The two compendiums produced for this event (covering the Anatolian and the Hijazi expeditions) address Turkish perception of the Arabs, and Arab perception of the Turks within the Ottoman sultanate, and the possibilities of a future Turkish-Syrian Federation after the war. Even though the language and ideological references of the expeditions are outdated today, they nevertheless reveal hidden agendas and concerns that were uppermost in the minds of the Ottoman leadership. Those concerns deal with the future of education within the Arab provinces and the issue of bilingualism; religious justifications of the war against the Europeans; the tenuous relationship between the CUP leadership and the Hashemites in Hijaz, and the relentless struggle against Arab separatism. The arguments against secession reflect the increasing significance of the Islamic bond that had gained ascendency over notions of secular Osmenlilik in uniting Anatolia with Syria during the war. They also demonstrate the centrality of Palestine and Kudus Serif (holy Jerusalem) in Ottoman attempts to win the hearts and minds of the Syrian intelligentsia.

The relationship between charity and feminism has often been posited in conflictual terms when treating the origins of the women's movement in the Arab East. The devastations of World War I led to the creation of a huge number of war victims and refugees, as well as major dislocations in urban centers. The earliest involvement of upper-class women in the formation of women's associations took the form of charity on behalf of war orphans and destitute girls. In examining the notebook of Adele Azar (who became known as "mother of the poor" in Mandate-period Jaffa), I show how, at the turn of the century, the use of family endowments and benevolent associations created the earliest forms of independent women's groups (chapter 7). We read her diary in light of the educational work—albeit in a colonial setting—of Halide Edip in Syria and Mount Lebanon during the war. The main focus of these projects, in Azar's case, was the teaching of destitute girls and their preparation for public employment. One of the major objectives of women's groups, not always declared, was to "save" native girls from missionary education that frequently led to their religious conversion to Protestantism and Catholicism. Although these associations emerged simultaneously in Syria and Lebanon just before and during the war period, the peculiarity of Palestine was the link between Rumi Orthodox benevolent associations and the emergence of a nationalist and secular women's movement in the 1920s. Azar's modest notebook shows that charity and pious foundations not only were *not* opposed to the evolution of a more substantial independent women's movement but also were often the very foundation from which these movements emerged.

Chapter 8 deals with the representation of Palestine in the photography of Khalil Raad. The early photographers of the Levant were almost exclusively Armenians, and Raad was one of the few Arab photographers who became prominent in this period. His work covered many subjects, beginning with commercial lantern slides of landscapes in the Holy Land; pictures of peasants dressed in "biblical costumes" posed in scenes representing the nativity of the baby Jesus and the flight of the holy family to Egypt; lepers begging by the walls of Jerusalem, and so on. The images indicate to what extent local artists had internalized the orientalist discourse of European photographers in their "documentation" of the Holy Land.

In the 1890s, Raad made a name for himself, in collaboration with his mentor Garbed Krikorian, as the major studio photographer in Jerusalem. This was a crucial source of professional reputation since it helped him gain the attention of Ottoman and German military officers, who often used their photographs for publicity and as cartes de visite. Raad's idyllic portraits of Ahmad Cemal Pasha, and Mersinli Cemal Pasha, the two main commanders of the Ottoman forces in Syria, appearing in relaxed family and social settings, were circulated widely during the war. They were often used to soften the harsh image of the former and to reduce the obscurity of the latter, known as the *kucuk,* or "lesser," Cemal. Raad's portraits of the two men helped him gain access to the inner circle of the Ottoman administration. His series of images taken during the war effected a major transformation not only in his career but also in the history of photography in the Middle East. Although many of these images were intended as propaganda for the Ottoman Fourth Army, exhibiting the prowess of army formations at the front and the technical preparedness of the armed forces (antiaircraft guns, signaling units, armed naval boats), his work also documented unknown features of military organization (such as underground factories and printing presses). Raad also documented the unseemly side of warfare, including the hanging of suspected deserters, and the work of so-called volunteer labor brigades, images of which showed backbreaking work in trenches undertaken by conscripted labor battalions.

These essays on the social history of Palestine at the turn of the nineteenth history are based the biographic trajectories of intellectual actors, some well known, and some (like Rafiq Tamimi and Adele Azar) raised from obscurity. All of them contributed significantly to the creation of Palestine as a cultural entity during and before World War I—before its delineation as a geographic region separated from Syria, at the end of the Great War. Their vision was framed by a conflicted engagement with the ideology of Osmenlilik (Ottomanism). The rise and fall of Osmenlilik, as a frame of post-Tanzimat civic identity, and as an imperial ideology during the rise of the Young Turks, has been the subject of considerable historical debate since the inception of the Arab literary revival of the nineteenth century, known as the Nahda. It came to designate widely contrasting facets of the relationship of the imperial center to Anatolia, the Rumeli, and Arab peripheries of the empire. In the earliest manifestation of Osmenlilik, as articulated by Young Ottoman rebels such as Namik Kemal, it heralded the adoption of a common citizenship for the various religious and ethnic communities of the sultanate that had a strong cultural core of Turkishness. It attempted to replace the bonds of an Islamic Umma with a new, multiethnic Ottoman Commonwealth (Umma Uthmaniyya).

In Syria and Palestine, as in the European provinces of the empire, Ottomanism had a variety of meanings to its adherents. To Ruhi al-Khalidi, the Jerusalem deputy and diplomat, it fulfilled the French Revolution's promise of modernity, equality before the law, and an end to Hamidian despotism.[17] In Khalidi—who wrote primarily in Arabic—we do not find any traces of Arab, Syrian, or Palestinian nationalist sentiments. If he could have used the term, he would most likely have called himself an Ottoman nationalist. His conception of Osmenlilik resonated with the early ideas of Namik Kemal, as well as of the pioneers of the Arab literary Nahda (Renaissance), most notably those of Butrus al-Bustani (1819–1883) and Nasif al-Yaziji, who diffused their ideas through a series of revolutionary circulars known as *Nafir Suriyya* and in their literary journal, *Al-Jinan*. Their notion of *al-'urwa al-'uthmaniyya* (the Ottoman bond) was a secular ideology that united Anatolia with the Syrian provinces in a common destiny and common citizenship *while preserving the cultural autonomy of Arabs*. To them, paradoxically, al-Uthmaniyya (Osmenlilik) was the best guarantor of the Syrian patriotic bond and the preservation of Arab cultural renaissance.[18]

During the second constitutional revolution, Osmenlilik became an attractive ideology to many Arab intellectuals, Muslim and Christian and Jewish, for different reasons. For those advocating an Islamic revivalism within the Ottoman commonwealth, which included Muhammad Abdo and Rashid Rida, it exemplified an Islamic cultural bond that responded to the challenges of European modernity within an accepted framework. For many Christian Arab intellectuals, fearful of the return to the sectarian bloodshed of the 1860s, it articulated a secular alternative to an earlier *dhimmi* (protected community) status. And for both, Ottomanism preserved the sultanate from the dangers of separatism that undermined the unity of the empire. In *Ottoman Brothers,* Michelle Campos examines how the new ideology was articulated in a new civic consciousness, uniting Jews and Christians with their Muslim compatriots (or at least elements in their respective intelligentsia) into a new "imperial citizenship" that countered the challenges of Zionism and Arab nationalist separatism.[19] A less-examined feature of Osmenlilik was its instrumental role in buttressing economic development during the period of the Ottoman debt crisis at the end of the nineteenth century. In his groundbreaking study of how the Ottoman bond worked at the institutional level, Jens Hannsen demonstrates how Levantine patrician families, such as the Malhamé clan, operated in alliance with state functionaries, to help finance industrial and commercial enterprises within the networks of the centralizing bureaucracy of Sultan Abdul Hamid. In this case Ottomanism brought Christian Arab entrepreneurs together with Turkish statesmen in an alliance that buttressed state reform against European colonial exactions.[20]

During the war years Osmenlilik was no longer primarily an ideology of common citizenship and legal equality. Under the strain of ethnic nationalism and the threat of secession, the Young Turks began to utilize the Ottoman bond in order to mobilize the Arab and other non-Turkish population in the defense of the homeland against European colonial ambitions. After their assumption of power in 1908, the CUP introduced a strong Islamic component into Ottomanism, both in the press and in the new educational curriculum, as an instrument for shaping the hearts and minds of Arab youth. As a consequence the movement began to lose its appeal as an overarching political source of identification for many ethnic and religious minorities. Many of those saw themselves as losing the protection of the *millet* system without benefiting tangibly from the new secular legislation.[21] With the Armenian massacres and the loss of Greece and large areas in the Balkan provinces, the new Ottoman leadership began to abandon Osmenlilik as a framework for a multinational imperial domain, in favor a residual commonwealth with Anatolia and the Arab provinces as the twin core of the sultanate.

Another source of alienation was the anti-Arab excess that accompanied the downfall of Sultan Abdul Hamid and his "Arab" circle of counselors (i.e., Sheikh Sayyadi and the Malhamé security network), which created a new schism between Arab Ottomanist circles and Istanbul. Ussama Makdisi has argued that Ottoman discourse on the Arab provinces was derivative of an orientalist imagination of the Orient (from the perspective of a Europeanized Orient in Istanbul) that reinforced and justified an actual colonial relationship between center and periphery. What camouflaged this new imperialism (new because it replaced a tributary decentralized empire) was the discourse on common citizenship and Islam as a common cultural bond.[22] But even though the war brought about a great deal of ethnic tension between officers and soldiers, the vision of Istanbul as the abode of the colonial masters was not one adopted by a significant group of Arab writers, as was the case in Greece and the Balkans. Within Syria and Palestine the majority of political and intellectual forces continued to operate within the framework of the Ottoman bond, championing various projects for decentralization and an inclusive autonomy. This ambivalence in the new conception of Osmenlilik can be gleaned from the work of Muhammad Kurd Ali, who, while persecuted by the military rulers of Syria for his dissident journalism, continued to exhibit adherence to the principles of Ottoman solidarity and to fight the proponents of Syrian separatism. Within Bilad al-Sham he also recognized that Palestine, while an essential part of geographic Syria, constituted a distinct political domain. When he organized the two "investigatory" expeditions to Gallipoli and Medina in 1915, he—together with Baqer Muhammad, Sheikh Ali Rimawi and many other Arab writers—expressly referred to their mission as a *Palestinian-Syrian* expedition.

Throughout the period of Ottoman rule in Syria, Palestine was a recognized geographic region in southern Syria, clearly delineated in the early maps of Peri Reissi (sixteenth century) and Kateb Celebi (seventeenth century) as the land centered on Kudus Serif (holy Jerusalem) and described in the large array of travel literature (known as *fada'il*) that commemorated the virtues of the sacred spaces of the Hebron of Ibrahim al-Khalil and the Jerusalem of Muhammad's ascension and Jesus's resurrection. The Ottoman administration inherited the early Islamic naming of Jund Filistin from the Ummayad, Abbasid, and Fatimid caliphates. But the region was not earmarked as a separate administrative unit before the establishment of the autonomous *mutasarriflik* of Jerusalem in 1876. In the last quarter of the nineteenth century, Jerusalem, as a province, became synonymous with Filistin as a country. This development was triggered by two military events: first was the campaign of Ibrahim Pasha to wrest control of Syria from the High Porte, and the establishment of an Egyptian administration in Bilad al-Sham. The peasant rebellions of 1834 against the army of Muhammad Ali in Palestine and the eventual evacuation of Ibrahim Pasha's troops compelled the Ottoman administration to refocus on extending the borders of Palestine to preempt new challenges over control of the Holy Land—especially those emanating from the European powers, now billed as the new "crusaders" by Istanbul. The second event was the creation of the "Palestine Front" (Filistin cebhasi) as a prelude to the military operation of World War I. To the south, the front extended deeply into the Sinai Peninsula, and in some military maps the southern borders of Filistin appear to be the western expanses of the Suez Canal. In the northern regions the logistic needs of the fourth and fifth imperial armies expanded the borders of the Palestine Front considerably beyond the frontiers of the Jerusalem province, reaching the contours of the Litani River in southern Lebanon.[23] Thus, by the beginning of World War I, Ottoman Palestine corresponded more or less to the political frontiers established by the British Mandate after the war, minus the Sidon subdistrict.

But identity and borders did not follow neatly from the delineation of boundaries. People of Palestine continued to identify themselves as Syrians, southern Syrians, and Shamis, and by their religious affiliations—Christians, Muslims, Druze, and Jews—depending on the context. Outside the region, they referred to themselves mostly as Ottoman Syrians (Aref al-Aref, Ali al-Rimawi), as Palestinians of Syria (Nassar, Sakakini), and increasingly as Palestinians (Issa al-Issa). But it was local identity, especially local urban affinities, as with the rest of the Arab East and Anatolia, that prevailed. Tamimi referred to himself as Ottoman and Nabulsi. Khalil Sakakini in America was a Syrian Jerusalemite. The Ottoman bond, Osmenlilik, persisted, but was the first to suffer and disintegrate during the war. By the war's end the ideational contestation was no longer between Ottomanism and localism, but between Syrian and Palestinian identities. The two categories that nourished and engulfed each other for over a century were now confronting each other and claiming exclusive domains.

Arabs, Turks, and Monkeys

THE ETHNOGRAPHY AND CARTOGRAPHY
OF OTTOMAN SYRIA

You have now become one nation on earth, Ottomans all—no
difference between Arabs and 'Ajam
No generations will divide you, and no religions will come
between you
Brothers together under our glorious constitution, joined
together by the Unionist banner flying high

Popular poem published in Beirut on the
eve of the declaration of the 1908 constitution

THE MONKEYS IN QUESTION were the Arab counselors of Sultan Abdul Hamid II. Ahmad Qadri, the Arab physician who was a founder of the Literary Forum in Istanbul in 1909 (and later, in 1911, a founder of the Young Arab Society in Paris), records an episode, in his Istanbul diary, that shook his faith in the continued unity of the Ottoman regime and its ability to maintain the loyalty of its Syrian and Arab subjects. He was taking an evening stroll in the imperial capital with his schoolmate and friend Awni Abdulhadi days after the proclamation of the new constitution of 1908. The city was teaming with excited crowds discussing the dawning of the new liberties and the end of the Hamidian dictatorship. The two Arabs (a Damascene and a Nabulsi), both of whom considered themselves loyal Ottoman citizens, came upon an agitated speaker attracting a large crowd. The speaker was a young charismatic officer by the name of Sari Bey, who was singing the praises of the new constitution to the crowds. Then he made a sudden turn and began attacking the supporters and lackeys of the old regime, using terms like "the Arab traitor Izzat" and the "Arab traitor Abul Huda."[1] The reference was to Izzat Pasha al-Abed, the sultan's private secretary, and Sheikh Abul Huda al-Saidawi, a religious scholar who formed part of Abdul Hamid's inner circle.[2]

14

Menagerie consultative...

FIGURE I. The Ottoman bureaucrats as monkeys. The 1908 Constitutional revolution ushered in press freedoms that allowed the publication of cartoons critical of the government and its bureaucracy, building on an earlier tradition of satirical caricatures, such as this one titled "Menagerie consultative" by Yusuf Franko Kusa, from *Types et Charges*, 1885.

It became customary in the oppositional press of Istanbul in this period to portray Hamid's Arab advisors as monkeys.[3] Abdulhadi and Qadri berated the speaker: "Why did you single out the Arab identity of Abdul Hamid's men, when there far more Turks among the supporters of the old regime?" It is quite likely that Qadri (though not Abdulhadi) was also upset because he himself sympathized with the regime of Abdul Hamid. Elsewhere he notes how the CUP overthrew "the last Sultan who conceived the Arabs as brothers in faith, inspiring Arab intellectuals to support an Ottoman patriotism," which had since disappeared.[4] Over the next several months he began to hear a revival of earlier derogatory epitaphs directed at Arabs, including such terms as *pis arap* (dirty Arabs), *siyah arap* (black Arabs), *çingene arap* (Arab gypsies), and *akılsız arap* (stupid Arabs).[5] Qadri reports that he was particularly hurt by these expressions because his father, Abdul Qadir Qadri, was an *amiralei* (colonel) in the Ottoman army who had fought valiantly in European provinces, and who was later appointed as military commander in Baalbak, Akka, and Basra.[6] Both he and his father considered themselves pillars of a multinational Ottoman order. Qadri identifies this episode, and the accompanying ethnic tension that emerged after the attempted coup of 1909, as a turning point in Arab relations with the Ottoman state. It led, in his view, to the determination of many active members of Arab literary societies in Istanbul to seek autonomy, and then separation, from Istanbul.

It is clear nevertheless that these ethnic tensions are conceived retrospectively, in the light of events that took place in Syria and Palestine during and after the war. The story that emerges from the Ottoman military's own sources tells a more complex, if not drastically different, story. One important such document is the *salnameh*-type (almanac-type) military handbook issued, for Palestine, at the beginning of the Great War.

Filistin Risalesi (1331 Rumi) is an astonishing document that disguises as much as it reveals. Ostensibly a soldier's manual issued for limited distribution to the officers (*hizme makkhsuslir*—"special services") of the Eighth Army Corps, the handbook is basically a demographic and geographic survey of the province that constituted the southern flank for the theater of military operations during World War I. It contains statistical tables, topographic maps, and an ethnography of Palestine. But it also contains two outstanding features that highlight the manner in which Palestine and Syria were seen from Istanbul by the new Ottoman leadership after the constitutional revolution of 1908. The first is a general map of the country in which the boundaries extend far beyond the frontiers of the *mutasarriflik* of Jerusalem, which was, until then, the standard delineation of Palestine. The northern borders of this map include the city of Tyre (Sur) and the Litani River, thus encompassing all of Galilee and parts of southern Lebanon, as well as districts of Nablus, Haifa, and Akka—all of which were part of the Wilayat of Beirut until the end of the war.

The second outstanding feature of the manual is a population map that identifies the populations of Palestine and coastal Syria by ethnic, communal, and religious identity. Contrary to what would be expected in light of later developments, the populations of Syria and southern Anatolia were divided not by nationality, linguistic grouping, or religious affiliation but by a combination of putative national and sectarian identities. Southern Anatolia is divided among "Turks," "Turkmen" (west of Sivas), and a category of "other Turks." Bilad al-Sham is divided into Syrians (Suri), and Arabs (east of the Jordan River). The rest of the population is made up of ethnic and religious minorities that overlap with these major national groupings: Maronites, Druze, Jews, Orthodox (Rum), Ismailis, Metwalis, and Nusseris. Another category that is dispersed in Palestine is "rural Arabs" (*arep kuli*) and "rural Druze" (*druz kuli*).

Filistin Risalesi was issued by the Eighth Army Corps to its officers. The Eighth Army for much its history was dominated by Mersinli Cemal Pasha (Cemal *kuchuk*), who in addition succeeded Ahmad Cemal Pasha (Cemal *buyuk*) in the leadership of the Fourth Army after the routing of Ottoman forces in Suez. In many ways the history of Palestine and Syria during the war years was dominated by these two figures: the first for his relentless war against Arab nationalists, and the second for his attempt to rectify the damage to Arab-Turkish relationships brought about by Ahmad Cemal's "campaign of terror." The Ottoman forces in Palestine were also led by three German generals, who were attached to the Ottoman command. Friedrich Kress von Kressenstein commanded the Eighth Army in 1917 (together with Cevat Pasha), and Otto Liman von Sanders was commander of the First Army at Gallipoli. The formation of the Yildirim Army Group in May 1917 by the merger of the Fourth, Seventh, and Eighth Armies (as well as the German Asia Group) was meant to save the situation in Palestine from defeat. The new Sa'iqa formation (Yildirim, or "Thunderbolt" in English) was led by Eric von Falkenhayn and Otto von Sanders. It was Mustafa Kemal Pasha (later Ataturk) who withdrew the Yildirim forces from southern Palestine when the front began to collapse.[7]

Ahmad Cemal took over the command of the Fourth Army from Zeki Pasha (Halepli) in November 1914 and established his headquarters in Damascus, moving in 1915 to Jerusalem's Mount of Olives. He had already established a name for himself within the new political-military elite before coming to Palestine. His name began to sparkle after the 1909 rebellion, when he joined the Action Army to suppress the Hamidian restoration movement.[8] As governor of Adana he was put in charge of suppressing "Armenian revolts" in the region. In 1911 he was appointed governor of Baghdad, again to deal with Arab tribal rebellions. He later joined the Ottoman troops in the Balkan War and was promoted to colonel. In 1913 he was among the inner leadership of the Young Turks who brought the CUP to power in the January coup d'état. He was appointed governor of Istanbul, where he engaged in an action to suppress opposition to the ruling party.[9] Just before the war, he was promoted to the rank of general and appointed minister of the navy—a position that he kept for much of his remaining political career. Before the war, Cemal was known for his pro-French sympathies. He held a number of talks with the French and sought an alliance with them on behalf of the CUP government, but was eventually forced to join Enver Pasha and Tal'at Pasha in concluding the Ottoman-German alliance.

It was soon after the proclamation of war, in November 1914, that Cemal was appointed as head of the Fourth Army in Syria. He already had a reputation as an "Arab hand" after suppressing the tribal rebellions in Iraq. When he arrived in Damascus, he was greeted enthusiastically by the Syrians. Ahmad Qadri, a leader of al-Arabiyya al-Fatat (the Young Arab Movement) and a medical officer in the Fourth Army, has described the progression of Cemal's relations with the Arabs. He quotes his maiden speech in Damascus in the plaza of the Ummayad mosque: "There is no conflict between Turks and Arabs in this struggle. We either win together or fail together." However, a series of events during the war led to the deterioration of his (and the CUP's) relations with the local population and to the start of the campaign of repression against the nationalists. The crucial factor was the failure of the second Suez campaign, and Cemal's perception of the Syrian soldiers as being responsible for that.[10] But the two direct issues were his interception of secessionist propaganda circulated by the Ottoman Decentralization Party, headquartered in Cairo, and news that Sherif Hussein was already negotiating an agreement with the British behind his back.[11] There were several interventions by Prince Faisal, along with Enver and with Tal'at Pasha, which seemed to have improved the relations with Cemal, but only temporarily.[12]

One factor in these vacillations was the fact that within the CUP there were several factions vying for power, not always coordinating with each other. This became clear before and during the war with the formation of the Teskelat-i Mahsusa (Special Forces) in 1911 under the command of Enver Pasha, originally to fight the Italian occupation of Libya. The Teskelat-i Mahsusa evolved by 1913 as an intelligence unit answerable only to the Ministry of War and designed to combat separatist movements in the empire. During the war years each member of the CUP triumvirate—Enver, Tal'at, and Ahmad Cemal—had his own personal Teskelat-i Mahsusa.[13] Cemal in particular used this security apparatus to combat both the Arab separatists and internal dissent in Syria and Palestine.[14] But he also tried to create a loyalist circle of supporters. Those included As'ad al-Shuqairi, the mufti of Akka; Prince Shakib Arsalan; Sheikh Abdul Aziz Shawish, head of the Salahiyya College; and Abdul Rahman al-Yusif, the director of the Haj Organization (Imarat al-Haj).[15] Their work was exemplified in initiating a campaign of Islamic mobilization for the war while justifying the repression of dissent against the war and against secessionist sentiments. In his

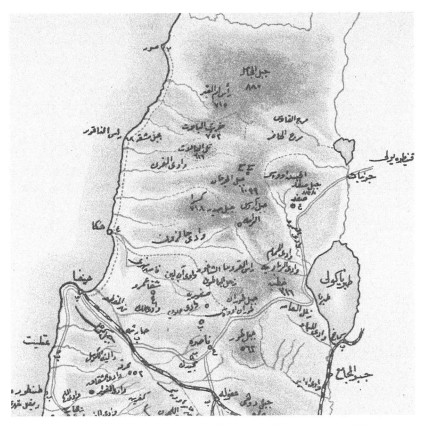

FIGURE 2. Map of northern Palestine, published in *Filistin Risalesi*. Military Press, Jerusalem, 1915.

campaign for Islamic mobilization Cemal received full support from the CUP leadership and from the Germans, who carried out their own campaign of Jihadist activities.[16] *Jihad Made in Germany,* by Tilman Lüdke, is a thorough record of Germany's disingenuous role in this campaign, showing a zeal among the Germans that far exceeded the intentions of the Ottoman leadership.[17]

But in the anti-Arabist campaign, it seems that Cemal was on his own, and in a number of instances he differed with Enver and Tal'at. Muhammad Izzat Darwazeh cites from the diary of Aziz Beyk, head of Ottoman intelligence in Damascus during the war years, to emphasize this deviation.[18] He explains the vehemence of Cemal's campaign against the Arab wing of the Decentralization Party (which, in program and action, was far from advocating a separation of the Arab provinces from Istanbul) as attributable to the latter's alliance with the (mainly Turkish) party of Freedom and Reconciliation (Hurriyat wa I'tilaf), when the latter conducted a briefly successful coup against the CUP government. When the unionists succeeded in restoring their rule, Cemal commenced his campaign against the autonomist movements and against what he saw as the seeds of "Arab separatism" in particular.[19]

Ahmad Cemal's military dictatorship of Syria had a lasting impact on the population's relationship with Istanbul. Hasan Kayali, who examined the internal documents of the CUP leadership, also suggests that Cemal's more extreme measures against the nationalist movement, including the Beirut-Damascus executions and the massive deportation of "hostile" elements from coastal regions to Anatolia, were not necessarily supported by the CUP leadership. In particular he suggests that the Turkification campaign instituted by Cemal in state schools and higher colleges in Palestine and Syria was a reflection of the centralizing and modernizing features of the new regime and was not particularly directed at Syrian or Arab nationalism.[20] Widespread rumors also claimed that Cemal was secretly negotiating a special status for the Arab provinces in a future Anatolian-Syrian federation.[21] Nevertheless, the damage engendered by Cemal's systematic campaign of repression was too extensive to mitigate. It brought about a rupture with the Ottoman regime in which the Syrian population began to associate natural disasters (famine, diseases, and the locust attack) with the policies of Cemal and, through him, with the central government.

When eventually, in September 1917, Ahmad Cemal resigned from his post at the southern front (ostensibly because of policy differences with von Falkenhayn over Suez), the opportunity arose to have him replaced by Mersinli Cemal Pasha as head of the Fourth Army. The latter also commanded the Eighth Army Corps, and fought in Palestine, Syria, and Transjordan until the end of the war. Thus when *Filistin Risalesi* was published, Mersinli was in command; but since we do not know who commissioned it and when, it could very well have the imprint of von Falkenhayn, von Sanders, and Ahmad Cemal Pasha on it.

COUNTRY MANUAL OR INTELLIGENCE REPORT?

As a military handbook, *Filistin Risalesi* can be compared to two genres of "country surveys." The first group are those military manuals issued by Allied forces during the war to help their officers manage their movements in enemy territory in the Syrian provinces. The second group of surveys is composed of Holy Land travel books, meant to acquaint pilgrims and visitors with the ways and manners of the Orient. A good example of the first genre is *A Handbook of Syria: Including Palestine,* issued first by British Naval Intelligence in 1915 and then reissued annually after the British conquest of Syria and Palestine.[22] Another is Harry Luke and Edward Keith-Roach's *Handbook of Palestine,* issued on the eve of the Mandate.[23] Luke later became deputy governor of Jerusalem immediately after the British occupation of Palestine.[24] Both books contain basic historical, geographic, and demographic data, as well as maps and diagrams of the country. The latter in addition contains practical information about transport, prices, and health precautions about the country, since it also targets the civilian visitor. But the ethnographic map is unique to *Filistin Risalesi.* Of the second genre, Holy Land travel books, we have two sources that seem to have lent themselves to the author(s) of *Filistin Risalesi,* especially the section on population types. One is Antonin Jaussen's *Coutumes des Arabes au pays de Moab* (1908), and the other is Harry Luke's *Handbook* mentioned above.[25]

In terms of its ethnic/political assessment of the local populations, *Filistin Risalesi* also has a British equivalent for Palestine. This is the series of intelligence reports prepared by the British army in Egypt during the war years. Those include "The Economic and Political Situation West of the Jordan," prepared by the War Office (1918), and intelligence reports prepared by the admiralty in Cairo.[26] Muhsin Muhamad al-Salih, who made an extensive survey of these intelligence reports, has concluded that that Palestinians were divided in their sentiments about the approaching Allied troops, but that there was nevertheless considerable support for the Ottomans, even in the final days of the war. To the extent that people welcomed British occupation of Palestine, their support was based largely on the alliance the British had with the forces of Sherif Hussein and with the Syrian nationalists, and on the promise to create a United Arab Kingdom after the war that would include the southern Syrian districts (i.e., Palestine).[27] Although the Ottoman and British assessments contained in the *Filistin Risalesi* treatise on Palestine, along with the War Office Reports on the local population, were meant to serve military purposes (orientation for soldiers and intelligence assessments during a time of war, including assessments of the potential loyalty and hostility of the natives), there are clear differences between the Ottoman and British assessments. Unlike the British reports, however, *Filistin Risalesi* was written in the manner of a monograph on a local population clearly seen as

Ottoman subject*s and not as a foreign population*. For example, the survey of the population mapped out in Palestine contained observations about local minorities and groups that existed in various configurations in all of Syria and large parts of Anatolia.

Still, these surveys in *Filistin Risalesi* are largely focused on geographic and demographic data that mirrors data found in European handbooks on Palestine. The topographic part relies on data that can be found in Holy Land surveys and uses a language and references that are common in these handbooks, including many biblical reference to the holy places. The survey of Palestinian history, in particular, relies on an eclectic reading of "main events": Canaanite, Philistine, Hebrew, Babylonian, Arab, and Islamic conquests. It is striking that either the word *conquest* (*fat'h*) or *occupation* (*ihtilal*) is used in reference to virtually all of these regimes, including the Ottoman conquest of Palestine by Sultan Selim in 1517. The only exception is the reference to the "liberation" (*tahrir*) of the Holy Land by Salah ed-Din in 1187.[28] In the religious communities of Palestine, the author focuses on the various minorities (Druze, Jews, various Christians, Matawleh, and Nuseiriyeen) in great detail. The minorities of Syria are included in the discussion of Palestine. Jews are divided into native (Arabic-speaking Jews), and eastern European immigrants (who spoke Yiddish and their native tongues).[29]

The military aspect of this document becomes clear, however, when discussing the topography of the country. The two central themes are the accessibility of the road networks and the presence of water sources for the armed forces. For example, locations that contain sufficient resources for sustaining an army division (*firqa*) are listed in the vicinity of Yazour, Wadi Haneen, Yibna, Isdud, Majda, and Ghazza (Gaza).[30] In the north, the authors list Ar'ara and Lajjoun.[31] In the center, they list Tulkarem and Deir Sharaf as containing enough water for an army corps (*liwa'*). The Jerusalem region is listed as very poor in water resources and to be avoided.[32] Road conditions are also given detailed attention. The main access roads usable for mechanized army divisions are listed as the Haifa-Nazareth Road, the Tulkarem-Nablus Road, and the Jaffa-Jerusalem Road.[33] Other roads, such as Zeita, Arrabeh, and Jenin, are listed as usable except for animal-driven units only. Yet another list is given for roads that are strategic but impassable for mechanized divisions, such as the Akka-Safad road.[34] Latrun and Nebi Samuel are listed as the places for panoramic surveillance.[35] Updated notations are given for roads that are being constructed or upgraded, such as the Julis-Latrun road and the Jaffa-Jerusalem roads, where seventeen military outposts were constructed by Thuraya Pasha, the *mutasarrif* (provincial governor) of Jerusalem.[36]

By contrast, the British War Office reports lack the ethnographic and topographic mapping that we find in the Ottoman documents. The central criteria for assessing the Palestinian region here were the degree of reliability of the local population and receptivity to the British presence. One hundred villages are surveyed in terms described as "very friendly," "friendly," "mixed," "not friendly," and "hostile."[37] Some townships, such as Qalqilieh and Safuriyyeh were singled out as "fanatical and hostile." Despite a tendency in these reports to portray the Christian population as being "more friendly," there were nevertheless significant exceptions. The populations of Akka (Acre), Tabariyya (Tiberius), and Affula (which was largely Jewish) were described as "unreliable" and, in the case of Akka, "hostile" (possibly because Akka politics were dominated by the Ottoman loyalist Sheikh As'ad al-Shuqairi). Nazareth, Haifa, Anabta, and Kufr Kanna were seen either as "friendly" or "very friendly."[38]

Much of the report is also preoccupied with describing social groups, families, and even individual leaders in terms of their political affinities and loyalties. Nablus, like Akka, was singled out as a city of pro-Ottoman sentiments and hostility toward the British. Among those whom the report named were the Ashour, Tuqan, Fahoum (from Nazareth), Abbas, and Abu Hamad families. Among the pro-British families listed were Hijjawi, Abdulhadi, and al-Dari. The Abdulhadis were described as influential, moderate in their views, and astute, but also as "ruthless toward their peasants, by whom they were hated."[39] Both Haifa and Jenin are portrayed as anti-Turkish cities, the latter mainly owing to its support of the Arab rebellions after the execution of Salim Abdulhadi, the brother of Jenin's governor, by Ahmad Cemal Pasha in 1915.

Muhsin Salih correctly suggests that many of these assessments were based on intelligence reports from local agents and, therefore, were not reliable. More likely, however, is that they were based on immediate temporal assessments during wartime activities. Salih quotes Nablus historian Ihsan al-Nimr, who himself came from a prominent Nablus family, for a different perspective. Nimr attributes much of anti-Turkish sentiment in Syria and Palestine during the war to the mistaken policies of Cemal Pasha. He gives credit to the local population for pressuring the Ottoman command to have him transferred to the Caucasus. Nimr also cites a number of meetings that took place in Nablus with Ottoman commander Fawzi Pasha, who denounced to the Palestinians the terms of the Sykes-Picot Agreement and the Balfour Declaration. Several pro-Ottoman demonstrations took place in Nablus after these meetings. After the appointment of Mersinli Cemal as commander of the Fourth Army, the local Palestinians began to cooperate closely with the Turkish command.[40] Nimr noted that after the conditions of the Balfour Declaration and Sykes-Picot Agreement became known, several hundred people from the Nablus region volunteered to fight with the Ottoman troops. He then adds a significant note: "It was this factor [i.e., opposition to Western colonial rule], *and not any sympathy for the Arab rebellion*—which was hardly felt in Nablus—that moved people to fight against the British."[41]

Thus, even though both sets of reports—the Ottoman and the British—tend to contain background demographic assessments of Palestine, and both are meant to serve military-intelligence objectives, they nevertheless diverge in the primacy of the intelligence function in the case of the War Office reports. *Filistin Risalesi,* by contrast, presents us with an elaborate monograph on social and ethnographic conditions in a province of Palestine, similar in scope to that of the regional *Salnames,* or to *Bayrut Vilayeti* (1914), the study commissioned by the local administration to record the social conditions of Beirut Province, authored by Muhammad Bahjat and Rafiq Tamimi.[42]

MERSINLI TO THE RESCUE

Several Arab writers contrast Mersinli Cemal favorably with Ahmad Cemal. Of those who left diaries and were active in the public sphere, we should mention Yusif al-Hakim, the Latakiyya judge and public prosecutor; Khalil Sakakini, who was released from his Damascus prison at the order of Mersinli Pasha; and Muhammad Izzat Darwazeh. All spoke of Cemal *kuchuk* (also known as Mersinli Cemal, in reference to his town of origin)as a man of clean military record, with "good intentions toward the Arabs."[43]

Mersinli Cemal's association with Palestine and Syria was as long as that of Ahmad Cemal, even though it is not recognized in the history of the war. He commanded the Eighth Army Corps in April 1914, before the war was declared, and served in Anatolia and Palestine. *Filistin Risalesi* was published by the Eighth Army Corps command during his tenure in Palestine. After Ahmad Cemal Pasha was retired from his command, in February 1918, Mersinli was appointed as commander of the Fourth Army in Syria and Palestine. Toward the end of the war, he saw a substantial amount of fighting in Transjordan (Kerak, Salt, and the Jordan Valley), as well as in northern

FIGURE 3. Mersinli Cemal Pasha with son and daughter, Jerusalem, 1915. Photographed by Khalil Raad. Matson Collection, Library of Congress.

Palestine. In both regions he had a positive reputation, which was often contrasted to that of the other Cemal by his friends and enemies. A number of Arab intellectuals from the period attested to the changed political atmosphere after Mersinli's appointment. Khalil Sakakini was in a Damascus prison when the general took command of the Fourth Army. Numerous entries from Sakakini's diary describe his communication with Cemal in which he sought to bring about his release from imprisonment (his imprisonment was the result of an order by Ahmad Cemal's head of security, Aziz Beyk).[44] When Sheikh Abdul Qadir al-Musaghar, acting as Sakakini's emissary, succeeded in this endeavor (on January 10, 1918), Sakakini wrote enthusiastically: "Cemal Pasha al-Sagheer [*kuchuk*] may be 'little' in his name, but he is great in his reputation. It is with commanders like him that nations are built. Everywhere he goes, people associate him with great love and respect."[45] One might detect a note of slavish hypocrisy here, except that it was inserted in his own private diary and was not meant for publication. Significantly, Mersinli himself was at pains to explain to Sakakini, in an apologetic note sent by his emissary, that his arrest and imprisonment has been a mistake.[46]

Those attitudes were also confirmed by the German command in Damascus. During this latter period, Mersinli Cemal had to coordinate with General Otto Liman von Sanders, and with Eric von Falkenhayn, who was appointed by Enver Pasha as head of the newly formed Yildirim (Sa'iqa) Army Group to replace Ahmad Cemal Pasha. Von Sanders had this to say about Mersinli in his memoirs: "[Mehmet Djemal Mersinli] knew the country of Arabia and the Arabs well from years of service in these provinces. The inhabitants trusted him, because he was considered wise and just. Several times he acted as their representative to lay their wishes before the government. He was beyond question a wise general who could be counted upon."[47]

Another important testimony comes from Sheikh Abdul Qadir al-Mudhafar, himself a leading member of the CUP and one of the few Arab close associates of Ahmad Cemal Pasha (the others included Prince Shakib Arsalan, Sheikh As'ad al-Shuqairi of Akka, and Sheikh Abdul Aziz Shawish, the head of Salahiyya College in Jerusalem). During the Suez campaign, Mudhafar was attached to one of the Fourth Army battalions in charge of religious mobilization. When Ahmad Cemal was replaced by Mersinli Cemal Pasha, he remained with the army and was appointed as mufti to replace Sheikh As'ad al-Shuqairi.[48] He remained loyal to the Ottoman regime till the end of the war, and (unlike Shuqairi) he continued to express pro-Ottoman sentiments even after the British occupied Palestine and Transjordan. According to Mudhafar, Mersinli was expressly appointed by Istanbul in order to control the damage to the Ottoman state brought about by the actions of Ahmad Cemal. In a diary entry, he quoted Mersinli Cemal Pasha as saying, "The arbitrary actions of Ahmad Cemal [against the Arab nationalists] were based on his own speculative prejudice, and not based on fact." Not exactly an accurate assessment, given Cemal's coordination of these activities with the Enver and the government, but still significant in that it signaled a policy shift. After his appointment he released several of the

Arab prisoners, including several who were awaiting execution.[49] Darwazeh, however, thought that these actions of reversal were too little, too late.[50]

OTTOMAN CARTOGRAPHY:
BORDERS AND FRONTIERS

Besides its military-logistic objective as a country survey, *Filistin Risalesi* is distinguished by its rich cartographic content, which includes separate political, topographical, and—most exceptionally—ethnographic charts. Most official maps of the Syrian provinces used the term *Palestine* as a designation for an amorphous region within the *mutasarriflik* of Jerusalem—that is, for the area bounded to the north by the *vilayat* (province) of Beirut, to the East by the *vilayat* of Surya, and to the south by Sinai (Tih Sahrasi).[51] *Filistin Risalesi* identified Palestine as including the *sanjaq* of Akka (Galilee), the sanjaq of Nablus, and the sanjaq of Jerusalem (Kudus Serif).[52] Thus it clearly extends the borders of Ottoman Palestine to include a substantial section of the Beirut Province, bounded by the Litani River. This resonates with European designations of the Holy Land and, to a lesser extent, with Jewish and biblical conceptions of Eretz Yisrael, which tended to cover a substantially larger area.

Ottoman cartography of Palestine and Syria has a rich history and resonance with both Islamic and European origins. The earliest sources showing detailed mapping of the Syrian coast were based on actual navigational drawings by well-known geographers-travelers. The most important were Peri Reissi (1465–1554), whose Mediterranean map in *Kitab al-Bahriyyah* (1528) continues to be an artistic masterpiece, and Kateb Celebi (1609–1657), whose *Tuhfat al-Kibar fi Asfar al-Bihar* (published 1729) constitutes the first detailed mapping of the Anatolian and Syrian provinces.[53] Celebi's work, moreover, contains elaborate descriptive and ethnographic material about these regions drawn partly from his own travels. His work confirms the restoration of the administrative boundaries used in the early Islamic (Ummayad) administrative units of Jund Filistin, a practice based on Roman-Byzantine practices.[54] Two Celebi maps from *Tuhfat al-Kibar* are of relevance here: the first is the map of the Mediterranean, which contains the names Iyalat al-Sham and Ard Filistin, most likely the first such reference in an Ottoman map. The second map is titled "Iqlim Jazirat al-Arab" and contains a more clearly marked "Ard Filistin" extending vertically for about half the

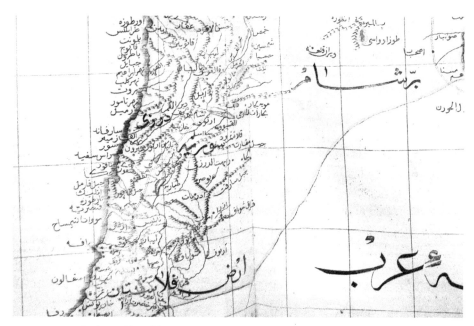

FIGURE 4. Ard Filistin (*detail*) by Kateb Celebi, first published in *Tufhat al-Kibar fi Asfar al-Bihar* in Istanbul in 1729.

Syrian coast. The text accompanying these maps describes the boundaries of Palestine, made up of the two sanjaqs of Gaza and Jerusalem: "In the southwest the border goes from the Mediterranean and al-Arish to the Wilderness of the Israelites [Sinai]. On the southeast it is the Dead Sea [Bahar Lut] and the Jordan River. In the north if goes from the Jordan River to the borders of Urdun as far as Caesarea."[55]

Celebi describes Palestine as the "noblest of the administrative divisions of Syria." He devotes many of his observations on the region, which he visited during his pilgrimage to Jerusalem and Mecca in the years 1633–1634, to a detailed description of the main urban centers, their populations, and their rituals. The bulk of his observations about Palestine concern Gaza, Jerusalem, and Hebron. In the latter he notes that the people are divided into two hostile factions: "the Yemenis or Whites (Aklu) and the Qaysis or Reds (Kizillu). When they clash, the Reds shout '*Ya lahu birr*' and the Whites shout '*Ya al-ma'ruf.*' These parties have survived from pre-Islamic times and retain the 'bigotry of ignorance' (al-Jahiliyya)."[56]

Commercial and military needs brought about new standards in nineteenth-century Ottoman mapping. This can already be seen in Mahmud Raif

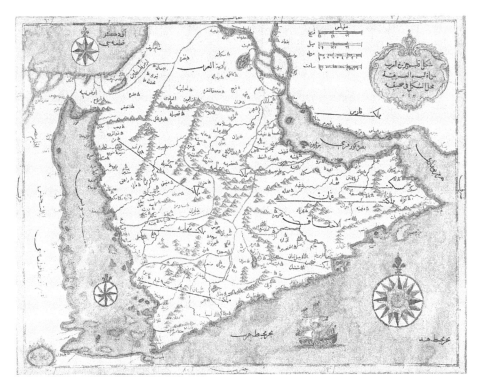

FIGURE 5. Kateb Celebi's map of the Arabian Peninsula and Palestine, first published in Istanbul in 1732.

Effendi's 1803 *Cedid Atlas,* published by the Istanbul College of Military Engineering.[57] The atlas constitutes a landmark document used in the new Ottoman reforms instituted by Selim III in the *Nizam-I Cedid,* aimed at bringing Ottoman administration up to modern standards. Although based on European sources (mainly William Faden's *General Atlas*), *Cedid Atlas* contained important Ottoman adaptations of geographic readings in the provinces. It also contained a substantial introduction by Mahmud Efendi.[58] Two maps of the Syrian districts contained references to both "Filastin" and "Ard Filastan" as part of Bar al-Sham.

In the latter map (Efendi 1803, 18) Palestine is drawn to show the region separating Ottoman Asia from Ottoman Africa. (This was, of course, before Muhammad Ali's campaign in Syria.) With the closing of the nineteenth century and the beginning of the twentieth, Ottoman maps become more instrumental, with the objective of making them usable for troop movements and for commercial activities. Anton Lutfi Beyk's 1891 map published by the

Khedival Society of Geography in Cairo is a specialized map indicating railroads in Syria and Palestine.[59]

After 1903 (1327 Rumi) the Government Mapping Department began to issue its own specialized maps, from which a highly stylized map of the Jerusalem sanjaq is available for 1904.[60] By 1912 a series of those maps, drawn to a scale of 1:200,000, was issued for the Syrian provinces by Dairesi Matbaasinda (Government Printing Press), of which two high-quality maps are available for the Jerusalem and Nablus districts.[61]

In all of these maps, as noted above, the administrative boundaries of the Jerusalem sanjaq, and later governorate (*mutasarifligi*), are not the same as the boundaries of the region of Filistin. The former was precise and delineated, the latter was fluid and undefined. The new, expanded use of the name *Filistin* by the Ottoman military authorities in *Filistin Risalesi*, therefore, is novel but not arbitrary. In Ottoman official correspondence there is a frequent application of the term *Artz-i Filistin* to the areas west of the River Jordan without confining it to the *sanjaq* of Jerusalem.[62] The Ottoman definition of the Holy Land as including Galilee in fact goes back to an earlier period—that of the Egyptian military campaign in Syria. In order to establish a unified command against the armies of Ibrahim Pasha in 1830, the Ottoman Porte took the unprecedented step of unifying the three *sanjaqs* of Jerusalem, Nablus, and Akka (i.e., modern Palestine) under the governor of Akka, Abdallah Pasha (1818–1832).[63] Both Butrus Abu-Manneh and Alexander Scholch trace the genealogy of this union to the point when, ten years later, in 1840, the sultan proposed, with the Europeans' blessing, that Muhammad Ali be named as "governor for life" of Akka and ruler of the southern *sanjaqs* of Syria, bounded by Ras al-Naqura in the north and Rafah to the south. This preemptive step—which made him the khedive of Egypt and Palestine—most likely was taken to ensure his reintegration into the imperial domain.[64]

The European powers pursued this plan for a separate Palestinian entity and, in 1872, succeeded briefly in gaining Ottoman consent to declare that "the *sanjaqs* of Jerusalem, Nablus, and Acre had been united to form . . . the province of Palestine."[65] Thuraya Pasha, then governor of Aleppo, assumed the governorship of the new province. But this proposal was short-lived and was revoked by a *firman* from Istanbul, which canceled the proposal and dissolved the new province of Jerusalem in July 1872, barely a month after Thuraya's appointment.[66]

Both the new grand vizier and the government were afraid that the new formation would tempt the European powers to intervene in order to control the Holy Land and put it under their protection. The Ottomans believed that dividing Palestine into two zones (*vilayat* of Beirut and the sanjaq of Jerusalem) would diffuse European influence.[67] Abu-Manneh provides a different interpretation. His view was that Istanbul was still reeling from the shadow of Egyptian annexationist designs. Only three decades had passed since the withdrawal of Ibrahim Pasha and his armies from Syria, and the High Porte believed that placing the province of Jerusalem under direct rule by Istanbul would create a barrier that would prevent another attempt by the Egyptians.[68] Whatever the reasons, this division of Palestine remained in place until the beginning of World War I.

OTTOMAN CONCEPTIONS OF PALESTINE: ETHNOGRAPHY

The Ottoman imperial regime viewed Palestine, in ethnic terms, as part of the Shami (Syrian) territories, which included, at the turn of the century, the provinces of Beirut, Syria, and the *mutasarriflik* of Jerusalem. In administrative terms the word *Palestine* was used on Ottoman maps of the period as equivalent to Kudus Serif *mutasarriflik*.[69] In narrative reports, however, *Filistin* was an amorphous term equivalent to *Holy Land* and often extended beyond, to the boundaries of the governorship, especially in its northern expanses. Being the land of Haram al-Sharif, as well as of Christian and Jewish holy places, however, added a special status to Palestine, which was augmented by the increasing presence of pilgrims from Europe (mostly Christians and Jews) and from North Africa and India (mostly Muslims).

In *Filistin Risalesi* the total number of Palestinians is assessed as "around 700,000" in 1331 (1915), which indicates that the anonymous authors of the treatise have added the districts of Akka and Nablus to the governorate of Jerusalem in their calculation.[70] Here we encounter two striking conceptions of native ethnicities: In the narrative descriptions of the peoples of the Holy Land, under the heading "Population" (*ehalisi*), the natives are presented as a mixture of Muslims, Christians, and Jews of various sects and denominations. In the ethnographic map that accompanies the text, however, the population becomes an amalgamation of broad nationalities that dominate the scene, and pockets of overlapping sects, as well as ethno-religious groupings that overlap with the nationalities. The map covers the bulk of the Syrian coast and southern Anatolia. The "national" groups are divided into Turks,

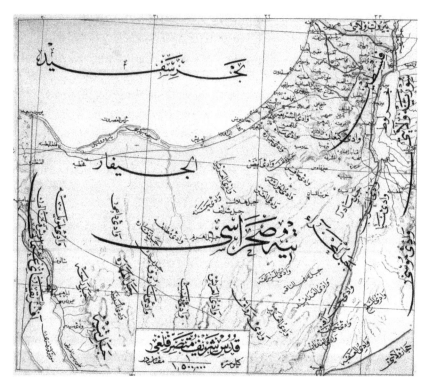

FIGURE 6. Ottoman Palestine, from the *Osmanlı Atlas,* published in Istanbul in 1912 (Tekin and Bas 2001).

Turkmen, Arabs, and Syrians. The "Syrian" population covers all of the of Palestinian highlands, Mount Lebanon, the settled population of Transjordan, and all the Syrian coast up to and including Iskandarun. The "Arabs" are the population east of Homs, Hamat, and Damascus and south of Gaza. Equally intriguing in this map is the distinction between Turks and Turkmen. "Turks" are the settled population of western Anatolia, *Turkmen* is the term used for the population living in the area roughly around Sivas and eastward. These major divisions of the population of the Ottoman Levant into Turks, Turkmen, Arabs, and Syrians are then interspersed with pockets of Druze, Ismailis, Jews, Maronites, Nuseiris, Metwalis, and Rum (Greek Orthodox). How should we interpret these divisions?

Contrary to common perception, the new Ottoman leadership did not divide the populations of Anatolia and the Syrian coast into Arabs and Turks. Rather, it assumed that the entire subject population belonged to the category of Ottoman citizens. The ethnic division was most likely made on a perception of ethnicity that distinguished between settled populations (Syrians and Turks) on the one hand, and tribal and semitribal populations (Turkmen and "other Turks" [*yakhoud Turki*]) on the other hand, who required a different military strategy.

Ottoman discourse on nationalism and ethnicity had preoccupied debates in the Ottoman press both in Istanbul and in the Arab provinces after the constitutional revolution. Within Syria and Palestine, the rising tide of nationalism became focused on issues of language and the use of Arabic in school curricula as well as in official correspondence (cf. Darwazeh 1993, Qadri 1993, and Husarī 1966). Unpublished war diaries indicate that soldiers and civilians were acutely aware of the identity of local governors and military commanders. "Arna'uti" (Albanian), "Suri," "Hijazi," "Bulghari' (Bulgarian), "Turki," and "Bushnaqi" (Bosnian) were common distinctions, although not necessarily implying negative distinctions.[71] As the war progressed, however, the usage of the phrases "oppressive Turks" and "Ottoman yoke" were increasingly heard, even though they did not mean the same thing, since the protestors identified themselves as Ottoman citizens.

The view from the imperial center, however, was different. In her review of the Ottoman revolutionary press, Palmira Brummett throws significant light on ethnic stereotyping in the waning years of Ottoman rule. Only the Greeks, Bulgarians, and Albanians were cast in ethnic political caricatures (mostly through dress).[72] Arabs were cast negatively only when the circle around Abdul Hamid's corrupt advisors (the "monkeys") was associated with the old reactionary order. Otherwise the "Arabs" were often seen as the victims of Italian and British imperialism (in Libya and Egypt), struggling to free themselves and (presumably) to restore Ottoman rule.[73]

This situation changed drastically after the Arab rebellion of Sherif Hussein in Hijaz in 1916, when Ahmad Cemal Pasha and his publicist Falih Rifqi (Atay) began to talk about the "Arab betrayal" and the "stab in the back."[74] A distinction continued to be made, however, between Syrians and Arabs, especially when Syrian soldiers had fought valiantly in the defense of Anatolia in Janaq Qal'a and Gallipoli (Janaq Qal'a [Turkish Canakale] and Gallipoli, located at the entrance of the Dardanelles straits, were two major battle sites during World War I). Both Brummett and Kayali note that distinctions within the press were made on the basis of regional, rather than ethnic affinities. In examining satirical cartoons, Brummett notes, "Other than in [the] anti-imperialist form, the 'Arab' is a bit hard to find in these Ottoman cartoons. He does not appear as a rabid separatist, demanding an

Arab nation from the new regime. He does not appear, as he will in a later era in the West, as a catch-all symbol of terrorism and trouble. Indeed, one can scan hundreds of Ottoman cartoons without finding a figure who can be irrevocably tagged as 'Arab.' For that matter, one can scan hundreds of cartoons without finding a figure tagged as a 'Turk,' except where 'Turk' stands as a synonym for Ottoman in general and particularly for an Ottoman as distinct from a European."[75] But within a few years, during the war, this identification of the Ottoman *with* the Turk started a process of differentiations and exclusions that led to the delegitimization of the term *Ottoman* as all-inclusive concept.

CONCLUSION: TOO LITTLE, TOO LATE?

The publication of *Filistin Risalesi* (1915) as a country survey by the Eighth Army Corps almost one hundred years ago calls for reflection and evaluation. This almanac is unique, since it is focused on a region, Filistin, that did not constitute an administrative unit in the empire. Palestine then encompassed the province of Jerusalem (which was a formal province) and substantial areas to the north (which were parts of another province, Beirut). The most significant aspect of this document is that it expanded the boundaries of Palestine to include Galilee and parts of southern Lebanon, up to the Litani River.

The Ottomans were cognizant of the ideologically alluring aspect of the Holy Land in the eyes of the Allied forces. They were also aware, through their German and Austrian allies, of Western imperial interests even before the release of the terms of the Sykes-Picot Agreement in October 1917. They certainly became alarmed, above all, by the Allied intention to turn the Arab provinces of the empire into French, Italian, Russian, and British zones. Thus, the redefinition of Palestine's boundaries was aimed in part at preempting this segmentation.

The fact that *Filistin Risalesi* draws, in much of its topographic and demographic data, on French and British military "country books" of the Holy Land and other Levantine regions does not make it "less Ottoman." The strategic planners in the Eighth Army Corps command used this information to create a manual meant to serve specifically Ottoman objectives—both military and civilian. This can be gleaned from the survey of water, agricultural, and road system networks and, more importantly, from the manner in which the local population, its religious and social composition, and its traditions were described and classified. *Filistin Risalesi* suffers from a degree of orientalist imagery in its conception of religious and ethnic minorities, and in the way ethnicity and religion are overlapped.

Beyond these conceptions, there is an assumption of Ottoman citizenship that sets this manual, and other similar *salnameh*-type almanacs, from British and French army manuals of "enemy territories" that I discuss here. The discussion of ethnic composition of the native population in Palestine, therefore, is treated here as an extension of social categories of *Ottoman* groups that existed also in Anatolia and Syria, though in a different population mix. A good example of this distinction is when the anonymous author of *Filistin Risalesi* discusses the Jews of Syria as being composed of local Israelites who were Arabic speaking, in contrast to Jews who were non-Ottomans pilgrims and migrants and who spoke Yiddish and Russian.

As far as the Arab population is concerned, the most important distinction made by the treatise is between Syrian (Suri) and Arab (Arep), with the former—including both urban Syrians and peasants—constituting the bulk of the coastal population. The term *Arab* was reserved for the "tribal" formations east of Salt and Hawran and extending to the periphery of the major urban centers of Iraq. Thus we have three categories of "Arabs" in Ottoman thinking during the war period: the Arabs of Hijaz and Iraqi tribesmen who "betrayed" the Ottoman state by allying themselves with the English; the Arabs of Libya, Egypt, and Morocco, who were seen as heroically fighting the Italians, French, and British imperialists to join their Ottoman motherland; and the tribal "urban" Arabs who lived east of Syria, and who were vacillating in their loyalty to the sultanate. An amorphous distinction was made between the Syrians (whose forces fought with the Ottomans in Gallipoli and Suez) on the one hand, and what might be called generic "Arabs" on the other, who were seen as untamed and unreliable. Clearly this distinction was an *ideological category* and did not always have conceptual coherence, since after the great Arab Revolt, many "Syrians" joined the Arab rebellion under the banner of Arab nationalism.

Enough Syrians (including Lebanese, Palestinians, and Transjordanians), however, remained within the ranks of the imperial order to lend some legitimacy to this distinction. It should be added here that this ambiguity about "who is an Arab" was not peculiar to the Turkish political and military elite. The word *Arab,* indicating Bedouins and tribal formations, was common to many, if not most, intellectuals in Egypt and Bilad al-Sham for much of the nineteenth century and the first decades of the twentieth century. From the perspective of the imperial capital (one hesitates to say "the Turkish side," since the Istanbuli intelligentsia was not entirely Turkish), the situation was equally complex. Despite Arab (as well as Greek and Armenian) nationalist attacks on the Turanic tendencies emerging within the ranks of the CUP, the idea of Turkishness, for much of the earlier period, was problematic for the new Ottomans. As Sukru Hanioglu states, "The young Turks refrained from formulating a nationalist theory involving race during the formative years of their movement.... There is little doubt that this was because, in the Darwinist racial hierarchy, Turks were always assigned to the lowest ranks."[76]

References to Anatolian peasants were infused with indications of backwardness in both the Arabic and Turkish lexicons. The contingencies of World War I changed all of this, since the Ottoman state, under CUP control, began to use Islam as a mobilizing factor against the allies, as well as a motif to undermine the legitimacy of Hijazi challenges against the secularism of the Young Turks and the new constitution. It was in this period that Muslim identity became paramount in Ottoman public discourse, *as a marker of citizenship,* and that the ethnicity of minorities became recognized as an indicator of separateness.[77] This was the prelude to the Republican construction of the new secular Ottoman-Turkish citizenship as having an Islamic core.

The political context of *Filistin Risalesi* was the attempt by the new Ottoman leadership to redefine its relationship to the Arab provinces, and to Palestine in particular. The failure of the Suez campaign, and the hardships generated by the war activities on the local population after 1915, including the impact of the coastal blockade against the Syrian provinces by the Allied forces, produced a backlash among Ottoman Arabs. This galvanized the forces that sought autonomy within the empire, and it encouraged secessionist forces to flaunt the idea of independence—with considerable French and British support. The ruthless behavior of the Fourth Army under Ahmad Cemal Pasha, as well as the brutal activities of Enver's Special Forces (Teskelat-i Mahsusa) among Arab nationalists—who were a minority at the beginning of the war—were decisive factors in the slide toward separatism. We have witnessed here how the Ottoman leadership sought a reconciliation with the Arab population after 1916, first by appeasing the Hijazi rebellion under Sherif Hussein and, later, by removing Ahmad Cemal and appointing Mersinli Mehmet Cemal in his place.

The style and content of *Filistin Risalesi,* which was drafted under the command of the Lesser Cemal (*kuchuk*), indicate that Palestine was a paramount territory in Ottoman civilian and military strategy, and that the

Ottoman leadership saw in the province a core region in the empire. Contemporary writings by Arab writers in Beirut, Damascus, and Jerusalem (soon to be expunged and forgotten) show that the appointment of Mersinli Cemal reflected a welcome shift in their attitudes toward Istanbul and Ottomanism, signaling the beginning of reconciliation and a new era of Arab-Turkish relations. But as Muhammad Izzat Darwazeh—himself a veteran supporter and member of the CUP—noted astutely, it was "the correct shift, executed too late."

THREE

The Sweet Aroma of Holy Sewage

URBAN PLANNING AND THE
NEW PUBLIC SPHERE IN PALESTINE

PALESTINE WITNESSED THREE major urban transformations in late Ottoman Palestine that took place in the context of European capitulations, indigenous reform, and war. I use here the term *triadic modernity* in reference to the regional network that linked three urban centers: Jaffa, the port city; Jerusalem, the provincial capital; and Beersheba, the new frontier garrison town. And I examine the emergence of a new public sphere in those cities from an earlier communitarian fabric.

This study draws on the important conceptual work on Ottoman Arab provincial cities by Hanssen, Philipp, and Weber in *The Empire in the City*. In particular it utilizes their approach to the production of urban space in "ushering in a process of acting, thinking, and feeling urban modernity,"[1] through an interchange between structural features (municipal planning, infrastructural investments, and the contingencies of war) and agency (the expansion of the public sphere, the emergence of notions urban citizenship, and the internalization of Ottoman modernism).

In *The Empire in the City* two analytical categories are introduced that are relevant to our understanding of Ottoman modernity. The first is the debate about Ottoman colonialism in the Arab provinces, which, following the work of Ussama Makdisi, refers to the centralizing policies of the post-Tanzimat period in which the new Ottoman bureaucracy began to mold the provincial areas in the image of a restructured Turkic-Ottoman state. This colonizing state was replacing the early Hamidian decentralized tributary state, which—according to this analysis—was autocratic, but decentralized, and did not exhibit ethnic Turkish hegemony, because it ruled through the mediation of local potentates.[2] The new centralized and centralizing Ottoman state was developing an Istanbuli urban prototype for emulation in the provinces.[3] It also created a subordinated vision of the Arab internal "other" that had to be incorporated into the new imperial domain.[4] This debate is especially relevant to an understanding of the planning of Beersheba.

A second analytical category that illuminates this discussion is the notion of agency in urban transformation. "In contrast to Celik's Istanbul," write Hanssen, Philipp, and Weber, "Arab provincial capitals were not merely a canvas on which political power was represented[;] their inhabitants also produced their own rhythms of change and adaptability within the pervasive and permeating power of Ottoman imperialism."[5] This emergent public sphere was propelled by investments and plans for provincial Ottoman urban centers, which often produced antagonistic features in the public domain. One of those developments was the emergence of new forms of urban identity, resulting from the first Ottoman constitutional revolution, and the replacement of a communitarian identity in the city.[6] It was accompanied by the growth of new forms of public assembly seen in the introduction of public cafés, theaters, music halls, and sport events.

Another feature of this public sphere emerged from the construction of modern institutions by foreign states, benefiting from the mercantile capitulations privileges, which favored the key European trade missions in the Levant. Following the defeat of the Egyptian campaign in 1841, France, Britain, Italy, Austria-Hungary, Russia, and Germany introduced a large number of denominational schools, telegraph and postal services, banks, trade outposts, and other institutions. The capitulations notably involved a patronage system that challenged the evolving struggle for Ottoman citizenship by allowing for the cooptation of Ottoman minorities, Jews, Christians, and Druze citizens in particular, but also a substantial number of Arab Muslims in the service of the European states.

The study of Ottoman urban developments in Palestine and greater Syria is essential to understanding the two major contested territories in the debate about modernity in the Arab East. The first one concerns the European claims (basically French, British, and Italian) about rescuing the "Levant" from the impact of Ottoman neglect and the destructive features of centuries of decentralized feudal appropriation of land rent, in which the provincial capitals were seen as static abodes of a local bureaucratic elite involved in siphoning the rural surplus. The major dent made in this oriental inertia was the innovation brought about in the coastal cities by European settlers and their mercantile clients from the local ethnic minorities. The second major contested territory in the modernist debate concerns the relationship between Zionism as a dynamic modernizing force through its urbanizing schemes, facing a traditional Arab society dominated by a parasitic urban elite dependent on rent capitalism. Here Bauhaus Tel Aviv is pitted against an idyllic Jaffa of the citrus effendis. A corollary of this dichotomy can be traced to the growth of the "planned" German colonies in Jaffa, Haifa, and Jerusalem, in the midst of Arab "spontaneous" habitat. It is striking in this context that the Zionist modernity is seen as a struggle against not only the traditional Arab-Islamic city but also the native Jewish communities that were immersed in communitarian enclosures. In this sense Tel Aviv as a prototype was perceived as a challenge not only to the "premodern" Arab Jaffa but also to the Jerusalem and Hebron of the old Jewish Yishuv.

COLONIAL ASSUMPTIONS ABOUT URBAN MODERNITY

Those features of Ottoman urban development were often forgotten, over-turned or—in some cases—superseded as the French and British governments began to forge their own systems of control in the Levantine administrations after World War I. Both colonial regimes behaved in Damascus, Aleppo, Amman, Beirut, and Jerusalem as if urban planning had to start from a void.

In the case of Palestine, the Ottoman army, having retreated from the southern part of the country, was still fighting the British army in the Jordan Valley and the Nablus region when Sir William McLean, planner and city engineer of Alexandria, was summoned in the winter of 1917 to prepare a city plan for Jerusalem. Within the course of five months, McLean's 1918 scheme was prepared, and it became the basis for all the subsequent Mandate plans for the city. Those include the 1919 plan by Patrick Geddes, the 1922 C.R. Ashbee plan (known as the Pro-Jerusalem Society scheme), and the 1930 scheme prepared by Henry Kendall, the chief city planner during the Mandate period and during Jordan's administration of the city after 1948. The "foundational" McLean scheme of 1918, as developed by Geddes in 1919 and the Pro-Jerusalem Society in 1922, had several key planning principles in it. Those principles rested on dividing the city into three "development" zones: the inner city, within the walls, was to be preserved and no modern buildings were to be built inside it; the city walls would become a green area, a garden city, framing the historic center; and all modern city expansion was to be regulated in the north and west of the city.[7] The restrictive measures adopted by the military government to buttress this scheme included guidelines stating that "no building should appear on the skyline of the Mount of Olives, . . . and no building [was] to be of greater height than 11 meters above ground."[8] No industrial buildings were allowed, and roofs and external building material had to be constructed from, or covered by, stone.[9]

The McLean plan became a benchmark for the colonial modernity of Jerusalem, separating what was heralded as the era of urban planning of the city, compared to the previous era of "administrative neglect."[10] Of the three Mandate planners, the most ambitious and ideologically motivated was Patrick Geddes (1854–1932). Geddes saw the urban planning of Jerusalem and Palestine as an imperial scheme rooted in colonial city-planning experiences in India. Unlike Ashbee and McLean, Geddes was also deeply committed to the Zionist project and saw the planning of Jerusalem as part of the scheme for Hebrew revival.[11] It was especially Geddes, but also Kendall, Ronald Storrs (the military governor of Jerusalem after the war), and Ashbee, who, in their review of the British presence in Palestine, made a point often repeated by others: namely, that the Ottomans had left the city and the country without any urban plans, and that the British colonial administration had to start from scratch.[12] Large portions of the urban planning schemes in Syria, Lebanon, and Palestine were later attributed to the Mandate period, with the assumption that the Ottomans left a tabula rasa in the occupied territories. As Vincent Lemire aptly put it: "The vulgate historiography concluded years ago that the Ottoman rulers were incapable of modernizing the urban networks. The colonialist ideology of the British mandate combined with Zionist discourse to reject the image of the Ottoman period as a modernizing enterprise. . . . [T]his is the condescending image of an 'immobile and complicated East,' the 'long slumber of Jerusalem' from 1517 to 1917."[13]

TABULA RASA? EARLY MANDATE PLANS
FOR JERUSALEM

These claims about Ottoman neglect of the provincial centers have been challenged effectively by several urban historians, beginning with André Raymond in his *Arab Cities in the Ottoman Period* and, more recently, by Zeynep Celik in her *Empire, Architecture and the City*.[14]

Yet despite the presumed originality of these measures for planning in Jerusalem and other cities in Palestine, virtually all of their main features—

as we shall see—had been adopted by the Ottoman administration of Syria and the *mutasarriflik* of Kudus Serif, after the adoption of the Ottoman Municipal Ordinance of October 1877, which defined "the authority, competence, budget and legal limits of the municipality."[15]

That Palestine was a recognized geographic region within the Ottoman southern boundaries, although not administratively delineated, is clear from Ottoman cartography, postal services, and government military manuals such as *Filistin Risalesi,* which was issued to officers in the field.[16] All of them refer to Palestine as a region south of Vilayat Beirut. For most of the Tanzimat period, Filistin was an area that corresponded more or less to the Jerusalem sanjaq, and—after 1874—it was established as an autonomous province (*mutasarriflik*) with special status, accountable directly to the High Porte. During World War I the Ottoman military began to use the term *Filistin* to refer to a wider area that corresponded to the area of Mandated Palestine and contained the districts of Nablus and Akka and parts of southern Lebanon.[17] For the purposes of this book, however, *Palestine* refers to southern Syria— the area that evolved as the southern flank of the empire during the Balkan Wars (1912–1913) and the Great War (1914–1918).

The three cities in question occupied a critical unity in Ottoman strategic planning. Jaffa, as the port city serving the Holy Land, was linked to Jerusalem by carriageway and railroad. It became the gateway for European pilgrims and trade, enhanced by the development of citriculture and the soap industry in the second half of the nineteenth century. Jerusalem was already the capital of the sanjaq of Kudus Serif, the seat of the most important religious court in the region, home of the mutasarrif (governor), and the site of major European capitulationary presence, which manifested itself in major urban investments in schools, hospitals, banks, consular ligations, and postal services. Beersheba was the new Ottoman city, planned, in 1900, to become the center of agricultural sedentarization of the Bedouin tribes and the market center of grain production in southern Syria. Linking the three cities was the extension of the Damascus-Medina-Hijazi rail line, which connected Jaffa to Jerusalem in 1892, and the Jaffa-Lydda connection to the Beersheba line, which was completed by Cemal Pasha during the war in 1915.

The second half of the twentieth century saw a major redefinition of the relationship between the central authority of the Ottoman Empire and its Arab regional centers. This was brought about in large part by the fear of losing these peripheral areas after the Egyptian campaign of Ibrahim Pasha (1831–1841) and the success of secessionist movements in the Rumi provinces, as well as after the loss of Greek, Bulgarian, and other territories. Along the eastern Mediterranean, port cities like Izmir, Beirut, and Jaffa were already locations of substantial growth and diversification propelled by Mediterranean trade, foreign investments, and the presence of foreign and local minority communities benefiting from the capitulations. This growth of coastal "Levantine cosmopolitanism" gave the impression that Ottoman modernization of these cities took place outside the domain of the central state in Istanbul, and that the inner cities of the Syrian littoral, such as Damascus, Nablus, and Jerusalem, remained static, conservative, and unchanging. This vision of Ottoman bareness, and the subsequent attribution of urban development to foreign investments during late Ottoman rule, has also been reinforced by nationalist historiography, both Arab and Turkish—which covered up many of the Ottoman achievements, and not only achievements in urban development discussed here—recorded between the end of the Egyptian campaign and World War I.

Recent research has demonstrated substantial schemes of urban planning and urban development in both the cities of the interior and the coastal cities. These schemes supplemented and complemented urban growth attributed to European capital investments and to ethnic minorities who benefited from the capitulation regime. Zeynep Celik's important work on Ottoman Imperial architecture has contributed much to our understanding of those late nineteenth-century urban developments. Although her work focuses on the interaction of French colonial urban planning in North Africa, and Ottoman parallel urban schemes in Syria and Libya, there is much in it that dispels the notion of bareness that had to be developed after World War I by the European powers.

Celik also demonstrates how Ottoman urban investments in infrastructure and in imperial ceremonial architecture (public plazas, *sabeels* [public water fountains], town halls, clock towers) marked and standardized an Ottoman style in the Arab provinces, using Istanbuli urban planning as a prototype. Stephan Weber, in a similar vein, describes how "Arab provincial capitals were sites of new and enforced manifestations of state presence. Freestanding administrative buildings, monuments, wide boulevards, and sumptuous squares created a vocabulary of a specifically Ottoman symmetry, regularity and order which enframed everyday conduct around markets, guilds, families and local, regional and international networks. At the same time, these cities functioned as bridgeheads for foreign interests in the region. Missions, schools, consulates, hotels, banks and insurance-, tourist-, and development companies established head offices in provincial capitals and branches in secondary cities or district capitals, and local agencies in smaller towns."[18] The first urban development plans appeared for Beirut (1876, 1888), Tarablusgarb (1883), and Damascus (1885), later such plans for other provincial centers followed.[19] Those schemes included large and diverse plans for public monuments, stations, and government buildings. The 1901 celebrations for the twenty-fifth anniversary of Sultan Abdul Hamid's ascension to the throne was an occasion for the launching of many of these schemes. A substantial number of Ottoman development schemes were investments in modernizing the military infrastructure of the state, and this included the development of railroad and telegraph lines. Standardized military barracks, imperial military schools, *karakolhanes* (police stations), and road networks were established throughout the Arab regions in order to meet the challenges—both military and economic—emanating from Egyptian and European imperial designs.[20]

THE TRIADIC GRID OF URBAN MODERNITY IN A FRONTIER LAND

Palestine was a central peripheral region, as well as a central Ottoman consideration. It was peripheral, however, in the sense that it marked the southern flanks of the Syrian provinces and did not initially produce significant tax revenue, and that it was not strategically located along the pilgrimage route to Hijaz. Soon after the loss of the Egyptian territory to the sultan in midcentury, however, it became a gateway to the Suez and Ottoman Africa. The Egyptian campaign also triggered Ottoman defenses in the regions south of Palestine, including Hijaz and Yemen. These defensive measures were accompanied by contested control over Jerusalem and the holy sites with the enhanced presence, and imperial ambitions, of the major European powers. The Ottoman shift signifying the increased importance of Palestine can be seen in the change of the territory's name from Sham Sherif (Holy Syria) in seventeenth- and eighteenth-century maps (for example, those by Peri Reissi and Kateb Celebi) to Kudus Serif (Holy Jerusalem).[21] Although Palestine was not a separate administrative unit in those designations, it was always marked clearly as "Filistin" or "Filastan" on those maps (beginning in the sixteenth century), as a region extending from the Galilee Mountains to the Sinai Peninsula. After the adoption of clearer administrative boundaries, marked on the *Cedid Atlas* (1803), Palestine shrank to encompass only the area south of the Nablus region.[22] It became more or less equivalent to the *sanjaq* (and after 1876, the *mutasarriflik*) of Jerusalem. Essentially Palestine became the southern region of Syria.

With the increased centralization and control of the Tanzimat state apparatus, urban Palestine, as in other Syrian districts, witnessed significant growth and a remaking of the public sphere. This process involved the creation of public plazas intended for military displays and imperial ceremonial performances. It also involved the creation of bourgeois domains of leisurely space: promenades, cafes, and public gardens.[23] Palestine also witnessed the decline of the *mahale* (city neighborhood) as the basic communitarian unit of social control and its replacement with citywide administrative networks. Ferdun Ergut examines this process in the context of new policing and surveillance practices of the Ottoman state.[24] This intrusive development contributed significantly to the redefinition of the public sphere and the blurring of lines of separation between what were considered private and public domains. The blurring of lines was manifested through the passage of administrative measures against public "deviance," such as vagrancy laws, and an enhanced role of the police in the licensing of trades and in monitoring and punishing what used to be considered private behavior, instances of which were now labeled "public crimes."[25] Vagrancy itself was a new "crime" that emerged as a result of urban pauperization, rural-urban migration, and class differentiation. Previously these "deviations" were dealt with normatively in the Mahale by the local imam, or *kadi*.[26] "Unseemly behavior," as well as violation of turf boundaries, was often resolved through the action of local *qabadayat* (neighborhood "tough guys."[27] Now the tasks of urban surveillance and control increasingly were handed to the police and those holding the newly introduced position of urban mukhtar.[28]

The regional urban development that constituted what I call a grid of triadic urban modernity to indicate that it involved purposeful planning and was regionally integrated to serve a new vision of a "frontier" development. These urban trends were enhanced by three significant new developments at the beginning of the twentieth century: first, the road and rail linking of Jerusalem with Jaffa, its port city, to facilitate the increasingly important pilgrimages to the holy city; second, the embeddedness of Palestinian and Syrian agricultural commodities in the European market with the rise of citrus (a coastal crop) and soap (an inland item based on highland olives) as major commodities; and third, the enhanced significance of Palestine as a frontier in the defense of the Ottoman realm from its southern hinterland and the dangers coming from British-controlled Egypt. No doubt these regional developments created a conflictual modernity. In the three cities examined, the process of growth involved both internal differentiation and regional disparities. The enhancement of Jerusalem as the capital of the province of Kudus Serif in 1876 gave new prominence, prestige, and power to the *ashraf* (city notables) and bureaucrats of the city over regional elites in an unprecedented manner. The increased centralization of bureaucratic power that accompanied the Tanzimat reforms eclipsed the regional status of Akka and Nablus. But in the case of Jaffa the regional disparity took a different trajectory.

JAFFA: CITY OF STRANGERS

Modern Jaffa is an Ottoman city par excellence. Mohammad Abu Nabbout Agha reconstructed the city after the destruction it suffered as a result of the plague and the Napoleonic army in 1800. Abu Nabbout, Ottoman governor from 1807 to 1819, aimed at creating a port city to serve the holy places that would rival Akka and possibly challenge his patron Jazzar Pasha.[29] After completing the fortifications of the city, he started an ambitious program of construction that established the major thoroughfares of the city, as well as two markets, two khans, port storehouses, and several light industries. He used his position as administrator of religious endowments to consolidate public properties under Waqf administration, building the Great Mosque and several *sabils* (water fountains). The main *sabil*, still bearing an engraved dedication in the name of Abu Nabbout to this day, was constructed within a municipal public garden. The establishment of public security, along with the commercial invigoration of Jaffa, under the rule of Abu Nabbout began to attract merchants and artisans, who bestowed on it the name Um al-Gharib (city of strangers), marking its hospitality to newcomers.[30] The completion of the city's monumental buildings marked Abu Nabbout as the ruler of southern Palestine.[31]

During the Egyptian administration of the city (1831–1840), Ibrahim Pasha undertook a number of engineering schemes. One scheme (an uncompleted project) was intended to improve the port facilities by creating an internal harbor at Bassa that would link to the external harbor via canal. Ibrahim Pasha created a number of "military suburbs" for his army at Abu

Kabir, Nuzha, and Darwish, which became working-class neighborhoods containing a large Egyptian population after the withdrawal of the Khedival army.[32] The main urban transformation of modern Jaffa, however, occurred after the adoption of the Ottoman Municipal Ordinance of 1877. This led to the removal of the city walls and moat (1879–1888), the building of the elite Ajami neighborhood (named after Sheikh Ibrahim al-Ajami), the expansion of the harbor and its docks, and the building of the customs house.[33] (Map 1 shows the new urban expansion of the city and the linkages established by the ordinance between the harbor area and the new orchard neighborhoods of Bassa and al-Ajami.) The Manshiyyeh Quarter was established in 1892 to house the railroad workers and technicians. That year also saw the building of the Jaffa-Jerusalem line, the first railroad in Palestine.[34]

On being appointed as the city's public prosecutor in 1912, Yusif al-Hakim, a Syrian attorney and judge from Latakiyya, noted the contrast between Jaffa's economic predominance and its political subordination to Jerusalem: "Jaffa is already larger than most district centers in the Ottoman sultanate. Its economic significance lies in that it is the only port for Jerusalem, linked by a major railway, with a substantial commercial base and a huge agricultural surplus. Its exports to England alone include two million containers of its famous orange yields. Its internal economy, however, is linked to the Nablus region, which is administratively part of the Beirut Province. By any criteria Jaffa should be the center of a *mutasarriflik* [province], if it weren't for the fact that it is subordinated to the governor of Jerusalem, who in his turn is accountable directly to the Ministry of the Interior [in Istanbul]. Nevertheless the Ottoman government has taken note of Jaffa's preeminence, by making it the seat of a special court to review commercial litigation, in addition to Jaffa's [new] Superior Court for Criminal Justice. Jaffa also houses all the major administrative departments in the [Jerusalem] Liwa, in addition to being the center for the command of the regular Sultanic Army."[35] Before the war, Jaffa was already the seat for the region's main newspapers, trade unions, theaters, and nascent political parties (the CUP, the Entente Party, and the Ottoman Decentralization Party).[36]

The early Ottoman planning of Jaffa, in contrast to that of Jerusalem, was accompanied by significant social differentiation. The development of agricultural capitalism in midcentury attracted a considerable labor force from the peripheral rural areas of the city, as well as from southern Palestine (Beersheba, Arish) and from Hauran. The military encampments in the city from the Egyptian period, Abu Kabir, and Sakanet Darwish, became working-class neighborhoods. At the turn of the century, the Manshiyyeh Quarter evolved as the habitat of rail workers and engineers, brought in to develop the Hijazi railroad under Ottoman-German partnership. In Jaffa (as well as in Jerusalem), the old city was increasingly deserted by a class of rising mercantile entrepreneurs and professionals, who built spacious mansions influenced by similar architectural patterns in Alexandria, Beirut, and Marseille, in the neighborhoods of al-Ajami, Nuzha, and Jabaliyyeh. By the first world war the substantial growth of the working class who held jobs in citriculture, railway work, and construction began to be reflected in labor protests and nationalist militancy.

The governorship of Hasan Beyk al-Jabi (1914–1917) saw another major thrust of urban expansion. Although the legacy of Hasan Beyk, a Damascene officer from Zabadani, is associated with the war years and the repression of Arab nationalists, his administration paid considerable attention to public construction. Al-Jabi built two major crossroads, Cemal Pasha (named after the commander of the Fourth Army, the virtual military ruler of Palestine during the war) and Nuzha Boulevards, which allow easy access from the port area to the flourishing orange plantations. He expanded the port again and undertook several renovation projects to beautify what became the "capital of the Palestine," as expressed by Egyptian urban planner Ali al-Miliji.[37] In addition to documenting the Ottoman planning schemes for Jaffa, al-Miliji himself prepared a detailed map for the city during the final years of the Mandate.

It is striking that at the beginning and end of the Mandate, two noted planners were summoned from Cairo. The first, McLean, was asked by the British military government of Ronald Storrs to provide a plan for Jerusalem; the second, Ali al-Miliji, was engaged by the Jaffa municipal government, headed by Yusif Haikal, to plan the future of Jaffa. By that time Jaffa was engaged in a "modernist duel" with the Jewish town of Tel Aviv, which had grown, in its northern territories, as the jewel in the crown of the Zionist project. Jaffa's Manshiyyeh Quarter—site of Hasan Beyk's road expansion and the construction of the country's first railroad network—became the seam line separating the Bauhaus modernity of Tel Aviv from the Levantine Ottoman modernity of Jaffa.[38] One of the biggest challenges in al-Miliji's schemes for Jaffa's expansion, undertaken during the Mandate, was how to accommodate the blockage of the city's urban space from Manshiyyeh-Tel Aviv in the north, and from the colony of Bat Yam in the southern approaches of the city.[39] Jaffa's Ottoman modernity was manifested in the creation of

FIGURE 7. Ali Ekrem Bey, Ottoman governor of Jerusalem, addressing Jaffa crowds during the celebration of "huriyya" (freedom), the popular reference to the celebration accompanying the promulgation of the new constitution, 1908. Wasif Jawhariyyeh Collection, Institute for Palestine Studies, Beirut.

imperial buildings surrounding the famous clock tower and its plaza. This process of urban aggrandizement was ushered in by the construction of the Great Mosque, built by Abu Nabbout in 1815, followed by the Saraya Building (also known as the Seray or Serail Building), which housed the city government, and the clock tower itself (1905) to celebrate the twenty-fifth anniversary of Sultan Abdul Hamid's ascension to the throne. Although modest in grandeur compared to public squares in other provincial capitals (Damascus, Aleppo, Izmir, and Beirut), Jaffa's very quickly became pivotal in galvanizing the city's population around political and cultural events.

In 1908, Jaffa saw the first major recorded political demonstration in celebration of the promulgation of the new constitution, ushering what was believed to be the onset of freedom of assembly and the press.[40] The rally was addressed by the liberal Jerusalem provincial governor (*mutasarrif*) Ali Ekrem Bey in front of the Saraya Building. Ekrem Bey was newly appointed and took his position with great zeal as an Ottoman administrative reformer and a champion of the new constitution. He was the son of the liberal Ottoman nationalist leader and writer Namik Kemal and referred to himself as Kemazade (son of Kemal).⁴¹ During the constitutional period and the restorative attempt to reinstall Sultan Abdul Hamid, Ekrem Bey used the new public arenas in the main cities, Jaffa and Jerusalem in particular, to mobilize for the new objectives of the CUP regime.⁴² He also used these occasions to promote his two policy objectives: to curtail Jewish immigration, and to monitor and combat the rise of Arab nationalist elements in Palestine.⁴³ Before that, he was instrumental in using public speaking in the new city of Beersheba to cement pro-regime alliances among the Bedouins.⁴⁴ A photograph of Ekrem Bey addressing the Jaffa crowds was preserved by the chronicler Wasif Jawhariyyeh and shows thousands of villagers and urban citizens teaming in the Clock Square.⁴⁵ The photo presents a sharp contrast to a similar event held in Jerusalem, which is dominated by pomp and circumstance and is attended by European consuls and town notables.⁴⁶ In the following years the same square became the rallying place for May Day parades and for anti-Zionist demonstrations protesting the Balfour Declaration, and as the starting point for the annual Nebi Rubeen (Rubin) procession.

The festival of Nebi Rubeen had as its destination the Shrine of Rubeen (Reuven of the Old Testament), which lay ten kilometers south of Jaffa. It was transformed during the governorship of Hasan Beyk, from a religious ceremonial for Jaffa and its satellite villages into a major urban secular event in which Christians, Muslims, and Jews celebrated the end of the winter season and marched to the sea, engaging in a monthlong respite from the hardships of work. It was a singular public event that brought together the rich, the poor, and various religious denominations in a carnivalesque celebration for the cities of Ramleh, Lydda, and Jaffa.⁴⁷

JAFFA VERSUS JERUSALEM: CITIES IN CONFLICT?

The notion of conflict between the "coastal metropolitan city" and the holy city is rooted in two analytical traditions, both of which have led to popular generalizations that are misconceived. The first we find in Scholch's contradistinctions between a "feudal" city dominated by imperial bureaucrats and a landed aristocracy that acquired increasing power and authority in the post-Tanzimat period, and the bourgeois city whose modernity was grounded in European investments and citriculture.⁴⁸ The second analytical tradition is rooted in a paradigm of cultural conflict, in which the "emancipated," cosmopolitan city is juxtaposed with the city of pilgrimage and religiosity.[49] This second paradigm was reinforced by a later dominant Israeli discourse that contrasted "worldly and secular Tel Aviv" with an otherworldly and religious Jerusalem—a discourse that was projected backward, from the antagonistic relationship of the two cities in the 1950s and 1960s, to the Mandate and late Ottoman period.

Both traditions have a kernel of truth in them. The contrast with the holy city recalls Ronald Storrs's assessment of Jerusalem as the "parasitic city" in reference to its religious endowments and nonproductive economic base.[50] It also explains the significant exodus of young professionals from Jerusalem to Jaffa (and of Jews to Tel Aviv) in search of a more emancipated lifestyle and employment. However, the analogy is basically false and unsubstantiated. Both Jerusalem and Jaffa developed significant conflict within their urban fabric as modern institutions evolved and the communitarian structure of the city began to give way to ethnic, religious, and class differentiation. Significant disparities emerged between the congested, poor, and "medieval" living conditions of the old city, and the regulated (and sometimes planned) neighborhoods of Talbieh Katamon, Baq'a, Yemin Moshe and Rehavia. The same is true of Jaffa and its rival Zionist city, Tel Aviv. But the contrast is essentially false and misleading, in that it posits two models of urban growth that are in conflict with each other. For the trajectory of urban growth and the modernization schemes implemented during the Khedival and late Ottoman administration of Palestine exhibited a substantial degree of complementarity between the coastal region and the inlands. Jaffa evolved and was seen as the port city of the Jerusalem province, essential for the development of its trade, pilgrimage routes, and linkages with Mediterranean commerce. Jaffa's soap industries and food processing plants were dependent on the agricultural products of the Nablus and Jerusalem mountains, just as the citrus exports depended on substantial investment by Jaffa bankers in the orange estates of Lydda, Ramleh, and Gaza. The existence of a network of economic mutual dependency does not negate the fact that disparity and a process of exploitation existed, but it was a disparity within these cities and not between them.

Similarly, the secular versus religious juxtaposition between Jaffa and Jerusalem (the religious and the profane) is false. In both cities we witness a syncretic religiosity manifested in the public celebrations of popular saints and their shrines (Nebi Musa in Jerusalem, al-Khader in Lydda, and Nebi Rubeen in Jaffa). We also witness the progressive secularization of the public sphere, discussed below, in which religious shrines and religious practices in the urban environment began to give way to public celebrations in which the religious elements became symbolic with little normative influence on the participants' behavior. Finally, we witness the nationalist appropriation of these ceremonials as the conflict between Zionism and the Palestinian national movement became polarized. These three developments occurred in tandem in both Jerusalem and Jaffa and reinforced each other. What helped create this misconceived contrast between the "holy and profane" cities was that the economic base of employment in the holy city was religious endowments and pilgrimage, while the economic base of Jaffa was agricultural capitalism, trade, and banking.

RAGHIB BEY: THE BRIDGING CAREER OF AN OTTOMAN URBAN PLANNER

Raghib Bey al-Nashashibi (1882–1951) provides us with an illustrious example of a local Palestinian notable whose political and professional career as an urban reformer and functionary bridged the late Ottoman period and the Mandate era. Having studied engineering and urban planning at the University of Constantinople (as it was called then), and having graduated in 1908, Nashashibi became the district and city engineer in the municipality of Jerusalem (1912), responsible for public works in the city and its environs. In 1914 he was elected to the Ottoman Parliament as a deputy from Jerusalem.[51] According to his biography by Nasser Eddin Nashashibi, which suffers from a measure of hagiography, Raghib Bey was the epitome of a new breed of political technocrat. As a district engineer in Jerusalem "he was [also] responsible for the rebuilding of Beersheba as an Ottoman frontier town. Later, as mayor of Jerusalem, he excelled as a planner and organizer. ... [M]uch of the layout of modern Jerusalem is due to him, as are many of its best buildings, including the municipality building." Ronald Storrs, the military governor of Jerusalem after the war, said of him: "As a planner he was hardly surpassed by competitors wholly without his other qualification(s)." During the Mandate era, Nashashibi was the longest-serving elected mayor of the city (1920–1934), succeeding Kazim Beyk al-Husseini; and in 1934, he became the leader of the oppositional National Defense Party. Raghib Bey exemplified members of the Palestine landed elites—discussed by Philip Khoury in describing Syria—who rose to prominence in the late Ottoman period and adjusted their professional and political fortunes under the Mandate.[52]

In his position as city engineer and planner he was singularly preoccupied with securing water sources for Jerusalem and its environs. The issue of water was a perennial problem for Jerusalem. Historically, it was related to the survival and physical security of the walled city, since invaders were able to subdue its defenses by prolonged sieges that cut off the city from its access to water resources in Silwan and the Bethlehem region. In the 1870s the municipality was able to repair the dilapidated conduits from Solomon's Pool south of the city to make potable water available. A 1894 report by the engineer Franghieh, head of public works in Palestine, refers to the restoration of the pools and their conduits by Izzat Pasha, governor of Jerusalem, with the use of taxpayers' money and, apparently, forced peasant labor.[53] In 1894, alternative sources of water supply were sought, including Ein Far'a and Ein Fawar, north of the city, as well as al-Arrub, near Hebron.[54] During his tenure as city engineer, Nashashibi began to develop the first two options; he continued to pursue the project during his 1920 mayorship of the city, but it was not completed until 1931.[55]

A major area of contestation during the period of Nashashibi's governance was the question of Jewish representation and the subsequent parameters of town planning. Under the Ottoman administration a distinction was made between Ottoman and non-Ottoman residents of the city, and the question of representation was resolved by confining voting and parliamentary representation to native citizens. With the growth of Jerusalem's migrant Jewish population at a significant rate, the municipal boundaries became a contested arena for the two issues of representation in the city council, as well as for drawing the municipal boundaries to include outlying Jewish communities. In the first case the question was whether to include, or exclude, non-Ottoman Jewish residents as part of the franchise; in the second case, the issue had to do with the delineation of boundaries.[56] In both cases Nashashibi (and before him Mayor Hussein al-Husseini, the last Ottoman mayor) had to walk a thin line between the official policy of accommodation to the civic rights of the Jewish residents, and the two mayors' opposition to the Zionist project.

THE PUBLIC PICNIC AND THE FOOTBALL GAME: READING THE NEW PUBLIC SPHERE IN THREE IMAGES

Aside from religious ceremonials (most notably the Nabi Musa, and Sabt al-Nur), which commenced on the public grounds in front of al-Aqsa and Holy

Sepulcher, respectively, official public ceremonials in Jerusalem were celebrated on the grounds of the Imperial Citadel, adjacent to the Jaffa Gate. A turning point in these public assemblies was the declaration of the 1908 constitution and the "freedom" marches that accompanied it, ending years of bans on spontaneous public assemblies. We have a vivid account of these demonstrations told by Governor Ali Ekrem Bey in a letter to his brother-in-law on July 24, 1908. Immediately after the announcement of the new constitution at the Saraya Building, Ekrem wrote, the Jerusalem crowds "wanted to declare their joy about the restoration of freedom. The day before yesterday there was a gathering in the square before the Imperial Citadel [Kisla-i-Humayun]. The joyful sounds of the city of Jerusalem, which has no equal in the world in terms of the variety of religions, communities, and races which it contains, were lifted to the sky in a thousand different tongues and styles. Speeches were made, hands were shaken. Marches were played. In short, all the appropriate things for honoring freedom were done. Later the people walked around Jerusalem until evening accompanied by the military band. The whole city was decorated by flags. The cries of 'Long Live the Homeland,' 'Long Live Freedom,' 'Long Live the Sultan,' were heard to the furthest corners of the city. . . . [A]mong us were the most prominent members of the 'Society of Union and Progress' in Jerusalem."[57]

Parallel to these manifestations of public assembly, urban Palestine witnessed another transformation of the public sphere outside the arena of ceremonious activities that can be attributed to a perceptible change in lifestyle. It is related, I believe, to the transfer of habitat to the neighborhoods outside the old city, as well as related to the change from leisure activities rooted in religious ritual to new forms of leisure activities. This transformation of a new physical space can be gleaned in three revealing photographs. The images span the beginning and end of World War I and are divided by the succession of two imperial rules—the end of the Ottomans, and the onset of the British colonial administration. These images were taken around 1910, 1912, and 1920, and although the first and last are separated by a decade, they were all captured in areas that are less than half a kilometer apart. Those locations are Bab al-Sahira, just outside Jerusalem's Herod's Gate; Jaffa Gate, near the western approach of the old city; and Sheikh Jarrah neighborhood, by Nablus Road. These three areas, located to the north and west of the walled city, witnessed the earliest modern expansion of middle-class habitat during the city's new extensions in the 1870s.

The first photo, taken around 1910 and attributed to the collection of Wasif Jawhariyyeh, shows a football game taking place next to the Muslim cemetery of Bab al-Sbat (Herod's Gate). The football field is surrounded by the new villas of Bab al-Sahira and Wadi al-Joz, where the city's notables began to move from the crowded city as a result of the enhanced security accruing from municipal innovations in road enlargement, creation of pavements, the placement of street gendarmes and the installation of street lighting.

The second photo, taken around 1920, depicts the "annual spring gathering of Jews, Muslims and Christians near the beginning of Nablus Road."[58] This photograph was taken in Sheikh Jarrah and shows a number of men and women milling leisurely between the olive trees on a clear spring day. The photograph accompanies the Jerusalem memoirs of British governor Keith Roach. In his recollections of his early tenure as commissioner general, Roach, nicknamed the Pasha of Jerusalem, complains of the excessive sectarianism that engulfed his administration of the holy city, and he recalls an earlier period of social concord and social amity at the onset of the onset of British rule. The memoirs are replete with references to sectarian strife, partly fueled by colonial myopia but often due to what he considers the factional nature of Palestinian society.[59] The accompanying "spring picnic" photo seems to identify this earlier period of social amity.

The photographs bracket a critical period in Jerusalem's (and Palestine's) urban transformation, in which the creation of a new secular public sphere emerged as a result of state intervention (planning, public works, electrification, security) and private initiatives (bourgeois housing development and mobility outside the city walls). This context of the period allows us to undertake an interrogative reading of the images in order to discern both the emergence of a new public space in the city and a rupture with the urban scape of the earlier decades. The features common to the two images are the emergence of "secular" space free from religious ritual; the mixing of men of women outside the domain of ceremonial processions; the new hybridity in attire for children and both sexes; and—most notably—the creation of a space for urban "leisure time."

In the first instance we have a sports event, itself a novelty in as far as a viewing public in the city is observing a game played by competing teams in a field designated for a nonreligious event. Virtually all the viewers, considering the direction of their gaze, are intensely involved in following the game. As in the second photograph, the public is decidedly middle class (judging from the attire). The dress code is hybrid (an amalgam of late Ottoman urban and European style) and shows significant variation for both men and women. Men's attire ranges from the traditional *qumbaz* and *laffeh* (head

FIGURE 8. Arrival of the *kasweh* (Ka'bah cover) from Medina, at the Jaffa Gate in Jerusalem in 1914. Matson Collection, Library of Congress.

turban) to European hats and trousers—but most men are wearing the *tar-bush*. A significant number of women in the image are wearing European clothes; few are wearing the traditional *mallayeh*. This is most likely a marker of their bourgeois standing. To appreciate this class factor, consider the third image, which was taken during the same period inside the city in a public square in which a markedly plebian crowd gives a more "representative" picture of the public dress code of the period. The occasion in this case is the arrival of the *kasweh* (the ornate cover of the holy Ka'bah in Mecca) from Hijaz in 1914. The Jerusalem public, and peasants from neighboring villages, are out to greet the mufti of Jerusalem and the Ottoman governor accompanying the *kasweh*. Here, both men and women are predominantly in *qanabeez* and *mallayehs*, with very few European men's hats and women's dresses. The variation in headgear is much richer here than in the previous two images and gives us clear indications about the social background of the men in the crowd. Aside from Ottoman soldiers in their drab uniforms, we note the urban effendis in *tarabeesh*, peasants in *hattas*, Ashkenazi Jews in European hats, and "Arab Jews" in North African fezzes. The *amamah* (religious headgear) is worn by Muslim clergy only. Here, too, we see a significant mixture of men and women in public space.

But there are significant contrasts with the football game image and the Sheikh Jarrah picnic, both of which display the new leisurely space. Here it is no longer possible to identify the dress code with any religious affiliation. In the second image the mixing of genders is freer and more relaxed, indicating the appearance of a new common bourgeois lifestyle. Most women in the second picture have adopted variations of European dresses, while most men are still wearing the *tarbush*. Barely a decade after the football game in 1910, most middle-class men are disheveled.

LEISURELY SPACE AND THE SECULARIZATION OF THE PUBLIC SPHERE

A contemporary ethnographic narrative provides us with an interpretation of shifts discernable in the photographic images discussed here. The football game photograph is attributed to the collection of Wasif Jawhariyyeh, who gathered several thousand images in his youth, from the late Ottoman and early Mandate period, in order to document contemporary events that he witnessed.[60] His memoirs, which accompany these photographs, are essentially a record of the modernity of late Ottoman Jerusalem.[61] Jawhariyyeh provided a profuse description of religious ceremonials for all three communities of the holy city. He also provided an extraordinary narrative of what can be called an urban syncretic tradition—namely, the engagement of celebrations of each community in the festivals of their other neighbors (Jews, Christians, and Muslims). Those narratives can be fruitfully utilized in understanding the residents' creation of a premodern synthetic urban culture of shared ceremonials while maintaining the communitarian boundaries of a separate social and habitat milieu. Within these narratives, however, we can observe the emergence of new practices at the turn of the century that go beyond syncretism, in the direction of shared social activities, that are linked to their religious origins while becoming secular in practice. Four significant public ceremonials illustrate this progression into secular space: the Feast of the Virgin Mary (July 31 to August 15, by the Julian calendar); the Festival of Shim'on the Just (al-Shat'ha al-Yahudiyyah); the Summer Outing of Sa'ed wa Sa'id (daily outing in July and August); the Festival of Job (Shat'hat B'ir Ayyub in April).

Until this period, public assemblies were mainly urban phenomena confined to market transactions (such as the Friday cattle market, *suq al-Jum'a*), to religious ceremonial processions, or to assemblies of military conscripts in times of war.

The Virgin's Picnic and Shim'on the Just

Regarding the old ceremonials, Jawhariyyeh makes the following comment: "They were all based on religious affiliation; without them the city's inhabitants would have died from grief, since they all used to live inside the walls of the old city and would close the doors of the city at sunset. Because the city was an exclusively sacred place, it was cluttered everywhere by convents, churches, mosques, *zawaya,* and synagogues, with no water, or spring, or river of any significance. And no sea or wooded areas. Thus these festivals were the only breathing outlets for the people of Jerusalem."[62] Of these festivals the most significant was that of the Virgin Mary, celebrated between July 31 and August 15. Jerusalem families would camp in tents by the Virgin's tomb on the eastern slopes of the Mount of Olives, near the Kidron Valley. The main focus during the holy fortnight was evening socialization and the exchange of drinks and food. After the termination of the Virgin's fast, the festival began with music and the consumption of alcohol (mainly wine and *araq*). According to Jawhariyyeh, "In the middle of the encampment you feel you are in a wedding celebration. You hear the *shubash* of the men [dance song] followed by the ululation of women. When men finish their *shubash,* the youth start shooting from their pistols and guns in the air, and this continues until midnight. In the morning shopkeepers, workers and clerks go back to their work, and return [to the encampment] in the evening."[63] The height of these celebrations was the Bramul (eve of the Virgin's birthday, on August 15). The Ottoman military orchestra performed for the public all day on the 14th and 15th, while the *mutasarrif* and town notables held a banquet in the main tent. (We have no record of the content of this music, but from Jawhariyyeh's description it was most likely to be Mehter military music). While most of the celebrants were members of the Christian Orthodox community, their composition began to change after around 1900. According to Jawhariyyeh, Muslims and Jews at the period began to join the encampment, which then extended from the mountain's slopes to Herod's Gate. On both sides of the street temporary cafes, bandstands, musical instrument sales booths (mainly selling flutes and *darbakes*), and children's playgrounds were installed.[64] After the Bramul of the Virgin the festivities acquired a more religious character, heightened by thousands of Russian pilgrims, who would pour into the site and engage in nine days of barefoot pilgrimage to the Maqam (shrine) of the Virgin Mary. Those processions were headed by the Orthodox priesthood holding the statue of the Virgin. Jawhariyyeh adds, "This festival was the equivalent of our sea, our public park, our cafes, and our cabarets, all wrapped in one event."[65]

Sephardic and Arab Jews celebrated the festival of Shim'on the Just (Shim'on ha Tsediq, site of al-Shat'ha al-Yahudiyyah) in Sheikh Jarrah neighborhood, near the Abu Jibneh Waqf land. This was celebrated twice a year, when, according to Jawhariyyeh, Christians and Muslims joined the Sephardic community in a public ceremonial, known in Arabic as Shat'hat al-Yahudiyyah (the Jewish Picnic). For the community, it involved an all-day performance of Andalucian music, which had a shared heritage of Muwasha'hat. Several musical ensembles performed; Jawhariyyeh identified the main performers as "Haim the Oud and Kaman [local violin] player, and Zaki al-Halabi, the Muwashah singer and Daff player, and unnamed women Khayakis."[66]

The Perennial Picnic in Sheikh Jarrah

The Picnic of Sa'd and Sa'eed was the only public celebration in Jerusalem devoid of any religious or national or official significance. The event apparently evolved with the expansion of the new neighborhood of Musrara and the improvement of public security in the city. The celebration grounds are identified as the Duzdar property, which abutted the olive groves of Hasan Beyk al-Turjman and was bounded by Nablus Road on the north. Jawhariyyeh identifies this event as a "perennial event" (i.e., year round), in which urban families would bring food and drinks, including alcohol, to relieve themselves from the congestion of the old city.[67]

Beer Ayyub (Job's Well) was a spring located on the eastern slope of the city's Silwan neighborhood. The overflow of the spring became a torrent that rushed toward the Dead Sea in good seasons. Jerusalemites celebrated the end of winter with communal visits to the spring. One unfortunate aspect of the spring's location was its proximity to the Jerusalem sewage pipes, which ran from covered outlets by the city walls eastward toward the village of Silwan. "Imagine dear reader," writes Jawhariyyeh, "men and women, riding their donkeys, and celebrating the spring on both banks of the water flow—

which to Jerusalemites was a virtual grand river. They would take their food in baskets, and encamp by the location. By the time the sewage pipes arrived in Silwan they became uncovered. There we were . . . celebrating and splashing our feet with pristine water [*ma'an zulal*] of B'ir Ayyub, surrounded by a bigger river of sewage and its overwhelming 'perfumes.' I have no doubt that every Jerusalemite who grew up with memories of Ayyub enjoyed the scene and the stench that came to be an essential part of it."[68]

The emergence of this new "secular" space was also being felt in the developments of new urban institutions energetically patronized by the public in Jerusalem and, to various degrees, in other regional townships, such as Jaffa, Nablus, and Haifa. These new spaces included the municipal park, the music hall/theater, the stone-paved boulevard for strolling, and the *odah*—the bachelor apartments used for the entertainment of the sons of the upper class.[69] In Beirut, in Tripoli, and in Jaffa, the planning of the *cornice* along the seashore became emblematic of a new Arab leisure space, which took its inspiration from Alexandria.

Within Palestine and in the Syrian provinces, a new intelligentsia was looking with enchantment at the pace of social change brought about by this modernity, invigorated by the preparations for the Great War. In the first work on the modern history of Palestine in the new century, Khalil Totah and Omar Salih al-Barghouti (the educator and lawyer) discussed the major changes brought about by the technological exigencies of war.[70] Wells were drilled all over the country and linked to pipes that carried potable water to the major urban centers. Railroads linked the north of the country to the southern front; a network of telephones and telegraph lines connected the country to the outside world. Postal services, which originated in consular European services, were now unified and replaced by the Ottoman postal services; roads were expanded to allow military vehicles, as well as automobiles and buses, to be operated. Public hospitals, clinics, and pharmacies were introduced in all provinces to combat malaria, cholera, and typhus epidemics during the war. In those construction projects the "volunteer labor battalions," basically forced labor, were crucial instruments. Recruits were released prisoners; men from villages, chosen by lottery; and men from the ranks of the urban poor.[71] Totah and Barghouti debated these modernities with a sense of anticipation of the great changes to come. Unlike Ottoman administrators like Hasan Bey of Jaffa, and Ekrem Bey, the *mutasarrif* of Jerusalem, who shared their exhilaration, Totah and Barghouti did not feel that the Ottoman state would survive these developments.

FIGURE 9. Aerial view of the Beersheba public square, 1916. Matson Collection, Library of Congress.

BEER AL-SABI': OTTOMAN PLANNING OF JERUSALEM'S IMPERIAL BOUNDARIES

Beersheba (Beer al-Sabi' in Arabic, Bir-I Sebi in Turkish) was conceived during the governorship of Ismael Kemal Bey on the foundation of the residual Bedouin market encampment and was meant to act, together with Amman in Transjordan, as a frontier town to control the nomadic tribes of southern Syria.[72] Built in 1900, it was the first "intentionally planned urban centre" in Palestine.[73] The agenda behind building the new city was, according to Zeynep Celik, "to establish control over the dispersed and unruly Bedouin tribes in the region by providing an official seat that represented the Ottoman state and by beginning to settle the nomadic populations in an orderly pattern."[74] The decision to build the city was made at the highest level in Istanbul, by an imperial edict in 1899, after an initial proposal by the city council of Jerusalem.[75] The state bought land for this purpose and commissioned two Jerusalemite architect/engineers, Sa'id al-Nashashibi and Raghib al-Nashashibi, to design the new town.[76]

Ottoman historian Yasemin Avci lists a number of crucial reasons for building the new town. Chief among them was a strategy to consolidate the border security arrangements in the province of Jerusalem against British expansion from Egypt, and against the British threat to the Sinai Peninsula after 1882. In this strategy, sedentarization of the nomadic population was thought of as a way to consolidate a solid population, which in turn would increase the revenue base for the state.[77] Another purpose was to separate the Negev Bedouins and their administration from the Gaza district and put the region, with Beersheba as the new center of control, under the authority of the Jerusalem governor, accountable directly to Istanbul.[78]

But there were two other important purposes: one was the improvement of collection procedures for a better system of land registration, embedded in the Land Code of 1858, which itself meant increasing the tax base from the Neqab area. Finally, the creation of Beersheba was aimed at creating a base for controlling rebellious tribes in the south.[79] Both Y. Gradus and Nimrod Luz suggest an increase in local dependence on the central government through "increased control over urban space" as the rationale for Ottoman policy in planning the city. Finally, all these sources suggest that, as war preparations loomed, an infrastructure for Ottoman military presence, and the provision of physical and economic resources for the military, were added reasons for planning the city.[80]

By 1903, the appointment of the new governor, the choice of engineers/planners, and the selection of public buildings for the city were determined at the highest levels. The new public buildings included the Saraya (the government building), military and civilian hospitals, police station, public schools, central mosque, and agricultural college.[81] The onset of the war accelerated the growth of Beersheba, since the city was the launching center for the Suez campaign. The city was linked to the Jerusalem-Jaffa road network by rail (1915), an asphalt road between Beersheba and Hebron, and a new bridge over Wadi Saba.[82] The Cemal Pasha Public Park was opened and then used as a site for ceremonial gatherings and for Ottoman administrators to address the people. Two new military airports, at Hafir and Iben (in Sinai), served the city and the region. Aerial photography by the nascent Ottoman air force and the allied German air force provided city surveys, showing the gridlike pattern of the city; a grid may have been deliberately used in planning the city.[83] In 1916 the government built a new printing press, which was mainly used for war mobilization; among other publications it issued was the newspaper *Juul* (Desert), which served the armed forces at the southern front.

Ottoman plans for the city were clarified in a memorandum written by Governor Ekrem Bey highlighting the registration of land as a basis for

FIGURE 10. The gridlike plan of Beersheba, 1916. Public Records Office, Kew Gardens, and Matson Collection, Library of Congress.

increasing revenue. The report, addressed to the High Porte, points out that the Bedouin population had refused to register their land for fear of taxes and conscription, which also meant that the census and state planning would be undermined. Ekrem noted, "There is almost no man in Beersheba who does not own land. Every man has a plot, be it as small as it may be. This way, if every plot is registered, then the name of the man[, too,] will be registered, as well as [of] the wife and children. In short, the registration of the land in Beersheba will be of benefit from all standpoints."[84] Ekrem himself maintained close contact with the city administration, appointing a *kaymakam* (deputy governor) and making the city the center of a new district.[85]

Celik reminds us of the significant schism that separated Ottoman planning in the new era from that of the pre-Tanzimat period. By the first decade of the new century, empire building had taken the region in a new direction. It "was crisscrossed by highways, rail and telegraph lines, and bridges, creating a connected network of settlements and incorporating them into a system."[86] Old cities were rejuvenated, and new ones, like Beersheba, heralded the modernist course of the relationship between Istanbul and the Arab provinces.

In 1906, Ekrem made a major speech to the new citizens of Beersheba in front of the Saraya building, introducing the new Ottoman policy in a mixture of paternalism and admonishment.

Arab Elders and Citizens:

I am your governor, your father, and your brother.
... Your land is vast, and with the most minute effort you may cultivate blessed wheat that will suffice not just for you alone but also for Jerusalem and the entire population of Syria.

I am here to explain to you the new order of Beersheba and, with it, the grants and favors that you have gained.... [A] big school for the study of agriculture is about to be built in Beersheba, because, although you are hardworking people, your lack of knowledge of land cultivation will render your efforts to work your land impossible. In this school, your children will learn sowing and harvesting. There your children will learn to read the holy book ... and the law of sharia and how to worship our Lord. Indeed, I will erect in Beersheba a clock and a tower so you will know the time for prayer and for work.[87]

The speech is a good example of the manner in which the post-Tanzimat Ottoman administration began to engage the population in civic politics while, at the same time, keeping a critical distance from the "masses." Devoid of any traces of the populism that would be associated with the Young Turk activism in Jaffa and Jerusalem in 1908 and 1909, the speech reflected the cautious manner in which authority looked at the new town—as the abode of an unruly and rebellious population that it was seeking to domesticate and sedentarize. One can feel the traces of a new policy of Arab-Turkish brotherhood in the defense of the common realm, tainted with a component of newly ascendant Ottoman imperialism.[88] But the speech also completes the policy of uniting the capital city with the port city and the new frontier capital, Beersheba, by means of roads, telegraph lines, and the newly constructed railway and its grand rail station, soon to be opened with great fanfare by Cemal Pasha and his generals. The clock and the tower—created with the purpose of regulating the tempo of "work, leisure and prayer"—symbolized the new modernity of Palestine and the Ottoman provinces.

CONCLUSION

The "triadic modernity" of Ottoman Palestine refers to the manner in which a regional urban network emerged at the end of the nineteenth century in southern Syria. The network involved a substantial amount of infrastructure (roads, railroads, and telegraphic communication) and created a complimentary system of defensive boundaries for the southern flank of the empire. Within this triad a new regional division of function emerged that had not existed before: the provincial administrative capital (Jerusalem); the port city (Jaffa) linking the province to external trade and pilgrimage; and the frontier garrison town (Beersheba). Within each city the Ottoman authorities, both central and local, created new public domains that echoed a vision of Istanbul modernity, adapted to local conditions. Public ceremonial architecture—such as the *sebils* (decorative public fountains), the government Saraya, telegraph monuments, and clock towers—was a collection of standardized Ottoman edifices that attempted to celebrate the centralized grandeur of the Tanzimat state and integrate the Arab provincial capitals within the Anatolian-Arab homeland. The construction of these features was accelerated and redefined by the onset of World War I. They also functioned as iconic structures for drumming up public support for imperial modernity and its constitutional reforms. During the constitutional revolution of 1908 and the accompanying agitation against the Hamidian dictatorship, these arenas became centers for popular mobilization.

While extensive social differentiation accompanied the growth and expansion of Syrian cities at the turn of the century, the popular conception of a Kulturkampf as involving a conflicted modernity in coastal metropolitan Jaffa and a bureaucratic religious domain in Jerusalem—and another such conflict between Jaffa and Tel Aviv—is erroneous. Rather, considerable ethnic and class conflicts emerged *within* these cities, not between them. These cleavages took the form of peripheral townships of working-class dwellings and itinerant labor surrounding the traditional *qasaba* (the original core area of a town or city) of the city (in the case of Jaffa), and the rapid expansion (after 1910) of planned and spontaneous middle-class habitat in the north and west of Jerusalem. Soon after the Mandate ended, much of the ethnic religious separation in habitat was translated in national struggle over land between Zionism and Palestinian nationalism.

The uses of public space have been discussed here in terms of novel mundane social practices (public-cafe patronization, picnics, street strolling, and attendance at public musical concerts) and of public political mobilization (public announcements, conscription campaigns, demonstrations, and public celebrations of events). At a more subliminal level a new public sphere was created in these cities through the transformation of ceremonials and syncretic religious ritual into popular secular practices. Here the examples of urban *mawasim*, such as Nebi Rubeen in Jaffa, and the processions of the Virgin Mary and Shim'on the Just in Jerusalem, demonstrate a ceremonial syncretism that was secularized by the decline of the ghettoized communitarian habitat in the old city. Ethnographic narratives of spring festivals (held in Beer Ayyub and Sheikh Jarrah) contribute to our understanding of this significant subversion and redefinition of the city public sphere in the years before the war.

I do not mean to suggest that extensive and rigorous urban planning was undertaken by the Ottoman authorities, but merely to indicate that there was a substantial amount of investment in public infrastructure in the period before and during the war, which belies the picture of neglect cultivated by British and French officialdom that is commonly cited in retrospective scholarship about the Mandate period. One area of contention is the absence of any significant attention paid to the creation of "green space" and public gardens in the three cities examined, in comparison to the grand imperial gardens created in Beirut, Aleppo, Damascus, and Izmir during the Hamidian period. There is no question about this neglect, but the context of this absence has to do with the size of the towns (the dominance of medium-sized towns in southern Syria) and with the existence of orchards and vineyards (and, in coastal towns, citriculture *bayarat*) in the heart of the cityscape. These orchards and vineyards also permitted substantial public access to urban agriculture. Until the first decade of the twentieth century, they defined the relationship of urban dwellers to "nature," as part of the urbanscape.

FOUR

———

A "Scientific Expedition" to Gallipoli

THE SYRIAN-PALESTINIAN
INTELLIGENTSIA DIVIDED

IN THE AUTUMN OF 1916, two years after the commencement of the Great War, the Ottoman leadership arranged for an expedition of writers, journalists, and religious scholars from the Syrian provinces to visit the Dardanelles front. The purpose of the expedition, according to the authors of the mission's report, was to examine firsthand the course of military operations in Janaq Qal'a (and Gallipoli), mobilize support for the Ottoman war effort in the Arab provinces of the sultanate, and enhance the bonds of Arab-Turkish solidarity. The last objective was an obvious reference to the rising tide of Arab separatist movements.[1] The main instigator of this expedition was Ahmad Cemal Pasha, governor of Syria and commander of the Fourth Army at the Palestine-Suez front, who carefully organized the group to include "opinion makers" from the region. The timing and composition of the group's mission was chosen to coincide with the recent military triumphs of the Ottoman forces in Gallipoli, and with Cemal's relentless campaign against Hijazi and Syrian dissidents.

The expedition was headed by Sheikh As'ad al-Shuqairi from Akka, mufti of the Fourth Army, a major activist in the CUP, and a supporter of Cemal's campaign against Arab nationalists. A few months earlier, on May 6, 1916, he had achieved notoriety by issuing a number of fatwas (edicts) in support of the execution of scores of Arab nationalists in Beirut, Damascus, and Jerusalem who had been charged with sedition and treason against the state.[2] The expedition produced a three-hundred-page report titled *The Scientific Expedition to the Seat of the Caliphate,* published in Beirut in 1916 and authored by Muhammad Kurd Ali, editor of the Damascene *Al-Muqtabas* (and one of the most prominent rationalist scholars in the Arab East) and Muhammad al-Baqir, editor of *Al-Balagh* in Beirut. A second report, *ArRihla al-Anwariyyeh,* published several months later and dedicated to Enver Pasha, addressed a subsequent mission to Hijaz and Syria to examine the conditions at the southern front and Syrian preparedness for the Suez campaign.

Scientific Expedition highlighted the role of a new class of intellectuals in the struggles over the national identity of the Arab provinces in the waning days of the Ottoman Empire. Although the term *intelligentsia* is an amorphous term, it does provide a useful reference to the emergence of a post-Tanzimat-era category of urban professionals who were embroiled in creating a cultural base for the contested identity of Bilad al-Sham. Those included the graduates of military academies, the graduates of mission schools, public officials in the regional civil service apparatus, and religious functionaries appointed by the state. They included substantial currents within the urban literati of the nineteenth-century Arab Nahda involved in private and public schooling, the theater, and newspaper production—discussed by Ilham Khuri-Makdisi.[3] They also included a sizable number of religious scholars in search of an Islamic modernist resurgence, who were taking their cue from the likes of Rashid Rida, Muhammad Abdo, and Jamal ed-Din al-Afghani. Many of them, but certainly not all, were actively involved in the political struggles over the destiny and direction of the Ottoman state after the constitutional revolutions of 1876 and 1908. During World War I they were substantially involved in the issues of European cultural hegemony, modernizing religious thought, and the use of Arabic (and bilingualism) in state administration and in public schools. They were also involved in land issues and the fate of the peasantry in an increasingly fierce process of land alienation, foreign settlement, and indebtedness, which had begun to shape the contours of the "national question" in greater Syria. Munir Fakhr Eddin refers to a segment of this Nahdawi group as a self-serving arriviste class—speaking for the national spirit of the peasantry and adopting a patronizing attitude toward the masses.[4] Members of this intelligentsia fell on both sides of the debate on the issue of Osmenlilik (Ottoman identity) and the question of decentralization and autonomy of the Arab provinces. A small, but vocal minority began to advocate secession from the sultanate. These debates constitute the background for the formation of the scientific delegation.

The use of the term *scientific* here is intentionally ambiguous. It has a dual meaning, referring to the scholarly character of the religious leadership of the group—Sheikh Shuqairi and his colleagues of Ulama' (sing. Alem, hence men of religious sciences), but also to the new modernist notion of positivist science, in deference to the investigative character of the mission. Most likely the use of *scientific* in the title was also an intentional device to deflect a propagandist impression of its reading.

Although the delegation's mission was to provide a platform for political mobilization and propaganda for the CUP leadership and its war campaign, the report is much more than that. Read almost a century after its publication, the collection of essays by leading members of the provincial intelligentsia sheds significant light on the conditions of Arab-Turkish relations during the war and on the state of internalized Ottoman identity in Syria. It also contains significant observations on Anatolian cities and villages during the war, on industries and crafts, on the conditions of Anatolian peasants compared to Syrian farmers, on military preparedness in the northern front, on the Turkish attitude toward Arabs, and on transport and communication roots. One of the most striking features of this report is the use of language as an instrument of national identity—and the expressed need to teach bilingualism (Arabic and Turkish) simultaneously in Anatolian, Rumi, and Syrian schools as a means of enhancing Ottoman citizenship in the empire. The report clearly suggests that Arabs and Turks are the essential core and the last remaining bulwark of Ottomanism.

A SYRIAN-PALESTINIAN EXPEDITION

The designation of the expedition as Syrian-Palestinian (*al-wafd al-Suri-al-Filastini*) is curious, since the composition of the group included a significant number of Turkish (Eintapi) Iraqi, Lebanese, Aleppine, Transjordanian, and other personalities. Furthermore, the eastern Arab provinces, which included Palestine and Transjordan, were known inclusively as Sem Serif (Bilad al-Sham) in Ottoman discourse. *Filistin* was a nonadministrative designation for the *mutasarriflik* of Jerusalem and its northern expanses. Why, then, the highlighting of the Palestinian component of this group? Filistin was continuously seen, at least after the campaign of Ibrahim Pasha in 1831, as a country *within* Bilad al-Sham, and often as a separate entity: "Palestine is the sister of Syria," proclaimed an Ottoman war report in 1915.[5]

In the case of the Syrian expedition, it seems that Cemal Pasha, the initiator of the group, was intent on promoting a sacred legitimacy, associated with Filistin as the Holy Land, and on buttressing Arab support for the Ottoman war effort and for the Ottoman principle as an alliance of Arabs and Turks. For this he chose Sheikh As'ad al-Shuqairi, the powerful imam from Akka, for its leadership. The group also included a large number of hardcore CUP loyalists, several of whom championed Cemal's campaign against the Syrian-Arab nationalists. Those included Muhammad Rif'ast Effendi Tuffaha, and Abdul Rahman al-Haj from Nablus; Sheikh Ibrahim al-Akki and Abdul Rahman Aziz from Akka, Muhammad Affendi Murad from Haifa; Taher Effendi Abul Suad and Sheikh Ali Rimawi from Jerusalem; and the poet Salim al-Ya'coubi from Jaffa (originally from Lydda).[6] The group was a mixture of educators, imams, and journalists, in addition to two poets.

By reviewing the membership of the expedition, one gets the impression that the Palestinians constituted the religious component of the group (led by Shuqairi), while the Syrians constituted the secular core (led by Kurd Ali). It should be remembered that the southern command of the Ottoman forces was located in Palestine (Gaza and Beersheba), and that the Sinai campaign against Suez was known as the Sina ve Filistin Cephesi (Sinai and Palestine Front). The Palestinian dimension of the group was highlighted through the speeches delivered by members of the expedition, and in responses made by Enver Pasha, Cemal Pasha, the prime minister, the crown prince, and Sultan Muhammad Rashad himself. The region evoked strong associations with both Haram al-Sharif and the southern front, where the conquest of Egypt was being planned.[7] During a discussion of the inspection of military workshops in the capital, the report makes reference to Palestinian and Syrian women involved in voluntary work for the war effort.[8] Once the expedition arrived at the Janaq Qal'a front, the group became known, however, as the Syrian delegation.

Two figures from the Palestinian delegation, Sheikh Ali Rimawi and Salim Abu al-Iqbal al-Ya'coubi, are worth examining here because they represent an Arab intellectual trajectory in which strong Ottomanist identities emerged after the Young Turks came to power. Significantly, both of these figures had substantive Islamic religious training and acquired considerable reputations in the Arab literary renaissance at the beginning of the century. Rimawi and Ya'coubi each demonstrated a dualist identity that may seem a contraction in retrospect—namely, a strong belief in Arabism, centered on the revival of the Arabic language as an articulator of the Arab renaissance, while maintaining an equally strong belief in Ottomanism as a political ideology.

Sheikh Ali Rimawi (1860–1919) came from the throne village of Beit Rima, in the Jerusalem *mutasarriflik,* well known for producing a series of Islamic scholars and Ottoman loyalists—and subsequently Arab nationalists, Nasserites, Ba'thists, and communists. After spending nine years acquiring religious training in al-Azhar (1899–1907), he started his career as a writer in the first journalistic enterprises in Palestine. The Ottoman authorities chose him to produce *Al-Quds al-Sharif,* the official gazette of the government in Palestine (1908–1913). He also became the partner of Jurgi Hanania, who had his own press and published *Al-Quds* (not to be confused with the similarly named *Al-Quds al-Sharif*), which is known as the first successful private newspaper in Palestine (1908–1914).

Al-Quds was an Ottoman-Orthodox paper—while Hanania defended the interests of the Greek Orthodox patriarchate against the rising tide of Arabization, Rimawi addressed issues emanating from Ottoman reform and educational policies.[9] Earlier Rimawi had launched his own paper, *Beit al-Maqdis,* in 1907, which was closed by the Hamidian censor. After the lifting of censorship, he started another Arab-Turkish paper, *Al-Najah,* inspired by the principles of the Ottoman revolution, which was billed as a "political, scientific, literary, and agricultural" weekly newspaper. According to Yehoshua, the real aim of the newspaper was to improve relations between the CUP government and Palestinian Arabs, who became discontented with the "empty and unfulfilled slogans of Ottoman freedoms."[10] He was particularly devoted to promoting the use of the Turkish language in Arab schools. An editorial that appeared in 1910 under his name, and which was titled "Arabic and Turkish Are Sisters: Why Are They Quarreling?" stated, "The next issue of *Al-Najah* will appear in both Arabic and Turkish together, as per the license of this paper. It will aim at serving the joint interests of the Arab and Turkish elements. For these two languages are sisters in the service of the umma and the nation, and we are today in the utmost need of solidarity and union for our common objectives."[11]

But Rimawi was not uncritical of the government. During his tenure at *Al-Najah* and *Al-Quds,* he published several essays attacking government spending on education, corruption in municipal administration, police procedures, the lack of amenities for journalists covering criminal cases, and the lack of accountability in the public budget.[12] Aside from his renown for his journalistic career, Rimawi was known primarily as a poet and teacher of Arabic literature. He taught Arabic and literature in a number of schools, including the German-supported Laeml School, for Sephardic girls. According to Yehoshua, he praised Jewish education in an article published in *HaHerut,* the organ of the Sephardic community in Palestine.[13]

Both the *Scientific Expedition* and its companion *ArRihla al-Anwariyyeh* are replete with the poetry he wrote in homage to the Ottoman armed forces and to Cemal Pasha, as well as to Enver, whose hagiography is unsurpassed, except perhaps by that of Salim al-Ya'coubi.[14] Much of this poetry is written in the style known as *adab al-mada'ih* in Arabic—eulogistic poetry that is highly stylized, effusive, and filled with feigned sentiments constructed spontaneously on the spot for political occasions or in praise of political leaders or patrons. In the case of Rimawi it was also ephemeral. With the defeat of the Ottoman forces in southern Palestine and the entry of the British forces into Jerusalem, he made a quick turnaround in his loyalties. The official *Palestine Gazette* issued by the British forces in the occupied territories published a poem by Rimawi celebrating the "emancipation" ushered in by the new British regime:

> This is the day when our shackles have been broken
> and our feet and thoughts are set free
> Oppression has been replaced with sweet justice
> And after the prolonged darkness our dawn has appeared[15]

It was as if his journalistic prose and his poetry belong to two different ideological domains. Unlike the rest of his comrades, however, Rimawi did not live to see the post-Ottoman era in Palestine. Within months he died from a bout of pneumonia in his village, Beit Rima.

In contrast to Rimawi, Salim al-Ya'coubi maintained his Ottomanist sympathies after the fall of Syria and the entry of the allied forces—a factor attributed by his biographer Sami Shehadeh to his Salafism.[16] Ya'coubi (1881–1946) was born in Lydda and, like Rimawi, was sent to study in al-Azhar for twelve years. During his Cairo years he emerged as a leading poet in greater Syria, for which he was nicknamed Hassan Filasteen after Hassan Ibn Thanbit, the prophet's poet.[17] On his return he was appointed as mufti of Jaffa, where he had moved his residence, and he established a study circle in the Manshiyyeh Mosque.[18] Ya'coubi joined the "scientific expedition" as an advocate of the Islamic Commonwealth (al-Jami'a al-Islamiyyeh). In his earlier poetry he dedicated a volume of poetry to Sultan Abdul Hamid, *Hasanat al-Yara* (1907), but after the 1908 revolution he became a strong advocate of the Young Turks.[19] Together with the mufti of Akka, Sheikh Shuqairi, he also supported Cemal Pasha's campaign against the Arab nationalists during the war. In 1916 he also issued a fatwa against Sherif Hussein for his insurrection against the Ottoman state.[20] During the scientific expedition, he distanced himself from the rhetorical propaganda of other participants, and he appears to have recited a two-line stanza in praise of Enver Pasha.[21] On the second trip to Medina, he composed another ode in support of the Ottoman campaign in Egypt.[22] Among his many comrades in the scientific expedition, Ya'coubi maintained vocal support for the Ottomans—for which he was severely punished by the British. One of his closest companions was Abdul Qadir al-Mudhafar, an associate of Mersinli Cemal Pasha, and they were both exiled to Sidi Bishir in Alexandria.[23] After the war Ya'coubi became close to the house of Ibn Saud and seems to have been influenced by Saudi Wahhabism. As imam of Manshiyyeh Mosque in Jaffa, he continuously agitated against Zionism and for the ideas of the Islamic Commonwealth.[24] He remained a staunch Ottomanist, even when there were no Ottomans.

The expedition's visit to the Ministry of the Navy in the capital was an occasion to sing the praises of Cemal Pasha. The two main speeches dedicated to the "great reformer" were made by the president of the expedition, Sheikh Shuqairi (speaking in Turkish), and by the publisher of *Al-Balagh* (Beirut), the Iraqi writer and publicist Muhammad al-Baqir (in Arabic). On this occasion, Cemal was likened to Sultan Salah-Eddin, who delivered Jerusalem from the crusaders, in the same manner that the speaker expected Cemal to liberate Egypt from the imperialist yoke.

In the report, Cemal's achievements are implicitly compared favorably with those of Tal'at and Enver, the leaders of the CUP, and even with those of the sultan himself. The report reads like a hagiographic account for the future leader of the Ottoman state. Cemal's historical achievements are discussed in terms of his political acumen, his military skills as a commander-strategist, his public works, and especially his educational reforms. In Syria, his administration was able to reform the divisive work of his predecessors. He created a new patriotism, which brought together Turks and Arabs.[25] His weekly councils in Damascus and Jerusalem ensured an open forum for the grievances of the public, without any mediation.[26]

The CUP administration modernized and transformed the face of Syria through Cemal's public works. It established a modern system of railroads that extended the Istanbul Damascus network to Haifa, Jerusalem, Jaffa, Beersheba, and Medina.[27] It paved thousands of roads linking the rural areas to the provincial centers, and the Syrian districts to Anatolia. Cemal's administration established public security in the major cities by introducing electrification and police patrols and by ending brigandage in the countryside.[28]

Together with Muhammad al-Baqir, Kurd Ali was the principal author of the *Scientific Report*. A Damascene scholar from a Kurdish-Circassian family that originated in Sulaymaniyyeh in northern Iraq, Muhammad Kurd Ali (1876–1953) was the publisher of *Al-Muqtabas*, one of the most influential (and most censored) dailies in the Hamidian period. His partner was Shukri al-Asali, who was later hanged by Ahmad Cemal's military tribunals in Alay, in 1916. Kurd Ali was also the founder of the Academy of the Arabic Language in Damascus and the author of the encyclopedic *Khitat al-Sham* (The Syrian Mapping)—a magisterial work on the social geography of Syria. The book was modeled after Ali Mubarak's *Al-Khitat al-Tawfiqiyya*. His authorship of *The Scientific Expedition* may well have been an attempt to establish his credentials as an Ottoman loyalist, since he spent years in exile in Cairo after his newspaper was suspended by the authorities. Years later he claimed that his work on behalf of Cemal Pasha and the expedition were imposed on him by Shuqairi and the Ottoman administration.[29] Nevertheless, his chapters in the report were reflective on the relationship between Arabs and Turks within the Ottoman Commonwealth.

In a biographic essay on the intellectual formation of Kurd Ali, Samir Seikaly traces his transformation through his journalistic career during the crucial years separating the rise of the Young Turks and the war years.[30] In 1906, Kurd Ali moved to Cairo from Damascus, where he published *Al-Muqtabas* as an organ of Islamic reform and regeneration (*al-islah wal tajdid*). He returned to Damascus in 1909, where he relaunched the paper as an instrument through which to propagate an Arabist cultural modernism in the context of Ottoman integration.[31] For Kurd Ali this revivalism involved a struggle for a synthetic culture that would borrow selectively from elements of European civilization, without losing its Islamic core, calling for what he termed a new Arab-Western civilization (*hadara 'arabiyya gharbiyya*).[32]

The relationship of this Arab revivalism to the Ottoman idea was much more problematic in the work of Kurd Ali. In the pre-Tanzimat period, he considered the Ottomans to be a barbaric nation (Tatars) consolidating its power by means of military organizational skills legitimized by the Islamic caliphate. Ottoman decline was rooted in the inability of Eastern societies to face the challenges of Western economic and technological superiority and in the feudal appropriation of peasant land following the Ottoman land reform of 1858. An important root of Ottoman backwardness was also what he considered to be the inadequacy of the Turkish language to adapt to modern civilization. In contrast to Arabic, "Turkish was not a language particular to a universal religion or to general scientific knowledge."[33] In the struggle for a synthetic Western-Arab-Ottoman civilization, Kurd Ali was skilled at distancing himself from imperialist schemes to control the Ottoman Empire, and especially its Arab provinces, while benefiting from European educational and technological advances.[34] He saw the necessity of defending the Ottoman realm, and the caliphate, as a means of preserving the unity of the empire and the Syrian lands. He looked favorably at European and Western educational institutions for the benefits they brought by disseminating a modernist pedagogy, but felt that only by strengthening native Turkish and Arab education could the Ottomans survive. For this reason he attacked the conversion of the teaching curriculum in the Jesuit college (St. Joseph's), and in the Syrian Protestant College, from Arabic to French and English in the 1880s.[35]

During the war years, Kurd Ali's views on language and cultural revivalism seem to have shifted in favor of a new synthetic Ottomanism. His trip to Anatolia and Gallipoli during the war made him rethink his cultural attitudes toward the Turkish ability to modernize Ottoman culture and society under siege conditions. His description of the industrial resourcefulness of Anatolian workers, often smacking of outright propaganda, and of the leadership's military preparedness was meant to dispel prevalent rumors of organizational disarray in the armed forces, as well as the Arab view of "Turkish laziness." While stridently opposed to Turkification as a state policy on the part of the CUP, he now began to favor bilingualism as an instrument of Ottoman unity.

One major purpose of *The Scientific Expedition* was to introduce the Arab reader to conditions in the Anatolian province and to report on the issue of military preparedness at the front. The richest ethnographic material in the report was written by Muhammad Kurd Ali.[36] Although the principle of common citizenship and Ottoman brotherhood permeates the compendium, all of its writers were aware of the Arab-Turkish divide, as well as the ethnic diversity that began to exhibit seditious features during the war. The report lacks reference to the racial tension and antagonism that began to surface, after the Hamidian restoration of 1909, against Arabs in Istanbul and other Anatolian centers—associating Arabs with the ancien régime and the reactionary advisers of the sultan.[37] According to Kurd Ali, "Our Syrian-Palestinian delegation was treated [in Anatolia] to an Ottoman generosity, an

Eastern hospitality, and Islamic brotherhood that attests to the mutual love and loyalty between Turks and Arabs—the two greatest components and intellectually advanced segments of the state."[38] In contrast to the Arabs, the Turk is described as more disciplined and law-abiding.[39] At the military front and in urban employment, the Turk defers to the judgment of his commander and administrator. In war he is willing to die for the cause—a hint, perhaps, about the high degree of desertion reported among Arab soldiers.[40] In matters of religion the Turk is mesmerized by the Arabs. They are seen as the source of blessedness and holiness. "Educated Turks are curious about the current conditions of the Arab lands, while traditional people ask about the past."[41]

Once in Istanbul, the expedition members were impressed by the degree of Europeanness of the capital, manifested in its magisterial buildings, wide and clean boulevards, and extensive transport system. A few years earlier, Kurd Ali notes, visitors would have been struck by the amount of filth and poverty in the capital. But now, in 1916, the lower classes were elevated and enjoyed a degree of prosperity that was trickling to other provinces as well.[42] In the central square one would think that one was in Budapest, Rome, or Marseille. The population was highly diversified in appearance and dress. The transport system linked Asitanah by sea and land to the various parts of the empire and the world. In matters of commerce, Greeks and Armenians controlled the city in the immediate past, but now this edge was disappearing as Turkish merchants and businessmen edged their way. "Those who follow financial affairs now acknowledge that the Turkish family is superior to the Rumi [Greek], Armenian, Arab, and Kurdish families. In general the status of the Turkish man is superior to [that of] his compatriots, and they [Turks] invest heavily in the education of their children. The proximity to Europe [or to European minorities in Ottoman cities] is a major factor in this judgment—thus Izmir is more advanced than Eskisehir, and Bursa is superior to Konya."[43]

The expedition to Janaq Qal'a is frequently described in the report as a form of investigative religious and secular tourism (*siyaha*), by which the authors meant pilgrimage. "Our tour from the lands of Bilad al-Sham to the center of the caliphate, and from there to the war front in Janaq Qal'a, combines the religious and civil features of tourism, for it strengthens the bonds of the religious and patriotic associations and helps us gain two forms of happiness: the worldly and the otherworldly."[44]

The tour helped, in his view, to bring together the two central components of the empire: the Arabs and Turks. It allowed each group to become acquainted with the life of the other. The war conditions also brought the

Ottomans to seek the friendship of the Germanic people, "whose leadership, unlike the government of the imperialist allies, has no ulterior motives over the Ottoman domains."[45] The war accelerated both the process of integration of the Ottoman peoples and their search for a modern status in the new world. It helped the Arabs and the Turks create a new synthesis—"a nation of East and West that combines the old and the new, which defends its domain by force to preserve its special character."[46]

Muhammad Kurd Ali devoted several pages to describing in detail the war industry, which was hastening, in his view, the independence of Anatolia from Western products. Within one or two decades, he anticipated, "we will have caught up with Europe and become an industrial and agricultural modern nation."[47]

THE TURKIFICATION OF THE ARABS AND THE ARABIZATION OF THE TURKS

The question of linguistic autonomy was a major bone of contention in the Arab provinces after the constitutional revolution. A recurrent charge made by Arab nationalists against the new regime concerned the imposition—by the leaders of the CUP and the young Turks—of a policy of Turkification in administrative, legal, and educational institutions. This issue was turned around by members of the scientific expedition, who saw it as a mark of progress and a move toward integration of the various ethnic groups within the context of Ottomanism. Muhammad al-Baqir, Abdul Basit al-Insi, and Hussein al-Habbal observed the increasing tendency among Turks to learn Arabic, and the ease with which Syrians were using Turkish as a language of communication. Kurd Ali was fascinated by the duality of linguistic usage in the border regions. "In Tarsus and Adana I was pleased to note that the majority of inhabitants speak Turkish and Arabic as a matter of daily use," he noted. "The best solution for the social-linguistic problem [*mas'lat al-lisan al-ijtima'iyya*] is for the Arabs to become Turkified, and for the Turks to become Arabized [*an yattatarak al-'arab wa yata'rrab al-atraak*]. . . . [T]his is inevitable, for Arabic is the tongue of Islam and is immersed in the history of Muslims, while Turkish is the language of politics and administration."[48]

Despite the use of the idioms *Turkified* and *Arabized,* it is unlikely that the author meant an ethnic integration of the two communities. Instead he seems to be advocating a policy of bilingualism. This becomes clear from the following paragraph, where he makes "policy recommendations." The ruling party (the CUP), he states, should implement a new educational policy in all Ottoman provinces—teaching Arabs Turkish "after they gain mastery of their own language," while Turks would similarly learn Arabic as a second language.[49] This measure would be a positive contribution to solving the issue of Ottoman ethnicities (*siyasat al-'anasir al-uthmaniyyah*). The expedition members note that in Anatolia there is no Arab problem, and no distinction is made between Arabs and Turks.[50] The assumption here is that this is a Syrian-Arab problem. For that reason Kurd Ali believed that educational leaders in the sultanate should move rapidly in implanting a policy of bilingualism: "for the biggest problem we face is ignorance of the other—our brothers in faith and citizenship."[51]

SYRIAN INTEREST IN THE DEFENSE OF GALLIPOLI

It was left to Sheikh As'ad Shuqairi, the expedition leader, to articulate the Syrian-Palestinian interest in defending the sultanate from collapse in the Dardanelles. He made his plea in a long speech delivered *in Turkish* at the Damascene theater named Cinema Janaq Qal'a, before a large crowd that included Cemal Pasha; Ali Munif Beyk, the governor of Mount Lebanon; Azmi Beyk, the governor of Syria; Midhat Beyk, the governor of Jerusalem, and many other civilian and military commanders. The audience also included Prince Faisal Beyk, the son "of our Lord Hussein bin Ali, the Amir of Mecca." This was on the eve of the latter's declaration of insurrection against the Ottoman leadership.[52]

Shuqairi begins his speech by referring to rumors of the impending collapse of the northern front, and what this collapse would mean to the integrity and safety of the sultanate as a whole. He goes on at length to demonstrate the massive diligence of men and women toiling in fields and factories to support the armed forces, which he and his companions had observed throughout Anatolia, and the invincible army that was mobilized at the Dardanelles in defense of the realm.[53] He mocked the rumors that prevailed in the capital and which indicated that the "Syrian people were indulging in their mundane pleasures and pastimes, impervious to the dangers that threaten the [Allied] conquest of the seat of the sultanate"—an oblique reference to Arab secessionist movements.[54] In organizing the expedition, Cemal Pasha had succeeded by bringing a selected segment of notable Syrians to

Anatolia and the front to dispel these rumors and bring a message of "union-ist" solidarity and support to the mujahideen in Janaq Qal'a. Shuqairi then attacked the "oppositionists" for suggesting that the members of the expedi-tion intended to engage in a slavish kowtowing before the sultan and his government in order to ingratiate themselves before the authorities. He reminded his enemies that their Ottoman loyalty had resulted in the material progress of the Arab provinces—which had resulted in the construction of roads, railroads, schools, and hospitals in Syria and had insured the protec-tion of the Holy Land from foreign conquest. Shuqairi was referring to expansion of the European presence in Palestine, and to the considerable increase in Jewish immigration from eastern Europe. In Jerusalem, he warned, Muslims were threatened with becoming a minority—but with the efforts of the great helmsman, this situation was being reversed. The estab-lishment of Salahiyya College, with hundreds of Muslim scholars undertak-ing advanced studies, was a milestone in this struggle for the Umma and for the consolidation of the Islamic Commonwealth (al-Jami'a al-Islamiyya).[55]

He then engaged his audience in publicly denouncing both the Arab sol-diers who escaped conscription and the citizens who criticized the formation of the *tawabeer al-amaleh* in Syria and Palestine. Those were the "volunteer labor battalions" that conscripted older civilians, as well as Christian and Jews, to dig trenches and perform menial labor at the front.[56] He reminded the audience that the Prophet himself had engaged in digging trenches in the war against Qureish.[57] Shuqairi ended his speech with a salute to Prince Faisal, "son of our lord and master the Sherif Hussein, the Prince of Mecca," who had mobilized his Hijazi forces in the ranks of (Cemal's) Fourth Army in the Egyptian campaign against the English enemies of God. "Salute to the Emir and his son Prince Faisal, and salute to the Hashemites and their allies."[58]

While Turkish-Arab brotherhood was the theme stressed by most speak-ers during the Syrian part of the expedition, once the delegation crossed to Anatolia, the idea of the Islamic association became dominant. This was particularly noticeable at the several receptions held for the Syrians by local branches of the CUP. In Istanbul, Habib Effendi al-Ubaidi, speaking on behalf of the CUP Central Committee (al-Markaz al-Umumi), outlined the evolution of the Islamic policies of the party. In part he was responding to the charges of secularism and abandonment of the caliphate leveled against the party. These were the two main attacks used by the Hashemites in justify-ing their break with the Ottoman leadership in 1916. During the Hamidian sultanate, Ubaidi announced, "The men of the party sought two major objectives: undermining the basis of despotism; and the establishment of the Islamic Commonwealth." The dissemination of these ideas was done in secret, he said, since the enemy had eyes everywhere. With the constitutional revolution, they openly began to attack the Hamidian dictatorship, but the period did not "allow for the assertion of our second objective, the enhancement of the Islamic Union."[59] With the passage of years, it became acceptable to raise the banner of the Islamic Union, and now it was the central feature of the party.[60]

What Ubaidi failed to mention was that the idea of Islamic Union preceded the CUP and was one of the major ideas propagated by Imam Jamal ed-Din al-Afghani and adopted by Abdul Hamid himself. It was later revived by the CUP, by both Cemal Pasha and Enver Pasha in particular, during the war to elicit sympathy from the Islamic communities inside and outside the Ottoman domains. In particular it was being used now to enhance the bonds of solidarity with Istanbul in the Arab provinces, and in soliciting support for the Ottoman war effort from India, Persia, and Indonesia. Cemal Pasha played a principal role in propagating the Islamic bond during the war as an instrument of mobilization. He did this through his educational work in Salahiyya College in Damascus and Jerusalem, but also in propaganda against the British and the use of Muslim troops from Egypt and India in the Allied campaign. He established the newspaper *Al-Sharq* (with a government subsidy) in Damascus, edited by Kurd Ali and Shakib Arsalan to propagate the idea of Islamic unity among the Ottomans.[61] According to Cicek, the main purpose of the paper was to counter the influence of the Arabist movement in Syria, which dominated the local press. But its content was to show the common fate of Ottoman Muslims in the imperialist campaign. It did this by emphasizing the need to rescue Egypt from the British yoke.[62] But it also had cultural content, showing the common interests of all Syrian Arabs in supporting the Ottoman state in its "civilizational mission" to restore the glorious past of Muslims and uplift the material condition of Syrian youth through education and scientific development.[63] After the rebellion of Sherif Hussein it devoted a significant portion of its coverage to the "treason of the Hashemites."[64] It is clear, however, that one of the major problems of *Al-Sharq*, as a propaganda tool for the CUP, was to maintain Arab support for the idea of Ottomanism while pursuing the repressive campaign against the Arab nationalists.

A few months after the appearance of *The Scientific Expedition,* Muhammad Kurd Ali authored a companion volume on the exploration of Hijaz titled *The Anwarite Expedition to the Hijazi and Syrian Lands.*[65] As the title indicates, this expedition report was mainly a tribute to Anwar, who hardly appears in the earlier report. But unlike the Gallipoli report, this tribute is lacking in an investigative analytical dimension, and it appears mainly to be publicity and a hagiographic salute to Enver. Years later Kurd Ali was to regret his association with this report and referred to it, in *Irshad al-Albab,* as "a superficial piece of propaganda."[66] This second report comprises a detailed description of Enver's tour of Lebanon, Syria, Palestine, Sinai, and Hijaz in January 1916 (Kanun Thani, 1331 Rumi calendar), accompanied in part by Ahmad Cemal, Mersinli Cemal Pasha (Eighth Army), and Hasan Beyk al-Jabi, the governor of Jaffa.

The report is a long tribute to Enver, as if it were giving him "equal time," to compensate for his neglect and marginalization in *The Scientific Expedition.* In Kurd Ali's report he is identified as the "Rising Star of the Ottomans" and the "Hero of All Ottomans."[67] In the special ceremony held in Damascus at the beginning of the second expedition, he is described by Abdi Tawfiq Beyk as the "Defender of Eternal Ottomanism" (al-Uthmaniyya al-Abadiyyah al-Mu'athama). The term used by Tawfiq Beyk was *Osmenlilik* in Turkish, and *al-Uthmaniyya* in Arabic. Curiously this is one of the few cases in the two reports in which the term is used in reference to the unionist ideology. Elsewhere the stress was on the Islamic affinity of the remaining ethnicities in the Ottoman lands.

Enver is credited here with four major achievements, which now seem to surpass the feats of Cemal Pasha:

- He was the main leader of the Inqilab Uthmani (i.e., the constitutional revolution of 1908).[68]
- He led the march on the capital on March 13, 1909, to smash the counter-revolutionary restoration of Abdul Hamid (*ikhmad shararat al-Raj'a alistibdadiyya*) and to remove the sultan from power.[69]
- He led the alliance of the Sanusi tribes in North Africa to liberate Libya from the Italian yoke.[70]

- As minister of war he led the defense against the British and European invasion of the Dardanelles and defeated the attackers during the onslaught on Gallipoli (no mention is made here of Mustafa Kemal).[71]

Compared to Enver Pasha, Cemal Pasha becomes (once the superlatives are tuned down) merely the "great reformer" and the future liberator of Egypt from the British yoke—an act that, of course, was soon to become a illusory dream.

THE PALESTINIAN EPISODE: THE CONQUEROR VERSUS THE REFORMER

In contrast to *The Scientific Expedition,* which contains detailed descriptions of the Anatolian provinces and the state of military preparedness in the Dardanelles, *The Anwarite Expedition* aims at showing popular support for the Ottoman leadership in Syria, in Palestine, and to lesser extent—despite the title—in Hijaz. The Palestine episode of Enver's trip is particularly extensive. Filistin, significantly, is referred to as the "sister of Syria," rather than as an extension of Syria.[72] Although Jaffa was not part of the itinerary, both Enver and Cemal made a detour at the beginning of their excursion at the insistence of the governor, Hasan Beyk al-Jabi. It transpired that Jabi wanted the CUP leadership to celebrate the new plan for what had emerged as Palestine's fastest-growing city—an urban facade for Ottoman-Arab modernity. Enver was asked to officially open the newly constructed Cemal Pasha Boulevard, described as the broadest street in greater Syria (thirty meters in width). And the parade involved tens of thousands of cheering celebrants, who marched past Ramleh Station, the Saraya Building, and the clock square and then joined in the public opening of Hasan Beyk's mosque in Manshiyyeh, at the border of Tel Aviv.[73] In the report, the mosque is identified as the New Jabi Mosque. At the outskirts of Jaffa the procession was halted by the city's famous orange groves, so that Cemal and Enver could pick and eat oranges from the tree.[74]

"Here is Palestine whose Arabdom was blessed by your presence / You, the most enlightened of creatures [*anwar en-nas*], Turks and Arabs."[75] Significantly in these salutations, Anwar is greeted as the *military* leader and Cemal as the great *reformer*.[76] The expedition's encampment in Beer al-Sabi' (Beersheba) and the visit to the military installations in northern Sinai (*tih sahrasi,* in Turkish) was a highlight of the trip. The city had become the pride of modern Ottoman planning, for a garrison town. The Hijazi railroad and asphalt roads linking the south of Palestine to the rest of Syria was seen as major engineering feats. "It is now possible to traverse the road between Bir Hassana and Beersheba in four hours. An engineering task which was concluded efficiently by the Fourth Army in record time, which rendered these desert roads that, until recently, could not be used by the most basic traffic."[77] The army corps of engineers is credited for installing artesian wells, railroads, military training facilities, and military airports (at Hafir and Iben)—"Our army is now fully prepared to march on Egypt and liberate it from the claws of the [British] occupier."[78] In Beersheba the tribal contingents from Hijaz arrived to greet the commanders and performed a ceremony of dance and singing "in their Bedouin dialects."[79]

The popular assembly that received the Ottoman expedition at the Medina station repeated, in organizational form, the demonstrations of support that had taken place in Damascus, Beirut, Jaffa, Jerusalem, and Beersheba. In Medina, however, the event took an archaic, almost medieval, form, perhaps because of the sacredness of the place and the attempt to confer religious legitimacy to the event. Here is how the *Al-Muqtabas* correspondent in Damascus described it:

> The assemblage moved forward in unison. The city's deputy governor, Jamal Beyk, and Bashir Beyk, the police commander, had mobilized the commoners and notables of the city, preceded by the sherifian *aghas* with their armed slaves and drums, followed by the permanent imams of the Prophet's *haram* and their instruments [?], then the main mujahideens of the *haram* wearing their uniforms and chanting *al-hamziyya* and *barada* chants—with their chants echoing in the whole city. Next marched the sherifian notables and the city's potentates, followed by the followers of the various Sufi orders [*mashayikh al-turuq*], led by Sayyid Hamza al-Rifa'i, head of the Rifa'iyya order. After those came the students of the *i'dadi* schools led by Hamza Effendi Wasfi and the teachers of the city holding the banners of victory adorned by silk frames. All were chanting patriotic stanzas in Arabic and Turkish.[80]

The visit to Medina was the final and pivotal event of the expedition. It was, significantly, portrayed as a rallying event in which the collective Syrian and Palestinian leadership came to pay homage to Enver Pasha and Cemal Pasha in their Egyptian campaign. After the speeches were made by the Hijazi notables the rally was addressed by the muftis of Beirut, Damascus, and Jerusalem, by Kamel Effendi al-Hussieni, and by the *naqib* of Damascus *ashraf,* Adib Taqqi al-Din, and the ubiquitous Sheikh As'ad al-Shuqairi.[81] The audience included a gathering of tribal members of the Hijazi tribes, as well as hundreds of pilgrims from India, Algeria, and Morocco. Shuqairi made a major speech about the requirement of jihad as binding on all Muslims in support of the campaign. Just before embarking on their return to Damascus, the two commanders appeared on the platform of the train station holding hands with "our popular prince" Emir Faisal, bidding farewell to the visitors.[82] Only the sherif of Mecca, King Hussein, was notable in his absence.[83]

The Medina event was clearly choreographed as a major event of mobilization and solidarity for the Suez campaign. Its main themes were tribal support, Islamic unity, and Arab-Turkish brotherhood in the crucible of the Ottoman war effort. The slogans of the constitutional revolution, of citizenship, and of Osmenlilik, had faded away.

The events described took place in the shadow of secret negotiations between the Allies and the Hijazi leadership, still nominally subject to Ottoman command. The expedition took place during one month, February 13 to March 15, 1916 (30 Kanunsani, 1331 Rumi calendar). Sherif Hussein declared his insurrection against the Ottoman state on June 27, 1916 (25 Sah'ban, 1334 hijri calendar). Less than three months separated the events of these rallies from the final rupture between Istanbul and Medina. The sherif of Mecca announced two reasons for the insurrection: the undermining of the precepts of the Islamic Khilafah by the secular command of the CUP, and the wave of repression against the Arab nationalists undertaken by the CUP leadership.[84] But it was clear from the announcement that it was the gallows of Beirut, Damascus, and Jerusalem that presented the decisive moment.

CONCLUSION: THE SYRIAN AND HIJAZI EXPEDITIONS IN RETROSPECT

The two expeditions, the first to Anatolia and Gallipoli, and the second to Syria, Palestine, and Hijaz, took place at a crucial junction of the Great War and the rising tension between the sultanate and the CUP leadership and secessionist groups in the Arab provinces. The earlier successes in defeating the British forces in Suez and Kut al-Amara, and the thwarting of the Anzac-British forces in Gallipoli, helped in creating the image of Ottoman resilience in the eyes of the Arabs. The first expedition succeeded in mobilizing some of the leading Islamic leaders, intellectuals, and journalists in the Arab East (Baqir, Kurd Ali, Shuqairi, Rimawi) to defend the Ottoman administration and Cemal's Pasha administration against their critics. These figures came from all the Arab districts of the empire, including a large and influential Palestinian contingent. They did this in the name of Osmenlilik (Ottomanism), the Islamic realm, common Ottoman citizenship, and Ottoman modernity and its material achievements in promoting development in Syria. But they mainly acted in defense of the Islamic Commonwealth—al-Jami'a al-Islamiyyeh.

These were obviously contradictory features of Ottoman claims for Arab loyalty, and the strain shows in the various contributions of the participants., which included speeches, poetry, and reports. Reports by some of the leading journalists and writers in greater Syria contained valuable observations about progress and military preparedness in the Anatolian regions. Despite the defensive tone of these reports, they should not be seen as apologias for a collapsing regime. They demonstrate that the Ottoman sultanate and CUP government had substantial support among the Arab population in the early war years. This support was independently monitored by British and French intelligence, which tracked popular Arab sentiment toward the Ottomans during the war.[85]

In undertaking a defense of the Ottoman leadership against Arab separatism, the authors of *The Scientific Expedition* outlined in detail the major developments undertaken by the government and by Cemal Pasha's administration in modernizing the school system and building hospitals and colleges. Particular attention is paid to Cemal's extension of the Hijazi railroad and telegraph lines linking central and southern Palestine to Syria, Anatolia, and Hijaz.

There is considerable focus in the expedition reports on the Hijazi attitude toward the sultanate. Prince Faisal and the Hashemites appear in the first expedition report as important supporters of the war effort. Their involvement was crucial for the CUP government because of their symbolic status as guardians of the holy places and as legitimizing loyalists of the Ottoman caliphate. Emir Faisal, who was on a solidarity mission in Damascus during this period, and Sherif Hussein are presented as partners in the Ottoman campaign against the British. In the second expedition report, the Hijazis appear to be more cautious. The Hashemites were described as vacillating in their support. Cemal's ruthless campaign against Syrian nationalists, including the execution of leading patriots in Beirut, Damascus, and Jerusalem, had alienated an increasing number of Ottoman loyalists in the CUP government. And even though, by the time these speeches were made, the Hashemites had already decided to secede from the Ottoman regime, the degree of their "betrayal" was not yet clear to Istanbul.

A third issue, which permeates the expedition reports, concerns the question of Turkification. Muhammad Kurd Ali presented the most sophisticated case for Arab support of an Ottoman commonwealth based on Turkish-Arab unity. He also made the most succinct plea for bilingualism as an instrument of integration in the empire. His contribution to the discourse of unity in the expedition contrasts sharply with his apologetic propaganda on behalf of Enver Pasha in *The Anwarite Expedition to the Hijazi and Syrian Lands (ArRihla al-Anwariyyeh)*. Turkification here appears as a linguistic issue—a matter of articulating a common Ottoman identity—and a question of political integration of the Arab provinces within the empire.

Contrary to subsequent accusations by Syrian and Arab nationalists, Turkification is not posited as a forceful imposition against Arab culture. On the contrary, the report proposes a parallel process of Ottoman integration through what it terms "Arab Turkification" and "Turkish Arabization," through the introduction of general curriculum reform in the Syrian and Anatolian schooling systems. The framing of these assimilatory schemes was the common Islamic bond within al-Jami'a al-Islamiyyeh. But these schemes are proposed here, mainly by Muhammad Kurd Ali and As'ad Shuqairi, as general guidelines for preserving the union against centrifugal currents, and no attempt is made to explain how they would be implemented or what their social ramifications would be. And no mention is made of the status of other ethnic or religious groups in the Ottoman domain, other than a single reference to Kurds, Armenians, Greeks (Rumis), and Bulgarians as constituent groups of the Ottoman domain.[86] Aside from Lebanon, where the delegates visited mission schools and speeches were made by local orators in favor of Osmenlilik, Christian Arabs were absent from both delegations, and the campaign against the Armenians was not even hinted at.

It was emblematic of the two reports that their chief author, Muhammad Kurd Ali, was a cosmopolitan man of Circassian-Kurdish descent, which may have been a factor in his strident adoption of Ottomanism and bilingualism as an instrument of national integration. His descent may have been a factor also in his sudden reversal of his national identity in favor of Syrian Arab nationalism. He was soon to regret his authorship of the report, which cast a dark shadow on his integrity as a scholar during the Faisali period in

Damascus. We note here the retreat in the discourse on Osmenlilik (Ottomanism, or common Ottoman identity), and the rise in the use of references to Islam, Islamic unity, and the unity of the Islamic bond in the sultanate. Not surprisingly, this discourse on the Islamic core of Ottomanism was also adopted by several Christian intellectuals in Mount Lebanon and Palestine (Najib Nassar, Suleiman al-Bustani, and others).[87] In Palestine, Zionism was a factor in dividing the local intelligentsia in their attitude toward the CUP leadership. In Nablus and Jaffa, for example, there was considerable support for the Hamidan restoration, deriving from a fear that the Young Turks were in favor of Jewish settlement, while the sultan was stridently opposed to land sale and colonization.[88]

FIVE

Two Faces of Palestinian Orthodoxy

HELLENISM, ARABNESS, AND OSMENLILIK

ISSA AL-ISSA, THE FOUNDER, PUBLISHER, and editor of *Filastin* (1911–1948), and Yusif al-Hakim, the Ottoman judge and district attorney from Latakiyya, present us with two faces of Arab Christian Orthodoxy in the late Ottoman period. Their lives intersected in two crucial years. In Jaffa, in 1910–1911), Issa al-Issa founded *Filastin,* the most combative and successful newspaper in modern Palestinian history, while Hakim was appointed district attorney for the burgeoning port city of Palestine. Both intellectuals later became significant members of the Faisali movement in 1919–1920, after the collapse of the Ottoman forces—Issa as private secretary to Prince (later King) Faisal, and Hakim as the minister of public works in the first Arab Syrian government.

Yet their Orthodox affiliation, and the struggle for the Arabization of the church against Greek clerical hegemony, led them to take opposite positions on the Ottoman regime and the constitutional revolution of 1908. Hakim was a firm believer in Ottomanism and in constitutional reform. He was involved in the struggle against the Hamidian despotism and became an enthusiastic supporter of the CUP and the Young Turks. Issa, on the other hand, had little hope for Arab-Turkish unity, was skeptical about the freedoms promised by the second constitution, and believed the CUP was basically a Turkish nationalist party with strong Zionist sympathies.[1] Together with Dr. Shibly Shamyyil and Haqqi al-Adhm—his friends while working in Egypt—he supported the Ottoman Decentralization Party, and later the National Defense Party, against the leadership of Haj Amin al-Husseini in Palestine.[2] In its initial years, however, *Filastin* had supported the CUP under the influence of Issa's cousin and second editor, Yusif al-Issa—whose Arabism was much more deeply rooted than his.

A contrast of the trajectories of the two lives, Issa's and Hakim's, sheds new light on the nature of Arab-Ottoman identity in the waning years of the empire, as well as on the formative years of Arab nationalist ideology.

OSMENLILIK AND THE FLUID YEARS

The period between the declaration of the 1908 constitution and the commencement of World War I (between *hurriet* and *seferberlik* in popular consciousness) was a period of fluidity in the formation and recasting of local identities in Bilad al-Sham. It marked the relative consolidation of an Ottoman imperial identity (Osmenlilik) within the ranks of the Syrian literary elites, played against a heightened contestation by Syrian, Arabist, and Arab nationalist movements. Throughout the latter part of the nineteenth century these movements had emerged as literary and political trends within an overarching Ottomanist identity. In a few cases, such as in the work of Butrus and Ibrahim al-Bustani, and of the group who published the *Nafir Suriyya* series of circulars, the Syrian-Arabist identity was seen as both a building block and a primary condition for the successful fruition of the Ottoman principle.[3] Syrian Arabism was seen as the agency for transcending sectarian conflicts in Mount Lebanon in particular, and in Bilad al-Sham in general; whereas an Osmenlilik consciousness was seen as the juridical guarantor of a new form of citizenship in the provinces, binding Anatolia to the countries of Hijaz, Iraq, and Syria.[4]

But the degree to which advocates of an Osmenlilik identity had gained a foothold in the provinces was never even or homologous. The earlier manifestations of Pax Ottomanica, according to Sukru Hanioglu, were the marginal ethnic and religious populations on the periphery of the empire's reaches—those who sought an ideology that superseded the *millet* system and allowed them to benefit from the new forms of citizenship.[5] The lack of a centralized and standardized system of primary education, coupled with widespread literacy, prevented, in the initial period, the desired diffusion of Ottomanist loyalties.[6] When the centralization of the educational and administrative systems did occur under the CUP administration, it was seen, and felt, as measures of Turkification.[7]

Hanioglu suggests that the solidity of the Ottoman principle was already weakened in Bulgaria, Serbia, and the remaining Greek areas (as well as in the Mediterranean islands where populations were mixed) as a result of the ascendency of Balkan nationalist separatist movements and the hegemony of the Greek Orthodox Church and its ability to convert communal religious consciousness into a nationalist identity. "Paradoxically," Hanioglu writes about the new Ottomanist identity, "the very reforms designed to create a coherent society unified by a common ideology, and a more centralized polity founded on universal, standardized laws, had the effect of exposing and deepening the fissures within the Ottoman state and society. Local resistance to the center's determined attempts to penetrate the periphery accentuated the fragmentation of identity throughout the empire. The unprecedented attempts to unify multiple religious, ethnic and regional groups only served to strengthen their splintered identities in defiance of central policies."[8]

This reaction to the centralizing thrust of late Ottomanism is relevant to an understanding of Balkan and Armenian nationalism but does not apply in the same manner to the Arab provinces (or to Kurdish nationalism). Here, Muslim elites integrated into the body of regional administrations were more secure in their status, partly because of their Islamic affiliation, and partly because of Istanbul's historical relationship to the Hijaz and Syria. Among Arab Christians, the dynamism defining their attitude to the state, in the manner analyzed by Butrus al-Bustani and the *Nafir Surya* group, was unique among the Rumi subjects. Orthodox Christians of the East had their own "national adversary," not in the Turkish Other, but in the hegemony of Greek ecclesiastical hierarchy. Eastern Arab Orthodoxy, in its rebellion against the Greeks, was also divided between those who (like Hakim) sought a common Ottoman cause with their Muslim compatriots (against European intrusions), and those who (like Issa) identified with Arab nationalism against pan-Turkic nationalism. There was no equivalent conflict in the Balkan provinces of the Ottoman state. In Palestine (as well as in Lebanon, for different reasons) the impact of the press, and its substantial diffusion in the 1908–1914 period, produced a much more substantial adherence to Ottomanism than in the Balkan, Bosnian, and Serbian hinterlands—is was obvious from the debates that raged before the war in the peripheral provinces.[9] An important feature of this debate is the extent to which the nineteenth-century Arab Nahda was pioneered by Mashriqi Arab Christians and Egyptians, as is the claim that, at least in its later stages, Osmenlilik ideology was reduced to a movement espoused mainly by Eastern Christians seeking an outlet from an increasingly Islamized Ottoman identity.[10]

Recent studies on religion and society in the Middle East have helped us transcend the earlier scholarship about sectarianism and the evolving

consciousness of the Arab Christians in relationship to the cultural renaissance (Nahda) of the nineteenth century, to Ottomanism, and to the origins
of Arab nationalism. These contributions, as Akram Khater and others have
argued, have liberated sectarian analysis from the *millet* paradigm, which saw
Arab Christians as either members of a perennial *dhimmis* or protégés of the
Western powers.[11] Ilham Khuri-Makdisi, in her study of nineteenth-century
intellectual currents in Beirut, Cairo, and Alexandria, demonstrated the
qualitative contributions of the Syrian Christian intelligentsia to the radical
features of the Nahda without resorting to resurrecting the pitfalls of the
Antonious thesis about the vanguardist role of the Christians as precursors
of a secular modernity.[12] And Ussama Makdisi has demonstrated that the
origin of sectarianism, particularly in Mount Lebanon, lies in a nativist
mobilization of a complex system of imperial intervention and Ottoman
reform, rather than an Islamic response to Western modernity.[13] In the littoral Syrian communities, as well as in Palestine, responses to sectarian interventions were quite different within the Christian communities, eliciting
clearer identifications with Ottoman, and later Arab, nationalist affinities.
In all of these studies we note that religious affiliation of the Arab intelligentsia did matter in *the formation of the new emerging identities,* but not necessarily along communitarian or sectarian lines.

The involvement of both Yusif al-Hakim and Issa al-Issa in the Christian
Arab Orthodox movement, and its renaissance at the turn of the twentieth
century, played a pivotal role in the formation of their Ottomanist and Arab
nationalist consciousness. Neither Hakim nor Issa, as was the case with tens
of thousands of their coreligionists, lived in "Christian neighborhoods" of
Syrian and Palestinian townships. And neither believed in the idea of a "protected community," since they both saw the capitulation and its association
with the *dhimmi* principle as a colonial enterprise, and welcomed the abolition of the *himaya* protocols that gave European citizens and their native
Christian and Jewish protégés extraterritorial privileges.[14]

The urban setting of their encounter was equally relevant to the creation
of nationalist consciousness and oppositional movements. By the turn of the
century, Jaffa was one of the fastest-growing port cities of the eastern
Mediterranean, with a sizable bourgeoisie and significant trade with Egypt
and Europe. In 1911, when Hakim started his career in Jaffa as public prosecutor, the same year that saw the launching of *Filastin,* the city had a population of seventy thousand people holding Ottoman citizenship, and a large
community of foreign residents involved in the city's trade.[15] Hakim noted

that the economic significance of the city was not properly acknowledged by the administrative powers conferred on it by the state.

> [Jaffa,] it should be remembered[,] is the only port for Jerusalem, linking it with a rail connection, [but] its trade connects the whole country together. The famous Jaffa oranges export two million boxes of citrus to Great Britain alone. It has extensive economic relations with the Nablus district, which belongs administratively to the Wilayat of Beirut. By right Jaffa should have been the capital of the Province [Mutasariffiyah], but since the governor of Jerusalem is responsible directly to Ministry of Interior in Istanbul [it was denied this privilege]. Nevertheless the Ottoman Government was cognizant of Jaffa's importance. It created a special court in the city to address commercial matters, in addition to an independent Appellate Court. Jaffa also houses several higher administrative departments, and is the HQ of a brigade [liwa] from the regular army.[16]

Both Issa and Hakim, who were proud members of the Rumi (Orthodox) Christian community, did not see themselves as members of a minority group in the Ottoman Empire. This negation of a minoritarian status was a product of their identification with the movement to create Ottoman citizenship out of the 'ra'yaa' (subject) principle that was transformed in two successive stages of the constitutional revolution of 1876 and 1908. But it ran deeper than that. Both men saw Christian Orthodoxy as part of an indigenous cultural tradition rooted in the Byzantine past of the Arab East, contradistinguished from Catholic Christianity associated with Rome and the crusades, and from nineteenth-century Protestantism.[17] The latter traditions, despite their substantial following among Christians of the East, were nevertheless religions of conversion and were contaminated in the minds of our authors, by the traditions of Ottoman capitulations to the Italian and European states. Orthodoxy, on the other hand, was the religion of Antioch, Jerusalem, and Constantinople (and of Alexandria, to a lesser extent)—seats of the Eastern patriarchates. Their Christianity was the religion of the Arab, Syrian, and Coptic masses, with important resonance for Islam and Muslim culture. It was the religion of the Ghassanids and the bishops of Yemen, framing and preceding the Islamic message. An implicit belief, shared by both Issa and Hakim, was that the majority Islamic culture was a derivative of Byzantine and Nestorian Christianity.[18] This belief was at the heart of their rejection of their minoritarian status.

Issa's and Hakim's Orthodoxy was defined in secular terms in relationship to their Ottoman (Hakim's) and Arabist (Issa's) self-conceptions. It was articulated as an indigenous marker of their urban identity in the struggle to Arabize the church and free it from control by the Greek hierarchy. At stake was not only the "national" question involving the language of the liturgy and prayer, which were of symbolic significance to the laity, but also the fate of the community schools, the language of instruction, and the disposition of church property and its revenue. In the case of Palestine, this property issue became pivotal also in relationship to Zionist land purchases and the ability of the Orthodox community to control its vast resources.

Hakim's loyalist Ottomanism and Issa's Arabism and eventual hostility to Young Turks were in large part the product of their protracted struggle to Arabize the Orthodox Church, which led them in two different directions. The success of this process in Syria (Antioch, Latakiyya, and Damascus) facilitated Hakim's integration in the bureaucracy; the failure of the process in Palestine contributed significantly to Issa's alienation from the regime and his involvement with the autonomy-seeking, and later secessionist, Decentralization Party.

AN ORTHODOX CHILDHOOD

Yusif al-Hakim was born in 1879 in Latakiyya. His father, Ya'coub al-Hakim, was the grandson of Spiridon al-Hakim [the doctor], the only physician in the city, hence his name, which remained a marker for three generations of physicians. Both Yusif and his brother Amin studied Arabic and mathematics with the local Orthodox priest, Father Mikhael, and his son Jiryis, at the age of four and five, but both soon moved on to study in the Latakiyya Anglican school headed by Master Ya'coub Jraidini.[19] Once Yusif finished his primary education his father chose to place him in the public (Ottoman) intermediate school (al-Maktab al-I'dadi), where all schooling was in Turkish, in contrast to the Arabic instruction in the Orthodox school. It seems that choice owed to the preference given in public employment to graduates of the I'dadi school.[20] This elicited protest by the Orthodox Bishop of Latakiyya, who complained that state schools tend to stress Muslim religious education and ignore the needs of the Christian community.[21]

Hakim's early education had a strong grounding in Quranic studies and Arabic grammar. We see this pattern in the early education of other Syrian and Palestinian Orthodox families, including that of Wasif Jawhariyyeh, Khalil Sakakini, and Issa al-Issa.[22] Upon graduation, Hakim was hired to teach Turkish in the local Orthodox church, with a salary of two hundred qirsh monthly, a post subsidized by the Ottoman authorities. This put him in a line of successive jobs working for the state, beginning with the job of court recorder in Latakiyya (1901), followed by that of deputy district prosecutor (1904) and a successions of judgeships in Jerusalem, Jaffa, and Tripoli (1905–1912). In 1913 he became the head of the "Turkish Bureau" (al Qalam al-Turki) in the autonomous government of Mount Lebanon, and deputy to the Armenian Ottoman governor Ohanis Pasha Qumnian.[23] During World War I he served as *qa'immaqam* in the districts of Kura and Batroun.

While he worked in the office of the district prosecutor, the struggle for the Arabization of the Orthodox Church raged in Syria. Although the conflict took the form of an Arab-Greek ethnolinguistic conflict (over the appointment of bishops, and the language of the church), it was in fact a struggle between the intelligentsia of the Orthodox community—or at least a segment of it who saw themselves as representing the Arab laity—and the Greek hierarchy over the disposition of church funds, control over the church's landed endowments, and the administration of the schooling system.

These issues first surfaced over the appointment of a new patriarch in Antioch in 1901, after the transfer of the old patriarch, Geranimus, to Jerusalem, with the Syrian communities in Damascus, Antioch, and Latakiyya supporting the installation of the Arab bishop Milatious Dumani, against his Greek opponent. The conflict, according to Hakim, involved members of the "new guard"—composing a majority of the Arab laity and Arab bishops and a substantial number of monks—against the "traditionalists," who insisted on the age-old custom of preserving the post for the Greeks. Those, according to Hakim, were supported by "the High Porte, the governors of Damascus, Aleppo, Beirut, and the Patriarchs of Istanbul, Alexandria, and Jerusalem, as well as the Bishops of Athens."[24] In 1902 the "young guards" secured a decisive victory against the Greek hierarchy with the election of Latakiyya bishop Dumani, who was of Damascene origin, to the post of the patriarch of Antioch and the Arab East. The High Porte issued a *firman* legitimizing the new Arab patriarch, with the result that most Greek bishops withdrew from Syria and Lebanon to the parishes of Palestine, which remained in Greek hands.[25]

Hakim himself was involved in this dispute in his capacity as an enthusiastic supporter of the Arabization of the church and as a protégé of the progressive Bishop Arsanius Haddad, newly installed bishop of Latakiyya. Hakim became special councilor to Haddad, using his skills in Turkish to facilitate the bishop's official communications to the Ottoman authorities. Hakim also encouraged the Syrian bishoprics to invite Russian scientific expeditions to Syria and Palestine, in support of the Orthodox schooling system. These Russian seminaries became a cornerstone of the Arab literary renaissance in Syria and Palestine before World War I.[26]

Throughout his career in the Ottoman legal administration, Hakim was supported by the Arabized church. He narrates in this regard how his demotion from his legal membership in the Latakiyya court was overturned through an intervention by the patriarch of Antioch. The case indicates that Hakim continued to enjoy and benefit from patronage by the Orthodox church under the new regime. But it also shows that given the choice between quick promotion within the hierarchy of the Orthodox establishment and service in the ranks of the Ottoman legal system, he chose the to stay in the Ottoman system and be supported by the church, rather than the other way round.

This encounter with the Orthodox church contrasts significantly from Issa's struggle within, and against, the Greek hierarchy. Like Hakim, Issa al-Issa (born in 1878 in Jaffa, one year earlier than Hakim) received his early training within the Orthodox educational system, but in reverse. He first studied at the Freres College in Jaffa and continued his schooling at the Greek Orthodox school in Kefteen, at the time one of the leading learning institutions in Ottoman Syria, under the direction of Bishop Gregarious Haddad.[27] When Issa was summoned for his "seditious" articles in *Filastin* in 1915, this connection proved useful. for he resorted to the same Bishop Haddad, now Patriarch Haddad, in Damascus to intercede on his behalf with the military tribunal in Damascus.[28] Unlike Hakim, however, Issa found that his continued relationship with the church was neither one of patronage, nor instrumental in his career. Bishop Haddad was either unwilling (given Issa's reputation with the Jerusalem clergy) or unable to intercede on his behalf. Issa received a sentence of three hundred days of imprisonment for his inflammatory editorials.[29] As Barghouti remarked in his biographical note, Issa came from a well-to-do merchant family and did not depend on Christian charities (on *talami deir al-Rum*) for his survival. He was able to challenge the church hierarchy vigorously and without recrimination. And he did so relentlessly. One of the most illustrative examples of this challenge was his scheming to facilitate the marriage of Khalil Sakakini and, later, two other Arabists, who were banned by the Greek hierarchy for their nationalist activity.

Issa al-Issa's character and his relationship to Orthodoxy were succinctly caught by the muckraker lawyer Omar Salih al-Barghouti in a very perceptive biographical essay. Barghouti refers to combative journalism and the continuous battles that *Filastin* provoked, not only with the Ottoman censor, but also with Issa's opponents. For those, Issa's pen is soaked with poison," and "he often causes them heart attacks . . . with his courage, amounting to the point of insolence."[30] Then Barghouti adds this observation about Issa's Orthodox identity:

> He comes from a family of [olive] oil and soap merchants. Their [private] wealth and prosperity was reflected on him gracefully, since the Issa family did not grow up eating convent black bread [baked for the Orthodox poor, *talami deir al-Rum*], nor did they live in the church's endowed denominational property [*wa lam yaskunu fi buyut al-awqaf*], which lent to his character dignity and strength. He is often accused of playing the Christian card in politics, but I know that he is secure and welcoming in his relationship with his Muslim compatriots. Nevertheless, he belongs to a Christian family milieu that hesitates in receiving Muslims in their households unless their women remove their archaic veils. And perhaps he is right in this matter.[31]

There are considerable implications for reading the social map of Ottoman Jaffa in these sarcastic references. Issa belonged to a mercantile bourgeoisie that freed itself from dependency on the charities of the Orthodox church, in the same manner that Hakim's employment in the Ottoman bureaucracy freed him, and his family, from relying on the patronage of the church of Antioch. The reference to *talami deir al-Rum* (the "black bread of the Orthodox convent") was evocative of the communal benefaction that bound the community to their church and allowed the church hierarchy a large measure of control over and influence on the laity. For urban Christians, there was of course more than bread involved in these transactions, in particular the housing of the poor on church property, and the provision of educational opportunities to the constituency. With the significant expansion of Ottoman public education, in the *nizamiyyah* schools, as well in educational opportunities available in Protestant, Russian, and Catholic schools, an important segment of the community gained access to avenues of mobility outside the church system.

Hellenic hegemony of the Jerusalem patriarchate contributed significantly and inadvertently to the emergence of a cultural renaissance that had a strong Orthodox component—much more so than in other parts of greater Syria and Egypt. There were two avenues for this distinction—journalism and the printing press, and Russian seminaries and teacher training colleges in Beit Jala, Tripoli, and Nazareth. The Russian seminaries, with the support of official czarist policies, sought a foothold in the Ottoman Empire on par with other imperial powers that benefited from the capitulations, and which patronized non-Muslim subjects under the guise of protection. Unlike the British and the French, however, who became patrons of Druze, Jewish, and Catholic communities, the Russians had to compete with the Hellenic institutional dominance of the Christian Orthodox community. Their instruments were the schools and seminaries, which contributed significantly to a secular Arab cultural renaissance—producing leading intellectual figures such as Mikhail Nu'aimi, Khalil Beidas, Bandali al-Juzeh, Kulthum Odeh, Khalil Sakakini, and many others. Some of those, such as Beidas and Sakakini, were also active in the nascent Arabic press. And it was in mass-circulating newspapers and satirical weeklies where al-Nahda al-Urthuduxiyyah al-Arabiyyah (the Arab Orthodox Renaissance), as it came to be known, made its mark.[32] Here we see that the editors and publishers of the leading newspapers that emerged after press censorship was abolished in 1908—*Al-Quds, Al-Insaf, Al-Asma'i, Al-Nafa'is,* and of course, *Filastin*—were noted members of the Orthodox community: Jurgi Habib Hanania (publisher of *Al-Quds*); Bandali Elias Mushahwar and Iskandar al-Khoury (owner and chief editor, respectively, of *Al-Insaf,* beginning in 1908); *Al-Asma'i* (published by Khalil Sakakini and Hanna Abdallah al-Issa, 1908); Khalil Beidas (*Al-Nafa'is,* political weekly, published in Haifa, 1908); Wahbeh Tamari (publisher of *Abu Shaduf,* satirical weekly in Jaffa, 1912); Emile Alonzo (publisher of *Al-Taraqqi*—named after the CUP—with Adel Jaber in Jaffa, 1909); and Issa al-Issa (publisher of *Filastin* in Jaffa, 1911).[33]

Al-Quds versus *Filastin*

Within the Orthodox community the struggle for Arabization is often portrayed as a perennial conflict between the Greek ecclesiastical hierarchy of the church and the majority of the Arab community in Syria and Palestine. The local Orthodox intelligentsia successfully propagated this view after

1908. Its main advocates were well-known community leaders and writers, such as Ya'coub Farraj, Khalil Sakakini, Yousif al-Bandak (publisher of *Sawt al-Sha'b*), and especially Yusif al-Issa and Issa al-Issa. Both Sakakini and Issa also argued that the Palestinian (and Syrian) Orthodox community constituted an oppressed majority controlled and manipulated by a clerical minority of the Greek and Cypriot priesthood.[34] At issue here were the revenue generated by the immense landed wealth of the church, the control of the network of Orthodox schools and colleges, and the disbursal of church welfare. Certainly the Orthodox real estate endowments (both Rumi and Russian) were immense in Palestine, far more numerous than the Muslim, Jewish and Catholic endowments put together.[35] There is little evidence, however, to support the argument for the perenniality of the conflict, which assumes that an essentially national (and nationalist) conflict emanated from the ethnic differences of the church's adherents. Hakim convincingly argues that the records of the church in the seventeenth, eighteenth, and nineteenth centuries show that elections in the church hierarchy and patriarchal succession were always subjects of controversy within the church, but not necessarily between Greek and Arab elements.[36] A good indicator of this "national" ambiguity can be found in the local histories of Christian villages and townships in Palestine, such as Musa Ibn Nasir's history of Birzeit; Shehadeh al-Khoury Ibrahim's *Tarikh al-Aranikah*, and Butrus Medabeel, *Histoire d'une localite et de sa mission Latine dans la Monatagne d'Ephraim.*[37] Nasir in particular narrates the intensification of conflict within the Orthodox church in the second half of the nineteenth century, and he explains it as a conflict within the community and not only between the patriarchate and the Arab parish churches. Both Medabeel and Nasir refer to "two parties" within Palestinian Orthodoxy—a party headed by Mikhael Yasmineh, Hanna Nasir Qurt, and a parish priest known as the Reverend Dawood. The opposing party, which championed the Greek patriarchy, was headed by Hanna Taqleh and a sizable number of parish priests. In the 1880s the a major issue in this conflict was the language of church liturgy, Arabic or Greek.[38] Musa Ibn Nasir narrates how the conflict between the two parties drove many adherents of Orthodoxy to adopt Catholicism when the Latin church presented itself as "above" factions. In Jifna and Birzeit, the new religion used schooling and soup kitchens to win converts—but it was seen at the local level as a movement sponsored by the French government to spread its influence.[39] Nasir himself deserted his Orthodox faith in favor of Catholicism, but was unhappy with its doctrines and was repelled by the cult of Mary and its "discouragement of a rational reading of the Bible."[40] He also narrates how the Orthodox peasants of the Bani Haritha region united with their Muslim neighbors to expel the Catholic priesthood from their towns.[41]

All of these local chronicles, by Catholic, Orthodox and Protestant scribes, written during the late nineteenth century, indicate the absence of an ethnic conflict within the ranks of Palestinian Orthodoxy, or at least suggest that the ethnic element of the conflict was a symptom of something else. More likely the assumption of nationalist conflict within the community was based on the emergence of a nationalist ideology and a sectarian development that was still embryonic in the early nineteenth century. Laura Robson suggests two important developments that either created or exacerbated this conflict: first was the growth of a sectarian identity out of the communitarian network of relations that prevailed among Ottoman Christians (and Jews) until the middle of the nineteenth century;[42] and second, the promulgation of the Ottoman Fundamental Law of 1875, which affirmed the [Rumi] patriarchate control over the church and its properties.[43] In both cases the conflict emanated from increased demands for community control of the church resources that accompanied the adoption notions of citizenship in the first Ottoman constitutional reform of 1876. During World War I and after, the conflict was further exacerbated by the loss of pilgrims' revenue from the Russian church following the Bolshevik revolution, and by the debt crisis of the Greek Orthodox Church.[44]

These demands were no doubt influenced by the precedents set by Balkan nationalism, in which religious movements (Bulgarian, Serbian, Macedonian, and Greek Orthodoxy) combined the demand for religious reform with the demand for national emancipation within the Ottoman Empire. In Syria this led to the successful reform movement in the Orthodox church, as well as the election, in 1899, of the first modern Arab patriarch. Sati al-Husary— the early ideological exponent of Arabism, called this "the first real victory of Arab nationalism."[45]

The seeming "nationalization" of Orthodox affinities in the late Ottoman period camouflaged a more hidden dynamic, a distinctly class and communitarian dimension that increasingly took the form of a nationalist conflict in which the High Porte, the CUP, and later, the British Mandate authorities took the side of the Greeks against the Arabs, or more likely the side of the Orthodox patriarchate against the claims of the local lay community to gain more control over the assets of the church. Yusif al-Hakim provides us with a different paradigm for understanding this hidden dynamic. His strong affinities with Ottoman reform and the CUP helped free him from seeing

FIGURE 11. Freedom, Brotherhood, and Equality—the Ottoman logo in the masthead of *Al-Quds* newspaper, January 19, 1911. Newspaper archive, Institute for Palestine Studies, Beirut.

the conflict in nationalist terms. More importantly, his family's involvement with the movement to reform the Antiochian Orthodox Church, and its successful "Arabization," provided a healthy background for and contrast with what was happening in Palestine.

Palestinian Orthodoxy, according to Hakim, benefited from important lessons from the movement to Arabize the Antiochian church. The Jerusalem patriarchate provided a vast network of support for the poorer members of the community—this included free and low-cost housing, free schooling, medical care, and welfare—exemplified by the distribution of the *tulum* bread. The ecclesiastical hierarchy maintained an effective working relationship with the Ottoman political elite, including local governors and administrators, during both the Hamidian period and the CUP period—all of which was at variance with the abilities of the Arabizing Orthodox intelligentsia.[46]

ISSA, HANANIA, AND *AL-NAFEER AL-UTHMANI*

The patriarchate was fully engaged in the ideological struggle against the Arab nationalists also. Their main instrument in this was the newly emergent

Arabic press. The Orthodox establishment owned the earliest printing press in Palestine, established in 1846 under the administration of Spiridon Sarrouf and his son Wahbe Sarrouf (1839–1913), who received their training in the Orthodox Theological College in Deir Musallabeh in south Jerusalem.[47] One of the earliest mass-circulating papers to represent the position of the Brotherhood of the Holy Sepulcher was *Al-Nafeer al-Uthmani* (The Ottoman bugle), published in Jaffa from 1904 to 1907 and in Jerusalem in 1908, by Elia Zakka, who moved to Haifa and continued publishing the paper under the shortened title of *Al-Nafeer.*[48] Zakka, who was trained in the Russian seminary in Nazareth, became an early Arab advocate of the Zionist project, which earned him the epitaph "the mercenary journalist" in the Arabist press.[49] Following the constitutional revolution, the patriarchate relied on Jurgi Hanania and his newspaper *Al-Quds*—which had its own separate printing press. Hanania was able to obtain an official license to publish in 1906 and became the main purveyor of nonreligious Arabic, Greek, and Turkish publications in the country, having issued 281 books by 1914, of which 38 were in Arabic.[50] Hanania (1857–1920) came from a well-established Arab-Ottoman family. His father, Issa Habib Hanania, was the only Christian judge in the Jerusalem Court of Appeals (Mahkamat al-Isti'naf), and his mother was the daughter of the artillery commander Topji (Tubgi) Pasha, a "Rumi" master general of the ordinance in Istanbul.[51]

In 1908, *Al-Quds* was the first private gazette in Palestine with a wide circulation. Hanania was able to enlist some of the best writers in Jerusalem for his paper. Those included Hanna al-Issa (who later published *Al-Asma'i*) and Khalil Sakakini, the founder of al-Dusturiyyeh College. His main editorialist was Sheikh Ali Rimawi (1860–1919), an Azharite scholar and poet who established his journalistic career as the editor of the Turkish-Arabic *Al-Quds al-Sharif,* the official Ottoman gazette in Palestine.[52] Rimawi strongly believed in Turkish-Arab unity as the core of Ottoman citizenship in Palestine, and this was reflected in the political line of *Al-Quds*. He later produced his own paper, *Al-Najah,* and wrote extensively in *Al-Munadi,* the anti-Zionist paper of Muhammad al-Mughrabi and Sa'id Jarallah.[53] But *Al-Quds* also became an instrument of the patriarchy against the nationalists.[54] Thus from its inception *Al-Quds* was a pro-CUP and pro-Greek platform at the same time.

It was largely against the success of *Al-Quds* that *Filastin* was established in Jaffa (1911) to articulate the demands of the Orthodox dissident intellectuals. Their main objectives: increasing the role of the Arab clergy in running the church; involving the lay Orthodox community in the administration of church endowments (waqf), which included an estimated annual revenue of forty thousand Ottoman pounds; and improving the level of Orthodox schools and colleges.[55]

In his book *Syria in the Ottoman Epoch,* Hakim suggests that the struggle within the church involved welfare provisions that the dissident intelligentsia (Sakakini, Farraj, Issa, and others) were unable to compete with. He also suggests that the Orthodox intelligentsia were divided between those who for a variety of reasons supported the establishment, whose organ was Hanania's *Al-Quds,* and those who coalesced around Issa's *Filastin.*[56] Thus Jerusalem (*Al-Quds*) was pitted against Jaffa *(Filastin)*; and the poorer communities in the villages and small towns—dependent on the Greek patriarchate for their welfare—were pitted against the rising professional Orthodox community who had been freed "from the convent *tulum*" and the charities of the patriarchate to make demands on the church.

But how to explain the Ottoman administration's siding with the Greeks against the Arabs? There are two explanations for this: the High Porte and, later, the CUP government were worried about the precedent of the Balkans, where demands for religious reform within the church escalated into secessionist demands from Anatolia. The Greek hierarchy in Jerusalem and Antioch was controlled by the Constantinople church and, therefore, constituted an establishment that the Porte could reach an understanding with; but the Arab Rumi laity was an unknown factor.[57] A more decisive factor, however, was property. The Orthodox landed endowments in Palestine were enormous, and the Ottoman administration was keen for these endowments to remain in the hands of a church hierarchy that could be administered and controlled from Istanbul. An Arab-controlled endowment would be subject to local forces that were potentially separatist and administratively segmental. By contrast, Antiochian Orthodox endowments were minuscule compared to those in Palestine, and thus the Arabization of the church involved neither the power struggles of Jerusalem, nor the nationalist dangers inherent in the Palestine church. Thus in Antioch and Damascus the situation allowed an accommodation that did not threaten the status quo as it did in Palestine.

"It was customary in Jerusalem during the Holy Week," Hakim narrates, "for the Patriarch to send a personal gift to his Muslim friends and senior administrators. The gift was specially baked bread and colored eggs. The head of the Jerusalem Court, Jamal Bey, called me and indicated that he refused to accept the gift, asking me to join the boycott. I refused to do so, indicating that my position [as public prosecutor] dictates that I remain neutral between the two conflicting parties. In addition, my religious beliefs and social graces compel me to accept the offerings of the Patriarch, simple as it is, as a special blessing from the head of the church."[58] Hakim's personal friendship with Yusif al-Issa, and his basic sympathy with the Arabization movement within the Orthodox community, did not sway him from observing the larger picture. He correctly did not view the movement in terms of an Arab majority against a Hellenic minority, but one in which a liberal and secularizing intelligentsia was challenging the authority of the patriarchate and the state; and his loyalties were clearly with the Ottoman state, though not with the patriarchate. And when the moment came he acted as a state functionary—swiftly suspending the press and sending to prison and exile his fellow Orthodox dissidents.

THE VIEW FROM ABOVE

The conflict within the ranks of the Orthodox community cannot be properly understood without taking the view of the ecclesiastical hierarchy, which had a strong (if often conflicted) institutional relationship with the High Porte. Greek dominance within the church, according to a recent study by Papastathis and Kark, was rooted in the notion of "Helleno-Orthodoxia," by which Greek identity is closely linked to Orthodoxy. According to this notion the Christian Orthodox populations of Syria and Palestine "were not [therefore] regarded as Arabs, but rather as a Greek 'Arabophones.'"[59]

> Since Orthodoxy is held to be the true faith expressing God's word, the Greek people are the "chosen" people, under whose guidance all the ecclesiastical centres (thus the Jerusalem Patriarchate as well) should continue to operate, as they have from their establishment. Consequently, the Greek nation is primordially their "rightful" owner. Two strategies were formulated within the Greek ecclesiastical apparatus for confronting the developing Arab Orthodox movement: a) absolute rejection of the Arab lay demands, which were viewed as subverting the Greek character of the Patriarchate and its religious "purity"; and b) the adoption of a controlled concession to the community of some secondary rights without putting at risk the institution's Greek character and centralized governing structure. The long-standing conflict between these two distinct schools of thought led to a series of crises within the Patriarchate from the end of the nineteenth century.[60]

As the demands for reform within the church and its Arab constituency escalated after the constitutional revolution, the Brotherhood of the Holy Sepulcher (i.e., the Greek ecclesiastical hierarchy) became more intransigent. The Arab demands for democratization and power-sharing became entangled with European interventions. Russian patronage of Arab claims, and Russian imperial rivalries with Britain and France, were crucial factors in swaying the Ottoman administration to side with the Greek hierarchy.

The battle for the Arabization of the Orthodox Church in Palestine, as in Syria, was exacerbated by the constitutional revolution of 1908. The Jerusalem Orthodox intelligentsia, led by Yusif al-Issa (Issa's cousin and the editor of *Al-Asma'i*) and Khalil Sakakini, founder of al-Dusturiyyeh College, made three demands on the church hierarchy: that they elect at least one bishop (out of twelve) from the ranks of the Arab laity; that they share the administration of the Orthodox endowment, whose annual income was estimated at forty thousand Ottoman pounds, with the Arab community; and that they improve the condition of Arab education within church schools and create an Arab Orthodox college of higher learning.[61] According to Yusif al-Hakim, the Brotherhood of the Holy Sepulcher (made up primarily of the Greek ecclesiastical hierarchy) in Jerusalem was alarmed by the success of the Syrian and Lebanese parishes in the Arabization of the church and mobilized a campaign within the Arab ranks to preempt a similar coup in Palestine. Their instrument was the influential *Al-Quds* newspaper, owned and edited by Jurgi Habib Hanania.[62] But Hanania was not alone—he carried with him a considerable number of Arab writers, both those who favored caution in dealing with the patriarchate, and those who felt that reforming the Brotherhood must come through the fulfillment of their demands regarding Ottoman decentralization.

The opposition resorted to *Al-Insaf* (Justice) and, after 1911, to Issa's *Filastin*. *Al-Insaf* (1908–1911) was published by Bandali Elias Mushahwar as a "literary, political, and satirical weekly" and seemed to have a single target—the struggle against the clergy of the Orthodox patriarchate in Jerusalem.[63] Jacob Yehoshua suggests that it was supported by the Russian consulate in Jerusalem, reflecting the earliest active intervention of Russian Orthodoxy on the side of the Arab nationalist movement.[64]

The most effective weapon in the hands of the Brotherhood, however, was the dispensation of charities and church services to the poorer members of the Arab community. Those included subsidized housing for members of the community on church property, schooling for their children, and daily distribution of free bread (*talami*).[65] The *talami* was not simply a symbolic feature of class division within the Christian community but a real material instrument in the allocation of influence and in winning the hearts and minds of the community. The hierarchy also cultivated strong connections with the local Ottoman administration and—through its links with the Greek patriarchate in Istanbul—with the High Porte. Hakim narrates in this regard how he, as judge in the Jerusalem Court of Appeals, refused to intervene in favor of one side or another, despite his declared sympathies with the Arabs.[66] It is clear from his diplomatic narrative, however, that the High Porte and the *mutasarrif* of Jerusalem refused to repeat the autonomous example of the Antioch church, thus ensuring the continued hegemony of the Greeks.

The respective Ottoman diaries of Hakim and Issa provide us with a rare moment of disclosure on these debates within the Orthodox community and among Arab intellectuals in general—since the issues raised by the Orthodox Renaissance movement became a general cause for the Arab public, pertaining to issues of land and secular education. They also constitute a window on how the two Arab Orthodox intellectuals reacted to the momentous events surrounding the fall of Sultan Abdul Hamid and the ensuing strains between Arabism and Ottomanism in the Syrian provinces of the empire. Issa's and Hakim's memoirs were written after the war, but both were based on diary entries recorded before the war.

ISSA'S ORTHODOXY AND ARABISM: INSPIRED BY A CHARLATAN

"My passion for journalism was not inherited," begins the memoirs of Issa al-Issa, "but Dr. Dahesh told me once that the spirit of a Chinese writer was reincarnated inside me.[67] And who knows? What I do know is that Dahesh Beyk was a big charlatan. My preoccupation with journalism did not begin with the establishment of the *Filastin* newspaper in 1911. It started in 1897, when as a student at the American University [in Beirut], I joined my friend Hafiz Abdul Malik in launching a small weekly magazine which we called *The Elite* [*Al-Nukhab*]. We used to print few [mimeographed] copies on gelatin and distribute them in the library for students to read. You may find some of those issues that have been kept by the library."

After moving through a number of itinerant jobs in Jerusalem (as secretary of the Iranian consulate in al-Quds al-Sharif, and *turjuman* [interpreter] in the Coptic Church), Issa moved to Cairo and became a correspondent for *Al-Ikhlas,* published by Ibrahim Abdul Masih, and an accountant in the customs department of the Sudan government in Cairo. He also worked as an inspector for the African Cigarette Company, owned by Qaraman, Deek, and Salti. The proclamation of the Ottoman constitution in 1908 brought him back to Palestine, where he found that the CUP had "replaced the autocratic rule of Abdul Hamid with a dictatorial rule of the Young Turks." He soon became involved, nevertheless, with the Orthodox Renaissance movement (al-Nahda al-Urthuduxiyyah al-Arabiyyah) through the leadership of his cousin Yusif. Yusif's brother Hanna was a member of the Orthodox delegation to Istanbul, which negotiated with the High Porte for the establishment of a mixed council in which the Palestinian Arab community would be represented, and for the provision by the patriarchate of the sum of thirty thousand Ottoman gold pounds annually for projects (social and educational) in the community. None of these provisions were realized, according to Issa, owing to the immense influence of the [Greek] patriarchate with the High Porte and its ability to fill the pockets of high government officials.[68] This triggered a series of protests and popular demonstrations among the Arab laity demanding the implementation of the adopted accords.

It was at this point that Issa decided to leave his job as an accountant and join the struggle against the church. Issa was explicit about the primacy of the Orthodox cause in launching his paper. This is how he describes the beginning of *Filastin:*

> My personal savings at the time amounted to seventy French pounds. I heard that a printing press was available for sale in Jerusalem. I traveled there and found a huge machine that was normally used for producing proofs. I bought it on the spot and had it delivered to Jaffa, where I had rented a store on Bustrus Street near the main post office. I bought a new set of print sets and had them fitted to the machine with help from the Wagner factory. On the first of January 1911, *Filastin* was launched to the public. My purpose in producing the paper was to serve the Orthodox cause above everything else. I organized an opening party for the newspaper in the biggest hotel in town, at which the major poets and literary figures in the country were present. Anybody who reviews the successive issues of *Filastin* from that date until the present will note that the Orthodox movement predominates on its pages.[69]

Zionism was the other major concern for the paper. Issa mentioned that after the adoption of the new constitution, the Zionists resumed their vigorous campaign to "buy Palestine" for the settlement activities in return for major loans to the Ottoman state. He noted that the ruling party, the Ittihad wal-Taraqqi Party (CUP), included major figures who sympathized with the project for a Jewish homeland. As a result of his adoption of the anti-Zionist campaign in *Filastin*, "the Jews began to see me as one of their bitterest opponents and continue to do so until the present [1948]."[70]

Issa devotes considerable space in his memoirs to the attempts by his opponents to buy off the paper. Those included the German consulate (in support of the Entente powers), the Zionists (in support of the settlement activities), and the local governor (Hasan Beyk al-Jabi). His noncooperation led to a legal campaign against *Filastin* by the public prosecutor (which involved Yusif al-Hakim) for "creating dissention among the population" (*al-Tafriq bayn al-ʻanasir*), as well as to several libel cases (most of them brought against him by Shim'on Moyal, editor of *Sawt al-Uthmaniyya*, a Zionist newspaper published in Arabic). *Filastin* was continuously being fined and suspended from publication as a result of these campaigns.

Issa refers to the involvement of Henry Morgenthau (1856–1946), American ambassador to the High Porte, who successfully intervened with Kamel Pasha, the prime minister, on behalf of the Zionists in 1913 to have *Filastin* permanently closed. The *mutasarrif* of Jerusalem, who sympathized with Issa, showed him the order from Istanbul to suspend the paper. Once it closed, Issa al-Issa left the paper in the hands of his cousin, Yusif, and carried the campaign from Egypt. The major newspaper in Egypt, *Al-Muqattam* (edited by Khalil Thabet, who was Issa's journalism professor in Beirut) refused to publish his protests against the closure. According to Issa, Nessim Mallul, coeditor of *Sawt al-Uthmaniyya* in Jaffa, had "bought off" *Al-Muqattam* on behalf of the Zionists by paying for five hundred subscriptions.[71] In addition *Al-Muqattam* regularly published a column on Palestine signed by an anonymous "Senior Zionist," possibly Moyal.[72] The paper allowed Issa on three occasions to reply to Moyal, but thereafter Thabet refused to publish his articles. Both *Al-Ahram* and *Al-Mu'ayyad* also rebuffed Issa. After several months the campaign on behalf of *Filastin* succeeded in reopening the paper, and Issa returned to Jaffa.

It seems, however, that Issa's position on Zionism, as with his vacillating attitude toward Prince Abdullah and the Hashemites, was not consistent. Rashid Khalidi, in *The Iron Cage*, suggests that Issa's anti-Zionism was largely motivated by his concern for rural poverty and peasant dispossession in Palestine.[73] Issa demonstrated this concern by sending a free copy of *Filastin* to every village in the Jaffa district.[74]

Filastin, in fact, had demonstrated this special focus on land issues and peasant poverty from the beginning, in 1911 and 1912, when the newspaper was still published twice a week. However, the regular column on village issues appeared under the title *Ras'il al-Fallah* (Peasant letters), which was signed by Abu Ibrahim. This was the Arabic pen name of Menashe Meirovitz, a Zionist *apparatchik* from Rishon Lezion, and an early member of the Bilu group.[75] "Abu Ibrahim" published a weekly column, often on a page that addressed land issues for *Filastin* readers. The main themes of his column were government neglect of the peasants, peasant indebtedness, and the need to parcelize the land and put an end to the backward *musha'* (communal) system of ownership. Frequently Meirovitz/Abu Ibrahim would refer to the positive achievements of the Jewish colonies, and sometimes to the German Templer colonists, as a model for Palestinian peasants. For example, in the June 23, 1912, issue of *Filastin,* Abu Ibrahim has an imaginary conversation with a local landlord, Sa'id Effendi, in which he demonstrates the benefits of land registration to the landlord: "So far not one village [in the Jaffa district] has been parcellized except Beit Dajan. The villagers there became envious of the achievements of the Jews of Iyoun Qara [Rishon Lezion] and decided to register the land as their Jewish neighbours did. Today their land has quadrupled its value. Beit Dajan villagers are now taking care of their plots using the latest European plowing techniques, etc."[76] In another article, on the need to improve the Jaffa Porte, he refers to the "millions of trees planted by German and Israelite colonists, which will soon be fruitful and exporting millions for fruit boxes."[77]

Issa al-Issa was aware of Abu Ibrahim's Zionist identity and his political position, yet Issa continued to publish Abu Ibrahim's column in a prime location of his paper. One explanation for this tolerance comes from the period in which these views were published. It seems Issa, while preoccupied with the social conditions of the local peasants, saw this as a manifestation of Arab backwardness. He may have been fascinated by the modernity of the German and Jewish colonial enterprises and, therefore, willing to overlook their Zionist activities.[78] By the time Issa wrote his memoirs, in the 1930s, the scope and meaning of Zionist colonization had become clear and he had solidified his position against them in his paper. In the early years of publication, *Filastin* paid considerable attention to issues of land, dispossession, educational reform, and government mismanagement, but the main issue remained that of Orthodoxy.

THE MARRIAGE OF KHALIL SAKAKINI: BANNED IN
JERUSALEM, PERMITTED IN JAFFA

A pivotal moment in Issa's battle with the ecclesiastical authorities involved the marriage of Khalil Sakakini, who was threatened with excommunication by the church and banned from marrying Sultana Abo (under the lame excuse of "preventing incest," since she was a distant cousin of his). We have two versions of the event. The first, by Sakakini, is detailed in his diary, in which he describes the episode as a punishment for his struggle on behalf the Orthodox community in Jerusalem for representation in the governing bodies of the church.[79] In Issa's memoirs, the story is transformed into a satirical mockery of the Greek patriarchate, albeit with a serious intent.

Sakakini had chosen Issa to be his best man (*ishbin*) in the wedding in Jerusalem. When the presiding priest did not show up, the assembled guests found out that the patriarchate had forbidden the wedding under the pretense that Sultana, the bride, was the adopted daughter of Sakakini's maternal cousin (in Khalil's version, she is described as his cousin five times removed). After a prolonged period of negotiations the patriarchate consented to the wedding on the condition that Sakakini would return the keys of Mar Ya'coub Church to the patriarchate.[80] It transpired that the Jerusalem Orthodox laity had rebelled earlier that year (1913) and seized, from the Greek patriarchate, the compound of what they considered to be the Arab church of Mar Ya'coub, adjacent to the Holy Sepulcher. They had handed the keys of the church to Khalil Sakakini for safekeeping and as a symbol of separation. Both Issa and Sakakini describe Mar Ya'coub as a "national [Arab] church" illegally occupied by the Greeks.[81] When Sakakini refused to submit to these conditions, Issa arranged for the marriage to be performed in Jaffa. Issa conspired with his cousin Yusif to have two local Orthodox priests arrested, apparently on some pretense, by the local gendarme, held incommunicado lest they be contacted by the patriarchate, and then brought to his house in Jaffa just before the wedding ceremony.[82] Issa writes,

> I had sent the invitations to the guests and prepared the drinks and food for the occasion. At the right moment I had the two priests released from their confinement and brought to my house. I immediately apologized to them for the arrest and explained to them the circumstances. The wedding ceremony was concluded smoothly, and we celebrated the event with great fanfare. The next day the wedding couple left for Jerusalem by train. On that same day

Filastin published an item on the front page under the title "What is banned in Jerusalem is permissible in Jaffa"![83]

Significantly these events overlap with Yusif al-Hakim's tenure in Palestine's courts, as a judge in the Jerusalem Court of Appeals, and earlier, as a public prosecutor in Jaffa.

ORTHODOXY AND OTTOMANISM: THE CASE OF THE STRAY PIG AND THE SANCTITY OF RAMADAN

Yusif al-Hakim chronicled his life in Palestine through the cases he had to resolve as a public prosecutor and then judge. The "case of the murdered pig" involved a stray pig belonging to the Spanish consul in Jaffa, the mufti of Jaffa, and the *Sawt al-Uthmaniyya* (the Zionist newspaper published by Moyal, an opponent of Issa al-Issa). The pig had entered the house of Mufti Tawfiq Effendi al-Dajani during the early days of Ramadan 1325 (May 1911). One of Mufti's men shot the pig dead to avoid any pollution of Ramadan's holiness.

At the turn of the century, Jaffa had two contending factions: a pro-Young Turk (CUP) party headed by Mayor Omar Effendi al-Bitar and the Dajani family; and an oppositional party headed by Hafiz Bey al-Sa'id, a parliamentary deputy from Jaffa and critic of Zionism and Jewish immigration.[84] Hafiz Beyk belonged to the Freedom and Reconciliation Party (Hurriyat wa I'tilaf), which pursued a campaign of Arabizing the administrative system in the Syrian provinces.[85] During the war, he joined the Ottoman Decentralization Party, based in Egypt, and was increasingly at odds with the new reformist regime in Istanbul.[86] Sa'id was also allied with Sadiq and Muhammad Ali, Sheikh al-Sawi, and the well-known lawyer Raghib al-Imam. The Spanish consul, angered by the killing of his pig, filed a complaint against the mufti with the police. Moyal publicized the case in *Sawt al-Uthmaniyya* in a manner that provoked the Dajani (pro-government) faction. Tawfiq Effendi al-Dajani and his allies mobilized the public against the newspaper for "insulting the mufti of Islam" and demanded, during a street demonstration, the punishment of the paper, its publisher, and its supporters, Hafiz al-Sa'id and his allies.[87]

It was at this juncture that Hakim, as public prosecutor was asked to intervene. The Turkish governor of Jaffa, Asef Beyk, was faced with the demonstration led by the mufti and his allies. "Asef Bey, accompanied by the commander of the Jaffa garrison, Abdul Rahman Pasha, was disturbed by the massive mobilization of the populace, who were angered by the attack on the Mufti, and wanted the Jewish publisher [Moyal] to be arrested, together with his Jaffite supporters [Sa'id and his allies in the Freedom Party], regardless of their status."[88] Hakim believed that the governor was coming to punish those forces opposed to the CUP, and that the "pig affair" was a factional fight between two sections of the Jaffa elite, who were using "the insult to Islam" as a cover to get to their opponents. He defused the situation by translating into Arabic the Turkish governor's speech, which promised to punish those who "disturb the public peace." "The government," the governor declared to the assembled Jaffites "will prosecute those who publish inciting news, and will pursue the figures behind them according to the law. However, the government will not allow the people to take the law into their hands. . . . [I]t is your duty as dignitaries to prevail on your supporters to go home. I expect you tomorrow to come to my office and file your complaints, bringing all supporting evidence. I will make sure that any breach of the law will be dealt with severely."[89] The following day, the governor filed a complaint against Moyal and his supporters, but the Bitar and Dajani factions did not pursue the matter, knowing—according to Hakim—that the new Ottoman law did not apply slander laws without clear evidence. Their target was the Entente Party not Moyal.

The "case of the murdered pig" demonstrates the growing strain in Palestine between the governing CUP faction and its opponents, in which the local military garrison, the governor, and the Zionists became involved. In this triadic struggle it is illustrative that Hakim, an Orthodox Christian government functionary and an active supporter of the CUP, chose to mediate the conflict in a manner that he thought would best serve the state, and not the party. He also saw that the claim of "insulting Islam and the Mufti" was a fig leaf used by the Dajanis and the local Young Turks Party to cover their actions against supporters of the Freedom and Reconciliation Party.

THE MURDER OF SULEIMAN HAIFAWI AND THE JAFFA GANGSTERS

Spring was a period of heightened alert in the ranks of the security forces in Jaffa and Jerusalem, since it brought tens of thousands of Russian, Greek, and

European pilgrims for the Eastern celebrations—vital for the economy of Ottoman Palestine. Hakim narrates the murder of Suleiman al-Haifawi in Jaffa to portray the anarchic situation of public security that he was brought in to control as the newly appointed public prosecutor (*na'ib 'am*). Haifawi, a landlord and public figure, was murdered in his orange orchard by a known gangster "of substantial connections" in May 1910.[90] The murder was followed by a period of gang warfare that compelled the authorities to intervene by hiring Hakim, who was already an established judge in Jerusalem, to deal with the issue of public security. Hakim describes at great length the measures (warnings, arrests, and heavy fines) undertaken by his bureau to deal with gangsterism without divulging the background of the causes of the gangsterism, or the particular details of the murder at hand. In the case of Haifawi's death, the murderer was a known figure, and his whereabouts were also public knowledge. He had escaped to Port Said and was, therefore, immune to prosecution by Ottoman law. Hakim organized a major campaign of pursuit, which involved extensive coordination with Egyptian police and border guards and ended with the successful arrest and extradition of Haifawi's murderer.[91] Hakim uses this case to illustrate his belief that the new Ottoman law was a basic tenant in establishing public security, but that it was marred by a weak and corrupt administration. It was also marred by continued discrimination against citizens that resulted from the terms of the capitulations, which allowed foreign nationals and native protégés of European powers to escape punishment. During the arrests that followed the Haifawi murder case, Hakim made sure that local Jaffa citizens were not treated differently from foreigners. "When I saw that local suspects were kept in jail, while foreign subjects where released, I summoned the police chief, Fawzi Beyk, and instructed him to make sure that all suspects be treated in the same manner, regardless of their nationality. . . . I explained to him the consequences of these capitulations on our nationals. And even though we may not ignore them or abolish them, at least we are under obligation to treat Ottoman citizens with a measure of dignity and respect."[92]

Hakim was not immune to opportunism, since he did not challenge the terms of capitulations and was merely trying to ameliorate its impact on the public image of the state. Nevertheless, he was confronted by a number of consuls, the French and British in particular, who questioned him on the status of their subjects before the law. He assured them that he was not challenging these laws, even though he was opposed to them personally.[93]

During his tenure in Jaffa as public prosecutor, and in Jerusalem as judge, Hakim pursued a campaign of Arabizing the language of the courts. He successfully petitioned the High Porte and the Appeals Court in Damascus to ensure that only Arab judges be appointed to Arab courts in Syria and Palestine. His success was proof "that the government in the constitutional period was responsive to calls for public reform—and they did not see [my campaign] as a form of nationalist bigotry in favor of the Arabic language."[94] Hakim's Arabism was congruent with his Osmenlilik, and the local administration in Jerusalem and Damascus reciprocated his loyalty. As a judge and prosecutor he rarely alluded to his Orthodox Christian affiliation, in the firm belief that his Ottoman identity was above any sectarian affinities. He was so secure in this conviction that he challenged the prevailing use of a law known as *al-fasaha al-lisaniyyeh* (law of insult), which severely punished any person who insulted the prophet Muhammad (and other "divine prophets") in public utterances. He was aware that many people used the law to exact revenge on their personal enemies on the basis of claims that were not always provable—and in particular, he recognized the sectarian abuse of that law. On May 22, 1911, the law of insult was modified.[95]

It was the case of the stray pig that brought Yusif al-Hakim to the path of Issa al-Issa. In early 1911, Yusif al-Issa and his cousin Issa al-Issa established the newspaper *Filastin* in Jaffa. Issa came from a family that had pioneered newspaper publishing in Palestine. His cousin Hanna had established *Al-Asma'i*, a biweekly literary-political newspaper in 1908 in Jerusalem with Is'af al-Nashashibi, Sheikh Ali al-Rimawi, Khalil Sakakini, and his brother Yusif.[96]

As district attorney, Yusif al-Hakim received a number of complaints from Zionists in the Jaffa community against Hanna al-Issa's *Al-Asma'i* and, later, *Filastin* for its relentless attacks on Jewish immigration and Jewish settlements in Palestine. The main initiators of these complaints were Shim'on Moyal and his wife, Ester Lazari, Palestinian Arab Jews of Moroccan origin, and Nessim Mallul, a Tunisian Jew who resided in Jaffa. They all belonged to the Society of Arabic Publishing, established in Jaffa to demonstrate Jewish affinities to the Ottoman state and to respond to Arab nationalist attacks against Zionism.[97] In the view of Moyal, Lazari, and Mallul, it was the Christian Orthodox intellectuals, represented by Najib Azuri, Najib Nassar (Haifa), and Issa al-Issa—and not the Muslim Arab leadership—who were hostile to the Zionist project.[98] Later on, Moyal and a number of Sephardic Jewish writers and publicists established the *Shield (ha-Magen)* and *Sawt al-Uthmaniyya* (Voice of the Ottomans) in Arabic, in response to *Al-Karmil* and *Filastin*. Issa al-Issa devotes a section of his diary to Ester Azhari (Lazari) and Shim'on Moyal and their role in the attack on *Filastin*. When Moyal made a speech in Jaffa attacking Mayor Bitar and Issa, the latter anonymously composed a "quintet," a satirical poem that he titled "He Who Knows Himself," and which included the following stanza: "We have known you as a charlatan, a crook and a liar, but now you claim to be a poet, a writer, but where is the rhyme?"[99]

Like Issa, Moyal and Lazari belonged to the Ottoman Decentralization Party, and, aside from the issue of Zionism, they were on collegial terms as fellow journalists. When Moyal found out who the anonymous author was, he came to Issa's office and told him that his quintet had become a "fisted fiver" in the ear.[100] It is significant that the Zionist leadership in Jaffa was made up of Sephardic intellectuals like Amzalek, Eliahu Chelouche, Moyal, and Mallul. All of them were Arab Jews. By and large, however, Palestinian Sephardic Jews were either opposed or indifferent to Zionism and were often accused by the Zionist leadership of being "assimilationists"—indicating their desire to be part of the Arab society and affirming their Ottoman citizenship.[101]

CONCLUSION: TWO FACES OF OTTOMAN EMANCIPATION AND THE ORTHODOX RENAISSANCE

An essential feature of Christian Orthodoxy in the Arab East is the consciousness among its adherents of its *indigenous character*. This belief applied to the Greek hierarchy in Antioch and Jerusalem, who considered themselves the nativist continuity of the Byzantine presence in the Holy Land, hence their rejection of the Arab designation of "foreignness" attributed to them. They implicitly believed the Arab Christian community to be Rumi Arabophones. The Arab and Syrian Orthodox communities in greater Syria equally adhered to this notion of indigenousness, regarding themselves as the residue of the population who did not convert to Islam.

Yusif al-Hakim and Issa al-Issa, the jurist and the journalist, were the products of the Arab Orthodox Renaissance (al-Nahda al-Urthuduxiyyah) of the late nineteenth century, which was centered in Latakiyya, Antioch, Damascus, Jerusalem, and Jaffa. They belonged to a generation that held great expectations in response to the promises of emancipation by the Hurriyat movement and the Ottoman constitution of 1908. Both intellectuals came from urban professional families that no longer depended on the protection and charity of the communitarian Orthodox system. As Omar Salih al-Barghouti put it, they were free "from the *tulum* of Deir al-Rum"— that is, they were free from the beneficence of Orthodox charities that bound the poorer members of the Christian community to the church. The two diaries of Hakim and Issa are crucial in highlighting the significant relationship between their Orthodox socialization and the development of their Ottoman/Arabist consciousness.

The Orthodox Renaissance movement, it should be remembered, became a cause célèbre within wide circles of the Muslim intelligentsia in Syria and Palestine. Many believed that it was an essential component for the development of Arab nationalist currents in the late nineteenth century. Sati al-Husary, the early ideologue of Arab nationalism, believed that the Arabization of the Orthodox Church of Antioch was a critical landmark and historical turning point for the triumph of Arabism in Syria.[102] Within the various currents of Arabist cultural movements in greater Syria, Christian Orthodox (Rumi) intellectuals often maintained stronger affinities with their Muslim compatriots than with their fellows who belonged to Catholic and Protestant communities.[103] This is clear from the intellectual circles frequented by Khalil Sakakini, Najib Nassar, Khalil Beidas, and Issa himself.

As members of the majority Christian communities of the Arab Mashriq, both Issa and Hakim rejected the minoritarian status adopted by many Christian middle-class intellectuals who benefited from the patronage of European cultural institutions and the system of capitulations—although in the case of Issa al-Issa, the writer continued to benefit from his earlier connections with European and consular institutions. The two men strongly believed in the nativist roots of Byzantine Christian Orthodoxy, and they took their citizenship (Ottoman and Syrian) as a mark of bonding with their Arab Muslim compatriots. Their Arabist identity mobilized them against the clerical hegemony of the Greek hegemony of the Antioch and Jerusalem patriarchates and led them to adopt radical secularist stances in Syria and Palestine. The success of that struggle in Antioch, and its failure in Palestine, were crucial factors in the different paths taken by Hakim and Issa toward Ottomanism and Arab nationalism.

After the constitutional revolution of 1908 their paths diverged in several important ways. Hakim continued to promote Arab autonomy within the Ottoman system. He believed that Ottoman constitutionalism was the best guarantor of an all-encompassing citizenship and had a strong working relationship with fellow Turkish jurists and administrators in Syria and Anatolia; and he believed in the leadership of the CUP, even when he became highly critical of Cemal Pasha's arbitrary rule in Syria. As a member of the Ottoman bureaucracy (judge, attorney, and public prosecutor) he remained an Ottoman loyalist. He fought against anti-Arab tendencies within the Young Turks and against the restoration of Hamidian despotism in 1909. His Ottomanism was secular, antifeudal, antiseparatist, modernist, and—at times—socialist. His Orthodoxy induced him to sympathize with the Armenians and the underprivileged; but, in defending the abuses suffered by both, he believed in the potency of Ottoman law. During the war he became actively engaged in countering Anglo-French interventions in Syria and Anatolia—which he regarded as colonialist and imperialist, and fought tenaciously against Christian separatism in Mount Lebanon. He continued to believe in the Ottoman principle even after the military defeat of Cemal Pasha and the Fourth Army.

Although Issa al-Issa belonged to the same social milieu as Hakim (both came from urban professional and mercantile families), his Orthodoxy moved him in a different direction. Like Hakim he had benefited from the limited educational opportunities provided by the church schools. He had studied under the direction of the Orthodox encyclopedist Issa Iskandar al-Ma'louf at Kefteen Orthodox Seminary—which at the time provided the highest level of Orthodox education available in the Arab East.[104] And, like Hakim, by virtue of his family's wealth he was freed from dependency on the communal resources of the church. That explains to a large extent his ability to rebel against the patriarchate. But unlike Hakim he developed a considerable distance from the Ottoman bureaucracy and maintained strong affinities to the remnants of the capitulation system. His early schooling took place at the Catholic Freres College in Jaffa, and his education continued later at the Syrian Protestant College in Beirut, where he acquired basic language skills in Arabic, Turkish, French, and English.[105] He began his professional career by working as a translator for the Coptic monastery in Jerusalem (1903–1904) and as a senior clerk in the Qajari consulate, Pashkarberdaz, taking care of the interests of Persian subjects in Palestine. Those experiences, as is clear from his diary, influenced his perception of the Ottoman authorities from the perspective of its privileged subjects and as a protégé of the ancien régime.[106] This attitude was reinforced during his later career, as a commercial agent in Egypt, where he became acquainted with a more combative press than existed in Syria and Palestine before 1908. His work with the consular corps in Jerusalem and with the press in Egypt no doubt had a major impact on his Ottoman politics. Once the constitutional revolution was launched, he returned to Palestine and joined the decentralization movement, adopting an ambivalent attitude toward Syria's continued bond within the Ottoman system. The Egyptian wing of the Ottoman decentralization movement—with which Issa apparently identified—unlike the Syrian one, took a secessionist position during World War I. Furthermore, his Orthodox identity, and his struggle for the Arabization of the church, convinced him that the Ottoman administration was solidly behind maintaining the privileges of the Orthodox patriarchate against the Arab laity. His early anti-Zionism and sympathy for the plight of Arab peasants pitted him, in endless litigations and court battles, against the Ottoman censor and the courts. All of which explains why Issa and his cousin Yusif were exiled to the Anatolian countryside during the war, while Hakim remained a pillar of the Ottoman establishment.

Hakim's memoirs during the Faisali period of the early period of Arab rule in Damascus reveal a balanced, though critical, view of the administration of Cemal Pasha. After the Faisali period, he remained critical of Cemal's administration, taking the position that it had undermined the principles of Ottoman rule, especially those that related to the autonomy and self-administration of Syria. Issa's views during the same period indicate that he did not take those principles seriously, nor did he believe that Palestine had a future within the Ottoman commonwealth.

Hakim's and Issa's intimate involvement with the Faisali regime in Damascus largely derived from their roots in the Orthodox community and their faith in the Orthodox Renaissance movement. They vigorously served what they believed would be an Arab nationalist, secular, and progressive regime that would maintain the integrity and unity of the Syrian provinces. In their minds it was the nonsectarian nature of that regime that guaranteed it would promote the best interests of the nation as a whole, and not only those of the Christian communities in Palestine and Syria.

SIX

A Farcical Moment

NARRATIVES OF REVOLUTION AND
COUNTERREVOLUTION IN NABLUS

THROUGHOUT MOST OF THE nineteenth century and all of the twentieth, the city of Nablus ("Little Damascus," a nickname coined by the medieval geographer Maqdisi) evoked images of soap, *knafeh,* and tolerance of homosexuality. The region surrounding the city was also a site of sporadic rebellions by the peasantry. The epitaph Jabal al-Nar, "the Mountain of Fire" (acquired during the 1936 revolt), was synonymous with the city of Nablus and its history, recalling the 1834 rebellion of Qasim al-Ahmad against the Egyptian armies of Ibrahim Pasha as well as a series of revolts that punctuated the Ottoman, Mandate, and Israeli periods after that.[1] Al-Ahmad's peasant rebellion is often seen, with some exaggeration, as a turning point in the formation of Palestinian nationalism and a separatist Palestinian identity. Little is known, however, of the city as a bastion of conservatism and a center for counterrevolutionary activities. Local historians have been keen at observing this other side of Nabulsi temperament, mainly through their preoccupation with the stable, the continuous, and the quotidian. In this historical note I examine a short and crucial episode when the city rallied *against* the overthrow of the autocratic regime of Abdul Hamid II and *for* the restoration of the sultanic dictatorship.

By most contemporary accounts the events accompanying the Young Turk revolution and the (re)adoption of the suspended constitution (Ikinci Mesrutiyet Devri) in April 1908 constituted a pivotal moment for the Arab provinces, and Palestine in particular. The revolution heralded the end of despotic rule by Sultan Abdul Hamid; it put an end to press control and press censorship and made possible a renaissance in publishing and dissemination of newspapers, books, and pamphlets; and it allowed for the freedom of assembly and, within limits, the formation of political parties in Syria and elsewhere—including parties calling for regional autonomy. Finally it reintroduced the system of qualified democratic participation of all regional and ethnic groups in parliament within the context of the idea of Osmenlilik—common Ottoman citizenship. Mass celebrations of Hurriet (the declaration of freedom) were widely reported and photographed in the public squares of Beirut, Damascus, Jaffa (in front of the city Saraya Building), and Jerusalem, but also in a large number of district centers such as Tripoli, Nablus, Latakiyya, and Zahle. Although regional officers orchestrated many of those celebrations, many were spontaneous expressions of support for the rebellion. Nevertheless, a number of accounts diverge from this seeming consensus on the significance of these celebrations and, in at least one case, Ihsan al-Nimr's history of Nablus, a strident position of dissent—a view of the revolution as a retrogressive event, a stab in the back, and even *a farcical moment*. The new regime under the aegis of the CUP and its successors in 1913 introduced, instead of freedom and decentralization, an increased centralization, standardization of bureaucratic governance, and Turkification of the administrative apparatus.

Revolutions are continuously being reexamined by historians, with the Ottoman revolution even more so in light of the circumstances of the Great War and the aftermath of the Sykes-Picot Agreement. The centennial recollections of the 1908–1909 events, and the attempts at restoring the ancien régime of the sultanate, leading to the devastating years of global war in Syria, Iraq, and Anatolia, have rekindled interest in how these events were written in local histories, shedding new light on what was happening at the regional level and in the countryside. Those momentous events were keenly observed by two local historians of Nablus: Ihsan al-Nimr and Muhammad Izzat Darwazeh. The significance of these histories lies, in part, in their claim that, in the context of the rebellion, Nablus possessed an exceptional status, as a bulwark of Hamidian support in Palestine. And it lies in part in their claim that, especially in the case of Nimr, the Young Turk "revolution" was a marginal, if not contrived, event as far as the local population was concerned. In addition, each of the two historians claims that his version of events, as we shall see, constituted a *national history* seen from a local perspective, rather than an isolated microhistory of a city.

What gives potency to these two accounts is the solid amount of investigation invested in them by the authors (who were political actors as well as self-defined historians), and the fact that they were both eyewitnesses and participants in the political struggles of the period. Despite the significant overlap in their accounts, Darwazeh and Nimr stood at opposite ends of the ideational divide in Ottoman Syria. Ihsan al-Nimr, a descendant of the most feudal of the landholding families in Nablus, was a solid supporter of the Islamic *salafi* currents and Hamidian Ottomanism; while Darwazeh, the plebian militant, adhered briefly to the ideals of the CUP and, subsequently, moved to the Ottoman Decentralization Party and (later) to the Freedom and Accord Party, also known as the Liberal Union Party (Hizb al-Hurriyah wal I'tilaf, or Hürriyet ve İtilâf Fırkası in Turkish). I examine Nimr's and Darwazeh's accounts here and contrast them with the view of the events from Jerusalem as recorded and analyzed by Ruhi al-Khalidi, a prominant Ottoman civil servant and deputy to the Majlis al-Mab'uthan (the parliament).

The Causes of the Ottoman Revolution (1908) by Ruhi al-Khalidi, published immediately after the event, was probably the earliest assessment of the rebellion and its potential impact on Palestine and the Arab provinces. The author saw the April events as the culmination of the post-Tanzimat struggle for democracy, constitutionalism, and decentralization of the state. On the centenary of the book's appearance, historian Khalid Ziadeh issued a retrospective assessment of its impact and the lasting legacy of its author.[2] Published as a series of articles in Rashid Rida's *Al-Manar* (Cairo), the book was released before the deposing the sultan in 1909, the seizure of power by the CUP, and the attempted restoration of the ancien régime. Khalidi uses the term *inqilab* (overturning) for the Ottoman revolution to distinguish it from *thawra,* which in his usage connoted agitation, mutiny, and insurrection. To him, *inqilab* accurately identified the all-encompassing structural and radical features of the movement, while *thawra* was a mere rebellion— short-lived, with little lasting effect. (Three decades later, the terms' meanings reversed in Arabic journalistic usage, but in Persian, Urdu, and Ottoman Turkish the term *inqilab* continued to mean "revolution.") To Khalidi, the movement realized the long-awaited restoration of the democratic freedoms and reforms launched by the first Ottoman constitution of 1876, and it was a vindication of the ideals of Midhat Pasha, governor of Syria, who came to be known as the "father of the constitution." Attacking the repressive state apparatus of Sultan Abdul Hamid (without directly naming the sultan as a culprit), Khalidi anticipates the ushering in of an era of federalism, constitutional freedoms, autonomy for the provinces, and guarantees of equality for ethnic and national groups. He (mistakenly) foresaw the Committee of Union and Progress as an advocate for decentralization. On the future of Palestine, despite his well-known criticism of Zionism, Khalidi compares the

صورة قوس الحرية باب القلعه ١٩٠٨ - القدس

FIGURE 12. Celebrating "huriyya" at Jerusalem's Jaffa Gate, 1908. Wasif Jawhariyyeh Collection, Institute for Palestine Studies, Beirut.

achievements of the German and Jewish colonies favorably with the corrupt Ottoman administration's handing of the fiscal debt.[3]

But not all Arab observers were enthusiastic about the events of April 1908 and the promises of the Young Turks. The historian Adel Manaa notes that partisans of the Committee of Union and Progress in Syria and Palestine had to exert themselves in order to mobilize public celebrations in support of the rebellion, while in inland cities, especially in Nablus, support continued to be expressed for Abdul Hamid and the ancien régime even after the deposing of the sultan. This was in contrast to the situation in Jaffa and Jerusalem, where local political figures and the intelligentsia were substantially, if not solidly, behind the constitutional movement. One reason for this divergence, as suggested by Manaa, was the considerable penetration of European economic and cultural interests in the coastal cities and the relative economic autarky of Nablus. Jerusalem and Jaffa, in addition, had large Jewish and Christian populations with important connections to Western official and charitable circles.[4] In both cities the majority of the Jews and Christians were Ottoman citizens. In the case of the Jewish population, Zionism had made few inroads except among those who were European immigrants—and both the Sephardic and Ashkenazi religious populations were largely anti-Zionist. In the case of the Christians, at least within the majority Orthodox community, the major issue was the dispute between the Greek-controlled patriarchate and the Arab laity. None of these issues, however, were relevant to the political struggles in Nablus, since both the Christian and Jewish (Samaritan) populations were marginal.

Khalidi's celebratory views on the 1908 events were meant as a general assessment of the Young Turk revolution. To understand what was happening on the local level requires an examination of the writings of local historians, specifically the narratives for Nablus made by Ihsan al-Nimr and Muhammad Izzat Darwazeh.

"I CAN HARDLY SEE [PALESTINE] ON THE MAP"

Nimr's family background and early education were crucial in molding his Ottomanist worldview. The Nimrs were a patrician family of tax-farming *aghas* in Syria and Palestine. His great-grandfathers served as guardians of the hajj routes (in the Karak region), and the family produced a series of judges and Ottoman bureaucrats (including the *daftardar,* chief waqf administrator of Damascus). The Nimr family was also one of the most prominent clans of tax-farmers (*multazimin*) in the Nablus region, but they lost their status as the region's major tax-farmers to their competitors, the Jarrars of Jenin and Abdulhadis of Arrabeh, during the life of Ihsan's father, Najib Agha al-Nimr, and his uncle Hussein Agha.[5]

Ihsan grew up in the Nimr family compound in old Nablus, where he received a traditional Quranic *kuttab* education with his sisters Shamseh and Nabiha, followed by his primary education at Maktab al-Khan and the Rashid Sultanic college. He received his secondary education ("the worst years of my life") at Najah College, where he was a student of Izzat Darwazeh, an agitator for "idealistic causes." As a student leader he was so self-confident that it made him insufferable. Ni'meh Ziadeh narrates an amusing episode where, after hearing him in a public debate, Darwazeh praised him as the "future orator of Palestine." "Nimr responded to this praise: 'I do not accept this title—if Palestine is large in your eyes, I can hardly see it on the map.' Darwazeh, then added—'[T]hen you are the orator of the Arabs [khatib al-Arab].'—'[N]ow I accept,' said Nimr."[6] He was expelled from Najah for his clashes with students and teachers over "religious issues and his zealotry" and continued his education at National College at Shweifat in Mount Lebanon.[7] He tried to study history at the American University in Beirut but was unable to do so, for financial reasons. Nimr was self-taught after that, or as Ziad puts it, "He graduated from his own university," which explains his eclectic style of writing. Nimr immersed himself in classical historical writings such as those of Ibn al-Athir, Ya'coubi, and Ibn Khaldun. After the Great War, he established contacts with Saudi scholars in Najd and adopted a Wahhabi perspective on religious interpretation. He read and internalized the work of Ibn Taymiyyeh, and Ibn Qayyim, and especially the work of Muhammad Abdul Wahhab and Suleiman Ibn Samhan al-Najdi. But he was also influenced by Islamic modernists whose writings he received from Egypt, including the works of Jamal ed-Din al-Afghani, Abdo, Kawakibi, Ghalayini, and Manfaluti. He also published extensively in Islamic journals such as *Al-Sirat al-Mustaqim* (edited in Jaffa by his friend Abdallah al-Qalqili) and *Al-Tamadun al-Islami* (Damascus) on the twin themes of the moral rearmament of youth, and Jihad.[8]

In ideological terms Nimr continued to adhere to an Ottomanist framework in his writing for many decades after the fall of the Ottoman regime. He remained politically active during the Mandate period, but refused to belong to any mainstream nationalist or Islamic party. Instead he was involved in local activities against Zionism and the British administration. In the 1920s he collaborated with the trade union movement in Nablus to establish the syndicate of Nablus shoemakers in order to combat the importation and sale of Bata shoes from Czechoslovakia—which he saw as undermining the local shoe industry. In 1929 he was arrested and sentenced to three-months imprisonment for leading anti-British demonstrations.[9] In 1933 he founded, in collaboration with Nabulsi nationalists, the Youth Party (Munadhamat Hizb al-Shabab) to combat Jewish immigration to Palestine. During the 1936 rebellion he escaped to Damascus and participated in the mobilization of Syrian volunteers, under the leadership of Fawzi al-Quwakgi, to fight in Palestine. With the failure of the rebellion, he returned and turned to the politics of Islamic moral rearmament, founding the Society of Islamic Guidance (Jam'iyyat al-Hidaya al-Islamiyyah) for that purpose, but failed to establish any branches outside Nablus. After the 1948 war, he withdrew from political activities and confined himself to writing local history. A writer who could "hardly see [Palestine] on the map" in 1917 ended his career seeing little outside the parameters of his native town.

NABLUS AS THE CENTER OF THE WORLD

Ihsan al-Nimr devotes almost a whole volume of his four-volume *Tarikh Jabal Nablus* to the events leading up to the Ottoman revolution, in July 1908, and their aftermath. While the rest of his magnum opus is based on a meticulous reading of the city's history from probate court records and from the family papers of the Nimrs and other city potentates, the volume is based on extended interviews with local participants, on city council records, and on his own eyewitness recollections of events.

Nimr's account of events in this section, in contrast to the earlier volumes of the Nablus chronicles, is a mixture of anecdotal narratives and polemical discourse against nationalist anti-Ottoman accounts. He reminds the reader that Ottoman rule in the Syrian provinces was not based exclusively or even mainly on Turkish personnel but also on a mixture of Arab, Turk, Circassian, Kurdish, Armenian, Rumi, and Jewish personnel. Nineteenth-century governors in Nablus were a succession of predominantly Arab figures: Dia Bey al-Masri was Egyptian, Sa'id Pasha was a Kurd from Damascus, Aziz Bey al-Azmeh was from Damascus, Hussein Bey al-Ahdab was a Beiruti, and Hulu Pasha al-Abed was also a Damascene.[10]

Cognizant of the rebellious nature of Nabulsis from the days of the Egyptian campaign, "the Sublime Porte began to weigh their appointments in the province [of] people of high caliber and expertise."[11] Nimr notes that Nablus was the center of the major peasant rebellion against Ibrahim Pasha's Egyptian rule in the 1830s. The rebellion was led by Qasim al-Ahmad from Jamma'in and succeeded in conquering Jerusalem in 1834. The rebellion brought into prominence the leadership of the Abdulhadi clan and their allies, and the demise of the Agha and Tuqan families. The wresting of Ottoman rule from the Egyptians led to the restoration of Nablus as the major economic center of Palestine and southern Syria, but only for a while.[12]

Support for the Committee of Union and Progress (CUP) in southern Syria (i.e., Palestine and Transjordan) seems to have been based in the Jerusalem district. Its leaders included the commander of the Jerusalem gendarmerie, Sami Bey al-Halabi, and Sheikh Musa al-Budeiri, a prominent teacher in the sultanic schools. The link with the Anatolian CUP was Amin Beyk, a clerk in the Jerusalem post office and the brother of Tal'at Pasha, the forthcoming minister of interior. In Nablus the local CUP was made up of middle government and urban clerks and of officers in the local armed forces. They established the first revolutionary organization in the country, known as Nadi al-Qalb (the Heart Club). The leadership committee was made up of Husni Bey, commander of the Nablus garrison; Amin Bey al-Squlelli, head of the Radif forces (military auxiliaries); Hajj Muhammad Abdo, the mayor of Nablus; and Abdul Fattah Malhas and Haydar Bey Tuqan, city merchants. They were subsequently joined by Ragheb Agha al-Nimr, who became the chief inspector of the party organizations in all of Southern Syria.[13]

When news of the revolt of the Third Army in Macedonia and the subsequent proclamation of the constitution in Istanbul reached Nablus in mid-April 1908, Governor Amin al-Tarazi refused to announce these events, as a mark of loyalty to the sultan. The decision to celebrate the event was made by the mayor, Hajj Muhammad Abdo, who initiated the celebrations from Nadi al-Qalb headquarters. The celebrations were muted in Nablus but wildly enthusiastic in Jerusalem, Jaffa, and Akka.

NABLUS IN SUPPORT OF THE RESTORATION

Within less than a year, while the new regime in the capital was consolidating its linkages and control over Syria, news of the April 18, 1909, countercoup (known as the March 31 incident, in reference to the Rumi calendar), and the announcement of the suspension of parliament and the restoration of the sultan's rule, reached Nablus. Nimr used the term the *restorative movement* in reference to the counterrevolution.[14] "With the formation of the Mohammadan Sharia Society [Jam'iat al-Shar'ia al-Muhammadiyyah] against the constitution,"[15] he wrote, "all segments of Nabulsi society rose, calling for the abolition of the constitution. The populace marched on the Nimr Diwan [compound], where they swore loyalty to Sultan Abdul Hamid and expressed their wrath against the CUP and cursed its leaders, Anwar [Enver] and Niazi. The movement was headed by Hajj Tawfiq Hammad and his party, against Mayor Muhammad Abdo and his [CUP] supporters."[16] The restorative movement was short-lived, and the rebels were soon restored to power after contingents of the armed forces, dispatched from Salonika by Mahmoud Sevket Pasha, defeated the insurrection and deposed Sultan Abdul Hamid.

Meanwhile supporters of the CUP in Nablus (still an underground movement), whom the Arabic press referred to as the "unionists" (Ittihadiyyun— i.e., "CUPers"), called for volunteers to fight for the constitutional government in the capital. The Heart Club became the center of mobilization, and in their initial enthusiasm the unionists telegraphed Istanbul claiming that sixty thousand volunteers were on their way in support of the revolution, presumably from Palestine. Of that number only five fighters, according to Nimr, materialized from Nablus, including the head of the population registry, Sa'ib Effendi, and Dhaher Effendi Abdo. By the time they reached Jenin the counterrevolutionary movement had been defeated, and they had to return to Nablus on foot, where they were mocked and pelted with stones and mud.[17]

Once the restorative movement had been defeated, the unionists moved to punish the supporters of the old regime and "restore law and order." The magnitude of support for the Hamidian regime can be gleaned from the amount of force used to discipline the city. Four battalions had to be brought to Nablus, according to Nimr, to suppress the supporters of the sultan and the Sharia movement.[18] Governor Amin Bey al-Tarazi was removed and replaced by Fathi Suleiman Pasha. An investigation committee was established to prepare a report and recommend punitive measures. As a result loyalist members of the Tuqan, Hammad, and Abdulhadi families were deported, and their kin were banned from public employment while the CUP was in power in the sultanate.[19] Nimr's reference to the four battalions might be an exaggeration and cannot be confirmed from other local sources, but his reference to the divisions in the city and the punishment meted out to the Hammad leadership is corroborated by Darwazeh.

CREDIBILITY OF IHSAN NIMR AS A LOCAL HISTORIAN

The story of the counterrevolutionary coup and its Nabulsi reverberations raises issues with the credibility of Ihsan Nimr as a local historian, both at the level of empirical details and with his interpretive schema. Nimr has shown considerable skill in the use of court records and family papers in delineating the social history of Nablus in the early and middle Ottoman periods (volumes 1 and 2). His work is exceptional in assessing the system of governance and the achievement of local independence by Nabulsi potentates,[20] in examining how common law (*qanun 'urfi*) was integrated with civil Islamic law,[21] and in interpreting how brigandage became a factor in consolidating a system of internal security in Nablus.[22] Despite his erratic and eclectic style, his work in these sections should be considered in the tradition of the Annales school of historical interpretation, of which he can be seen as an unconscious practitioner.

Nimr's work is particularly valuable, as well as original, in his depiction of the autonomy of Jabal Nablus and southern Palestine during the era of military fiefdoms (*timar sipahi*) in the eighteenth century, and of its linkages to the administration of hajj (pilgrimage) routes.[23] Much of later work in his monumental *Tarikh Jabal Nablus* deals with the triadic struggle during the Tanzimat period between the central Ottoman government on the one hand, and, on the other, the feudal lords (*shuyukh al-nawahi*) who controlled the collection of the agricultural revenue, such the Jarrars of Sanur and Abdulhadis of Arrabeh, and the urban aristocracy of Nablus, the Nimr-Aghas and the Tuqans in particular. A turning point in this conflict was the Egyptian campaign of Ibrahim Pasha (1830–1840) typified by peasant rebellions (led by Qasim al-Ahmad) and the rise of the Abdulhadi clan as a hegemonic force in the Nablus province. The restoration of Ottoman rule in Syria (1841) introduced an era of centralization of government control and the weakening of rural feudalism in favor of the urban potentates, a landlord class that integrated its rural wealth with investment in manufacturing (textiles, soap) and merchant capital.[24]

Nimr traces the incidents of 1908 and 1909, discussed here, to the establishment of the city's first advisory council (*majlis al-ishara*), in 1848, in line with Ottoman urban municipal reform. It was this advisory council that evolved into the elected municipal council of 1869, which became the arena of conflict between the central government in its attempts to increase rural revenue and the reconstituted urban elites of Nablus, who resisted these incursions. Beshara Doumani's pioneering work on the history of Jabal Nablus provides an important interpretation of Nimr's convoluted narrative of these events.[25] "[Nablus urban] notables used the council to bargain with the Ottoman government over the boundaries of political authority and tried to promote their own interpretations of the meaning of citizenship, identity, custom, and tradition. The central government had little choice but to cooperate. It could not even replace the tax-farmers with a salaried expatriate bureaucratic cadre of its own, much less abolish the tax-farms as the reforms publicly intended to do."[26]

One feature of this conflict between the central government and the city's elite was the ability of the potentates, Nimr keeps reminding us, to interpret the High Porte circulars and bend government directives in the interest of the local elites. They also succeeded, much more so than in Jerusalem and other provincial centers, in ensuring the appointment of local figures, rather than outsiders, to the administration of district affairs.[27]

Nimr's work begins to suffer, nevertheless, in his handling of the post-Tanzimat era, in particular his treatment of the second constitutional era, which led to the events of World War I in Nablus. His account of this period is dominated by a Manichaean opposition between the forces of law and order (Hamidian rule) and what he sees as the secular and destructive CUP. He highlights this opposition in terms of a factional conflict between segments of the Nabulsi elite—pitting the Abdo and Malhas families against the Tuqans, Nimrs, and Abdulhadis. The closer he gets to the events of 1908–1912 (the fall of the CUP), the more he relies on his personal recollections and interviews with local informants, rather than on court records and municipal records. The dizzying lists of personal actions and personal careers, and the rise and fall of family fortunes, are cited with little reference to social content or social referencing—their context is either assumed to be self-evident or explained simply as an abandonment of the Ottoman Islamic bond. Thus his extensive personal interviews with "actors and participants in events," a major strength of Nimr's historical contemporary narrative, are rendered as an incoherent pastiche of family squabbles. Framing all of this incoherence is a likely recognition, on the author's part, of the decline in the status and power of the Nimr family fortune as a leading base of Ottoman administration in Nablus.[28] Therefore, in illuminating the local history of Nablus for this period, we are lucky to have an alternative account in the work of Muhammad Izzat Darwazeh.

IZZAT DARWAZEH'S VISION

In his account of Nablus (and Palestine) during the second constitutional period and World War I, Darwazeh offers a keen integration of biographical trajectories with a class analysis of the forces involved. Like Ihsan Nimr, Darwazeh, a copious diarist and chronicler, was an eyewitness of the great transformations at the local scene, albeit a more adult and, therefore, engaged observer. In addition, Darwazeh, a junior officer in the Ottoman postal civil service, was involved directly in the apparatus of governance and as a partisan in the momentous political struggles in Beirut and Nablus. He was an active member of several Ottoman oppositional groups, the CUP, the Entente Party, and, later, the Faisali movement and the Istiqlal Party, of which he was a founding member.

Darwazeh seeks to understand the Nabulsi social struggle by examining the new social formations of the city's elites. The turn of the nineteenth century posed challenges to the region's feudal families—the Tuqans, Abdulhadis, Nimrs, and Qasems—who continued to amass wealth by controlling the region's landed estates in the post-Tanzimat period. The main arena for this struggle was the city's municipal council, which witnessed in 1911 the defeat of Bashir Tuqan, "representing an alliance of the city's feudal elements,"[29] by Hajj Tawfiq Hammad (1863–1934), a significant figure in city politics. The mercantile bourgeoisie of Nablus coalesced around the party of the Abbasi Society, named after Abbas Effendi al-Khammash. The Abbasi Society, and later the Hammadi Society, as it became called, united the forces of the Zuaiter, Shak'a, and Masri families and a small faction of the Abdulhadis family.[30] Tawfiq Hammad was the head of the Provincial Registry (Katib Qalam al-Mutasariffiyah). In addition he was appointed as head of the Nablus Council and, shortly thereafter, was elected to the new Ottoman parliament. His party was able to rally the rising "antifeudal figures" in Jenin, Tulkarim, and Qalqilieh (that is, in the whole region) against the influence of the Tuqans and the Nimrs. Their power was mobilized against the CUP in Palestine, which, according to Darwazeh, was supported by military officers and the cadres of the Ottoman civil service.[31]

The power of the Hammadi Society, the "bourgeoisie party," as Darwazeh calls it, rested on Tawfiq Hammad's leadership and organizational skills in bringing a wide network of commercial interests together against the old guard (the Tuqans and their allies). They were able to compete successfully for the collection of the rural land revenue (*daribat al-'a'shar*, or tithe) which was now collected by public auction, after the dissolution of the tax-farming system, or—more accurately—after the *iltizam* system was no longer in the hands of feudal landlords.[32] Their ideological position was strongly supportive of Sultan Abdul Hamid and the short-lived countercoup aimed at restoring the caliphate in 1909. Later, most of their members joined the Ottoman Decentralization Party.[33] An anomaly in this class analysis of Nablus's politics was the alliance between the Hammadi Society and the Abdulhadis of Jenin, headed by Sa'id Pasha and Hafiz Pasha Abdulhadi—arguably the feudal family with the most extensive landholdings. Darwazeh refers to this anomaly as a paradox (*mufaraqa*). The alliance was a power tool in the hands of the Society, he claims, but one that created few problems:

> For the Abdulhadis were the spearheads of the feudal forces. Sa'id and Hafiz [Abdulhadi] were the most powerful figures in the Jenin area. . . . [W]hat was more surprising is that the family did not object to being a cornerstone in the antifeudal party. Their power and status was so entrenched that they did not object to the deal. They saw their alliance with the Nablus-based Society as an instrument in their own factional conflicts with other feudal forces in the province. It seems to me that Salim al-Ahmad [their nephew] had a basic role in resolving these contradictions and providing intellectual formulations for the Abdulhadi involvement [in the antifeudal campaign].[34]

Darwazeh's interpretation here is both sophisticated and penetrating. While utilizing a materialist and Marxist frame of analysis, it suffers, nevertheless, from a certain degree of reductionism, by collapsing class categories into political forces, especially in trying to explain the "anomaly" of a feudal family in the Nabulsi party of the bourgeoisie. One reason behind this apparent paradox is Darwazeh's failure to see that large segments of the Palestinian landed elite had already become commercialized and "bourgeoisified" through investing much of their land revenue in industry (soap, sesame oil, cotton), creating new avenues for their wealth and new professional horizons for their family members. Still, his general analysis is astute and lends coherence to the nature of the political conflicts in Nablus, which Ihsan al-Nimr subsumed under a Hamidian/anti-Hamidian rubric.

THE "FARCICAL MOMENT" RETOLD

In Darwazeh's account of the rebellion, which is described in derogatory terms by Nimr, it was the restoration of Hamidian despotism, and not the rebellion, that was the farcical moment. In June 1907, Izzat Darwazeh was appointed as a clerk in the Nablus Post Office, in charge of telegrams (a sensitive post requiring security clearance), with a monthly salary of three hundred piasters. His father had to pay thirty Ottoman pounds (a bribe he euphemistically calls *ma feeh al-Naseeb,* "their anticipated share") to those in charge of the postal directorate to secure the appointment.[35] He remained in his job until 1914, when he was promoted to deputy head, and witnessed the momentous events that engulfed Nablus during the rebellion. One of his tasks was to intercept proscribed newspapers and journals received by clients in the city and confiscate them. The list of banned publications was distributed weekly.[36] This gave Darwazeh a chance to read and disseminate dissident material mailed from Cairo and Europe, as well as radical Arabic broadsheets that were sent from America.

On July 24, 1908 (the 4th of Tammuz 1324, by the Ottoman Mali calendar), Izzat received a circular telegram addressed to the Nablus *mutasarrif* announcing the imperial decree of Sultan Abdul Hamid "activating al-qanun al-assasi," the constitution. During the next few days the "Nabulsi street," as Darwazeh calls it, was flooded with the leaflets of the Committee of Union and Progress and red-and-white banners bearing the party's slogans: Freedom, Equality and Brotherhood (Hurriyat, Musawat, Ukhuwat). The CUP club (which Nimr called Nadi al-Qalb) at Nablus's eastern gate, next to the post office, became a magnet for Nablus youth.[37] Darwazeh joined the party at the age of nineteen, along with his friend and comrade Ibrahim al-Qasim Abdulhadi: "Ibrahim was a great orator. He would address the gathered masses in the plaza of the Saraya in the Nabulsi dialect, explaining the meaning of the Dustur and its implication for justice and brotherhood, as well as a marker against corruption and nepotism."[38]

He remained close to Ibrahim during the war years, when they both became members of the Entente (Liberal Union) Party and the Decentralization Party. Here is how Darwazeh describes the events of March 31, 1909 (billed in his memoirs as *thawrat al-mashayikh,* or rebellion of the religious orders). Recall that Darwazeh at the time was a postal clerk in the Beirut Ottoman post office, soon to be transferred to Nablus.[39]

On March 31 1325 [April 13, 1909] the postal authorities in the capital [Istanbul] communicated to their colleagues in Beirut and elsewhere that a group of religious sheikhs commanded by Darwish Wihdati [Dervish Vahdeti] conducted a movement against the constitution, the CUP, and their government. They were able to win the support of segments of the religious public, as well as army officers in Asitanah [Istanbul]. Their demands were to annul the constitution, dissolve the parliament, expel the "atheist" CUP, and apply Sharia law as the constitution of the realm. They were able to eliminate several ministers and deputies. CUP members went into hiding. Sultan Abdul Hamid, who was obviously behind the movement, responded to all their demands and invalidated the parliament and the constitution.[40]

Darwish Widhtadi was a Cypriot militant, the leader of al-Jam'iyyah al-Muhammadiyyah, and the editor of *Volkan,* an Istanbuli Islamic newspaper.[41] The movement replaced a large number of governors in Anatolia and Syria with Hamidian loyalists. Festivities were announced throughout the sultanate to celebrate the restoration of the sultan's rule. In Nablus the restorative movement was led by Hajj Tawfiq Hammad and his followers. They held a number of mass meetings in the city's neighborhoods and compelled the inhabitants to swear allegiance to the sultan and Islamic Sharia. "They accused the unionists of apostasy and atheism [*al-kufr wal il-haad*] and of being enemies of the caliphate."[42] Both Ihsan al-Nimr and Darwazeh attended these meetings, the former as a supporter, and the latter as a critical observer. Izzat Darwazeh noted that similar meetings took place throughout Palestine and Syria.[43]

When Omar Mahmoud Shawkat (Arabic spelling of the Turkish Sevket) led the Romeli army against the counterrebellion in Istanbul, deposed the sultan, and restored the parliament, the CUP sent a call to its regional branches to march on the capital in support of the revolution. Ten people from Nablus, according to Darwazeh (five according to Nimr), were the vanguard of the march from Palestine. They were led by Yuzbashi Amin, head of the Nablus garrison; Halim Abdul Baqi (the future prime minister of Hajj Amin's all-Palestine government and the leader of al-Istiqlal Party); Abdul Fattah Malhas; and Raghib Shaheen.[44] When they reached Damascus, the "revolutionary forces" were already in power and the support group went back to Nablus. The new government began a process of suppressing followers of the Hamidian regime in Palestine and Syria. New governors were appointed. Hajj Tawfiq Hammad and his followers were arrested and exiled to Beirut. Bashir Tuqan was appointed by the Turkish governor of Nablus, and Fathi Bey, as the new district governor of Jenin in charge of liquidating the influence of the Hamidian order in the region. The CUP government embarked on a major campaign of ensuring the success of its supporters in the new parliament. In the case of Nablus this brought back the influence of the Tuqan family—with Haydar Tuqan taking the position of his deceased cousin Bashir Tuqan.[45] In this process the CUP used a substantial amount of "vote rigging and intimidation," according to Darwazeh, since the opposition was still popular among the populace.

Darwazeh suggests that the conflict in Nablus, and Palestine in general, was between two wings of the local elite, that the Restorative Movement was based on the new mercantile elements (Hajj Hammad and his party), while the constitutional anti-Hamidian movement derived its leadership from the old feudal elements (the Tuqans and their followers). This was a major reason why the radical opposition to the ancien régime turned against both factions and moved in a nationalist direction, supporting the Decentralization Party and eventually the nationalist Istiqlal Party—of which Darwazeh would soon become a leading member.

DARWAZEH'S REVOLUTION IS NIMR'S FARCICAL MOMENT

Ihsan al-Nimr perceived the collapse of the Ottoman order as rooted in its misconceived modernization attempt, ending with the decline of the autonomy of the provincial administration, not only in Nablus but in all the Syrian provinces. The periodization of this collapse is not clearly delineated in his monumental history *Balqa and Jabal Nablus,* but he does suggest that the abolition of decentralized control by local landlords (*shuyukh al-nawahi),* which saw the hegemony of the Nimrs, the Abdulhadis, and the Tuqans, gave way to competitive bidding for tax-farms by new social forces who sought personal enrichment in tax-farming and had no compassion for local peasants and their plight. He notes that until the end of the fourteenth hijri century (last third of the nineteenth century), rural taxes were still collected by local feudal lords and *sipahis.* These lords maintained social bonds with the peasants and made sure that their households were productive and above the subsistence level.[46] This process was destroyed by the Tanzimat state in its relentless search for increased revenue and in the institutionalization of tax-farming in the form of open competitive bidding.

> With the demise of Emirs of Jabal Nablus and its feudal sheikhs, a new generation of [commercial] entrepreneurs entered the scene, and *iltizam* [tax-farming] became a bidding process. The newly rich families began to displace the ruling mansions [*buyut al-hukm*] in the tax-farming auctions. Gradually, finance feudalism replaced prebendal feudalism [*al Iqta' al-mulki*], with important consequences. For those new landlords lacked consensual control [over the peasants] and began to use the whip of the gendarmes and police elements to enforce the collection.[47]

Nimr lists the mode of enrichment by the tax-farmers and the addition of new taxes (*werko,* animal head tax, and personal income tax) as measures leading to the pauperization of the Nablus peasants. The gendarmes were now enforcing not only the collection of the tithe but also the debts on behalf of city merchants and moneylenders—leading to the practice of corvée in response to nonpayment and to widespread corruption. He quotes the dean of al-Nimr lords, his cousin Mahmoud Agha al-Nimr, as noting, "What destroyed the Ottoman state was the gendarmes and their ruthless financial exactions."[48]

Nimr paints an idealized picture of the old feudal order and laments its demise, as exemplified by the demise of his own family—the Aghas—and their allies. His lamentation, however, is grounded in an acute sense of loss and suffering by the peasantry and the urban poor. He quotes peasant complaints cited in an official report by his Nabulsi compatriot Rafiq al-Tamimi, author of *Wilayat Beirut,* about the difference between the CUP period and the Hamidian regime: "The constitutional gendarmes are a thousand times worse than the police force of the despotic [Hamidian] period. For the old police used to be recruited from the members of neighboring clans, who were known for their good manners and conduct."[49] Nimr adds, "Their [titular] commander was Uthman Beyk, an outsider, while the actual commander was his deputy, Abdul Karim Agha al-Nimr, who was a local and familiar with the local traditions and economic conditions of the people."[50] In the new era the police force turned to wide-scale bribery and pillage to supplement their incomes.[51] The local governor began to recruit "rebels and gangsters," presumably as a means of domesticating brigands, into the police force. Those, in turn, resorted to cruel methods of exacting justice that turned people away from the new regime and undermined the legitimacy of the entire Ottoman state.

Thus Nimr attributes the alienation of the people from the Ottoman state to administrative measures taken during the constitutional period, and not particularly to the regime of Cemal Pasha and the war economy, as observed by Darwazeh and others. During the war, these measures introduced and exacerbated hostility to measures of Turkification and to anti-Arab sentiments emanating from the imperial capital.[52] In Nimr's narrative, however, the Nabulsi population, in general, remained loyal to the Ottomans despite the repressive measures undertaken by Cemal and his officers. This was the case even after Jerusalem and southern Palestine fell into British hands. Nablus became home to the relocated Ottoman central military command, which was supported by the German air force.

Nimr describes several meetings in the city called by commander Fawzi Pasha to rally the retreating army and prepare for the defense of the remaining part of southern Syria. He cites the exposition of Allied schemes in the region, including the Balfour Declaration and the Sykes-Picot Agreement, as a main reason for the renewed popular support for the army.[53] Several hundred deserters, and new local recruits, were organized into a new Salah ed-Din battalion. Schoolchildren were taught to sing in Turkish the words *Türkler ve Araplar kardeştir—paylaşılan bir vatan var* (Turks and Arabs are brothers—they have a shared homeland). This new situation, according to Nimr, delayed and overturned the thrust of the anti-Ottoman nationalist forces, "for people became aware of the impending danger and [recognized] that Turkish rule is much more tolerable than the plans of the Allies."[54] In December 1917, he pointedly noted that "the Arab rebellion of Sherif Hussein and his Syrian nationalist allies had little support in Nablus.[55] But this new revival of Ottomanism was short-lived. With the collapse of the Bulgarian front, orders were given for the withdrawal of the Ottoman forces from Syria and Palestine.

The claim that, in Nablus and other parts of Palestine, the Arab revolt had little support is verified by several historians, including Darwazeh. It contributes to our understanding of the exceptional situation in Nablus that set it apart from Jaffa and Jerusalem, and it explains why the Ottoman army was able to retain its foothold in northern Palestine for more than a year after the fall of the southern front.

CONCLUSION: LOCAL HISTORY AND
THE ISSUE OF EXCEPTIONALISM

The narratives of two local historians of Nablus, Ihsan al-Nimr and Muhammad Izzat Darwazeh, provide two contrasting views of the events that surrounded the constitutional revolution of 1908 and the subsequent collapse of the Ottoman sultanate.. The value of local history here lies in uncovering processes that explain the larger picture that took place in the Syrian provinces, at the regional and global levels. It also highlights the exceptionalism and the nuances of provincial forces that undermined what later became the established Arab nationalist narrative.

A major conceptual issue in the historiography of individual cities is the question of exceptionalism. This is a recurrent theme in local histories; they highlight the particularism of concrete local identities and isolate the degree of integration of local social organization in the web of national and global connections. The question is: to what extent are the particularistic social features of the urban scene—which are necessary for examining urban ethnography—rendered as exceptional and sui generis?

In the case of Nablus, the accounts of Nimr and Darwazeh are radically different in their approaches. One highlights the exceptional character of Jabal Nablus and its ruling forces in terms of the city's autonomy (Nimr), and the other in terms of particular class configurations in the late nineteenth century (Darwazeh). Darwazeh raises the curious issue of how segments of the old feudal classes decided to side with the revolution, while the "bourgeois party" took the side of Hamidian restoration. In Nimr's analysis, his exceptionalism is related to his perception of Nablus's enhanced autonomy within the Ottoman administrative apparatus; its ability to maintain the prolonged hegemony of its patrician families over the rural areas; and the ability of the city's elite to convert agrarian revenue into commercial and industrial wealth and to resist the encroachment of the centralized bureaucratic power of Istanbul over local affairs. In many ways this was true of several Syrian provincial centers, including Damascus and Aleppo, but more so in Nablus. The narratives of Darwazeh and Nimr define the defiance on the part of the city's local council and its ruling families as of paramount importance. This particular configuration of urban power allowed wealthy families not only to effectively siphon the rural surplus but also to mediate the relationship between peasants and urban landlords in defense of the Ottoman realm. Nablus was able to retain a substantially higher portion of the rural revenue than other districts in Palestine, allowing for noticeable growth in its commercial and industrial production while effectively integrating the fiscal reforms of the post-Tanzimat period.

After the fall of Jaffa, Jerusalem, and Beersheba in December 1917 to the Allied forces, the relocation of the Ottoman central command in southern Syria, from Jerusalem to Nablus, was not an accident of geography. Nimr and Darwazeh explain how and why Nablus remained loyal to the sultanate even at the height of Cemal Pasha's dictatorship—a support that was both ideological and military. It allowed the Ottomans to retain their control of northern Palestine and southern Syria for almost a full year, until November 1918.

Three narratives of the 1908–1909 revolution and counterrevolution are discussed here, by writers who claimed the city of Nablus as their city, two as native sons and the third as a person who spent his formative years in the city.

Nimr and Darwazeh were scions of established city families. Ruhi Yasin al-Khalidi, a well-integrated member of the imperial bureaucracy, came from a notable Jerusalemite family that traces its origins—by some accounts—to Mardah in the Nablus district, and he concluded his primary education in the Nablus Maktab Rashid school. This was during the tenure of Midhat Pasha, the progressive governor of Syria, who appointed Ruhi's father, Yasin al-Khalidi, as a judge in the Nablus court.[56] Nimr belonged to the leading feudal family of the city—the Aghas—whose hegemony was declining because of the Ottoman fiscal reforms. Muhammad Izzat Darwazeh, then a minor civil servant in the postal authority, belonged to a new professional and mercantile strata that benefited considerably from the new educational system and its reforms.

The social origins and class rankings of these three writers (imperial bureaucracy, landed elite, and professional petty bourgeoisie, respectively) sheds light on their perceptions of the constitutional revolution. But their diagnoses of events cannot be explained, much less deduced, by their class affiliations. Khalidi's *inqilab* provides an overarching and historical overview of the causes of the Ottoman revolution that is both utopian and positivist. In his view the second constitutional revolution performed, or rather attempted to perform, for the Ottoman realm what the French Revolution did for France: it ushered in its modernity by overthrowing feudalism and absolutist despotism in an Islamic, reformist garb. To him, Islamic reform allowed the Ottomans to avoid the class violence of the French revolution. His perspective was an imperial one, and Palestine was a footnote in this scheme. His distance from the region at the moment of writing (he was by then the Ottoman consul in Bordeaux), and his early death, in 1913, prevented him from examining the changes exacted by the revolution at the local level.

Nimr and Darwazeh provide an antidote to Khalidi's abstract and triumphalist conception of the constitutional movement, having witnessed the unfolding events of the revolution, and the "counterrevolution," on the ground. For both chroniclers, local history was a window on the larger forces transforming Palestine and Syria at the end of empire. It attempted to examine the exceptional status of Mount Nablus while underscoring the manner in which these local forces signified the death of the old order.

The focus on the politics of ruling elites in Nablus allowed both Darwazeh and Nimr (to a lesser extent) to transcend the pitfalls of localism in "local history"—that is, the isolation of the city's social structure from the political economy of it regional setting. This can be seen in a number of references to the city's external links:

- Nablus was called Little Damascus by Maqdisi in the tenth century, a term still used today, in large part because the city was administratively part of the Damascus Vilayat, and not the Jerusalem *mutasarriflik,* for most of the Ottoman period. Trade, architecture, cuisine, and marriage bonds within the patrician families continued to enhance the Damascene link.

- Both Darwazeh and Nimr note the absence of Arab nationalist politics (as opposed to Arabist cultural consciousness) in the main divide in the city's politics. Syrian separatist politics were either marginal (Darwazeh) or absent (Nimr). Nimr particularly noted that in the war period (1914–1918) the Arab revolt and the Faisali movement had no following, as noted above. Political movements, open and clandestine, such as the CUP, the Entente (Liberal Union) Party, and the Decentralization Party, were all Ottoman currents—with the exception of the Wahhabi influences.

- The Nablus elite was well integrated into the imperial Ottoman bureaucratic regime through appointments of local administrators, deputies to the Majlis al-Mab'uthan, and judges, in addition to civil servants (employees of the gendarmerie, municipal government, and schools), the bulk of whom were local people. Tension between Nablus and Istanbul continued to simmer over the choice of tax-farming allotments (*iltizam*) and the allotment of tax shares. Nimr refers to another main source of conflict, the use of the Ottoman gendarmerie in the forceful collection of taxes. In the late nineteenth century, those gendarmes were recruited increasingly from tribal police forces in the Balqa region.

But Nimr's and Darwazeh's accounts differ in a substantial manner. Nimr's assessment of the revolutionary movement of 1908–1909—that is, the successful attempt at overthrowing the Hamidian regime, and the unsuccessful attempt at restoring the sultanate—as a "farcical movement" was a figure of speech. It was meant to highlight the failure of the CUP coup, despite its apparent success, to penetrate power relations in the Arab provinces and Nablus in particular, a failure that he saw as being vindicated by the fall of unionists from power in 1912. Palestinian and Arab nationalism, to him, were retrogressive forces that helped the British and French to control Syria and paved the way for Zionism and the severing of Palestine from the sultanate—

which to him was the only guarantor of the sultanate's survival. Nimr's cosmology was heavily influenced by his Wahhabi sympathies, and he emerges as a consistently antinationalist, Ottomanist, and Islamic historian.

Darwazeh, in contrast, saw the contestation of power between the unionists and the Hamidian forces as a real conflict, manifested in Nablus as a social and political struggle between the old feudal patrician families and the merchant and shopkeeper class. His analysis of the 1908–1909 events is highlighted by his focus on the rise of the antifeudal forces in Nabulsi politics and the role of what he calls the "bourgeois party" of Hajj Tawfiq Hammad. What Nimr saw as a struggle between Hamidian and anti-Hamidian forces for the salvation of the Islamic domain, Darwazeh correctly assessed as a conflict between two wings of the local elite. He was troubled by the "messiness" of local class politics, which he considered to be an anomaly, owing to the presence of significant landed forces (the Abdulhadis, whom he saw as the "most feudal" of the feudal forces) at the vanguard of the "bourgeois party." Those were the precursors of the Masri and Shak'a family business imperiums, which continue to dominate politics and the economy of Nablus to this day. What Darwazeh may have missed was the manner in which landed interests became enmeshed in industrial and commercial investments as land revenue declined as the major source of wealth and status. To him, the triumph of the modernist forces of the Ottoman revolution, which he enthusiastically supported as an activist in the CUP and, later, in the Entente (Liberal Union) Party, was a pyrrhic victory, because it was undermined by Turkification and centralization. Unlike Nimr, Izzat Darwazeh refused to ally himself with either the Hamidian regime or its local opponents in Nablus and Palestine. As the war progressed he quickly shed his enthusiasm for the CUP unionists and the Liberal Union Party and gave up all hope in the continued Ottoman presence, joining the Faisali movement for the independence of Syria and Palestine.

SEVEN

Adele Azar's Notebook

CHARITY AND FEMINISM

THE NOTEBOOK OF ADELE SHAMAT AZAR (1886–1968), "mother of the poor," as she was known in wartime Jaffa, is an autobiographic narrative of her struggles on behalf of destitute women in the early twentieth century, written in the form of an extended letter to her grandchildren. The notebook is illuminating in that it sheds light on the linkages between endowed charitable associations, the schooling of girls, and early feminism. It also dwells on the engagement of the Arab (Rumi) Orthodox movement in the creation of independent nonsectarian women's associations. Azar's struggle on behalf of women, like that of her contemporaries Qasim Amin and Huda Sha'rawi, is permeated with a modernist discourse. Her early life and schooling in Jaffa indicates her indebtedness to the Protestant and Catholic mission schools, from which she was later to disengage.

> I was born in Jaffa, Palestine, in 1886. My parents, Niqola Beshara Shamat and Asine Yousef Ghandour, were renowned for their piety. Being the only child, my parents sent me to school at the age of two. My school, known as Miss Arnot's Mission School, was established under the supervision of Ustaz Constantine Azar, located in the Ajami neighborhood, where we used to live. . . . [A] friend of the family used to pick me up from home every morning and take me there, thus the love of learning was ingrained in me at such a tender age. . . . [A]fter finishing the intermediate education at the age of 14, I was transferred to St. Joseph's, also in Jaffa, to study French. I had barely finished my first year, in 1899, when I was engaged to Mr. Afteem Ya'coub Azar. In 1901, two years later, we were married.[1]

Yet Azar's name is virtually unknown in the annals of the Arab and Palestinian women's movement. She does not appear in the chronicle of the history of early feminism covering the first half of the twentieth century,[2] nor in the major compendium of activists in the women's movement for the first half of the twentieth century, published by Faiha Abdulhadi in several volumes.[3] She is also absent from Ela Greenberg's groundbreaking work on female education in Mandatory Palestine, *Preparing the Mothers of Tomorrow*, even though she was a primary force in the creation of local schools for females at the end of the Ottoman era.[4] Among the multitude of writers on the women's movement, I could find reference to her work only in the writings of Asma Toubi (*Abeer wa Majd*) and Ellen Fleischmann (*The Nation and Its "New" Women*).[5] Fleischmann cites the Azar work as a source for a nascent feminist movement at the turn of the century.[6]

There are two reasons for this absence. The first is a predisposition among feminist writers (radicals and avant-garde) to treat charity and charitable associations as outside the domain of the women's movement—or at best, as a precursor to the involvement of middle-class urban women in philanthropic activities that undermined an autonomous consciousness for women.[7] There is also a tendency to subsume Orthodox women's groups, of which Azar was a pioneering advocate, within the constellation of sectarian and missionary associations. My objective here is to challenge these assumptions and to demonstrate how the work of Azar and her contemporaries in the schooling of destitute and working-class girls was a revolutionary episode in the creation of the women's movement at the turn of the century. A major obstacle in this regard is the limited and incomplete nature of the sources of our knowledge of Azar and her period. Her notebook is a fragmentary and truncated record of her life. Furthermore, her papers and those of her associates were obliterated by the war of 1948, as was the whole population of the city that gave rise to her work and ideas. To fill the gaps we are compelled to examine published material from the press, the proceedings of meetings and conferences from that period, and interviews with surviving members from early women's associations such as the Arab Women's Union, the Orthodox Women's Association, and the In'as al-Usra Society.[8]

In examining the sources on the history of the women's movement and the emergent feminist consciousness, it is useful to distinguish two types of writings—those of authors who wrote about women in a new vein, and those of authors who were actively engaged in groups and associations on behalf of women. The former includes the work of a group of literary figures and intellectuals whose careers took off during World War I, such as May Ziadeh, Sadhej Nassar, Malak Hafni, Kulthum Odeh, Anbara Salam, and Asma Toubi. The latter includes the work of the "doers"—activists, patrons, and

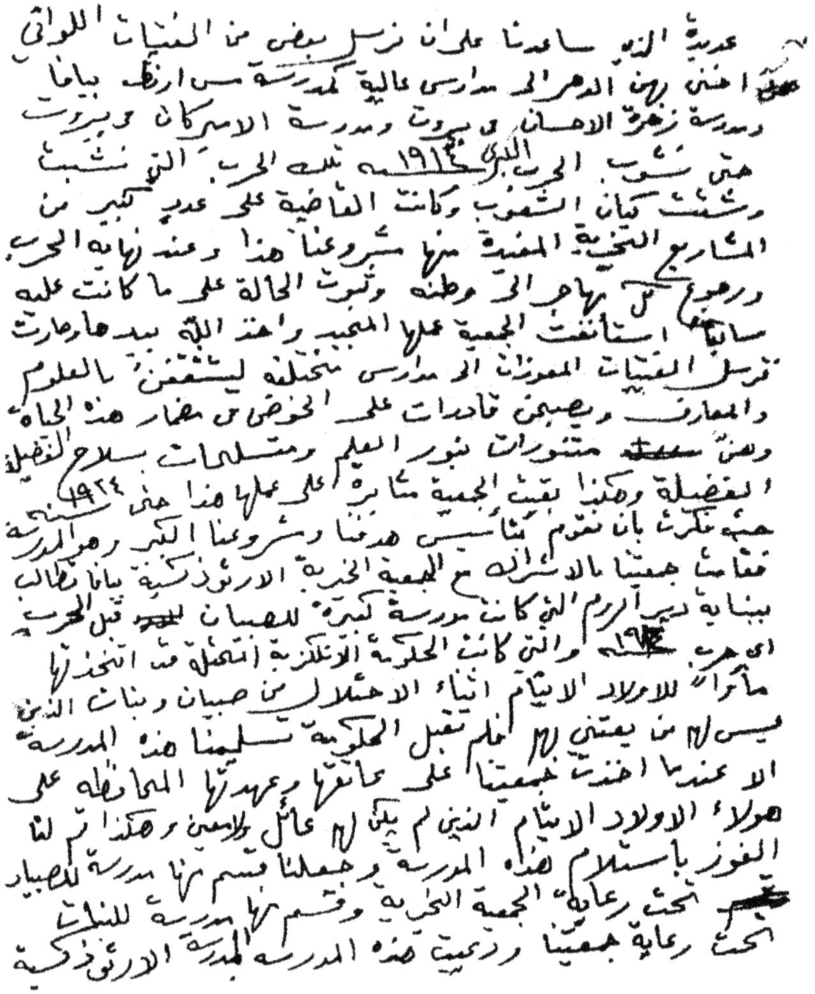

عديدة الزهرة ساعدنا على ان نرسل بعض من الفتيات اللواتي
اخترن زهرة الزهر الى مدارس عالية كمدرسة مس ارنط بيافا
ومدرسة زهرة الاحسان في بيروت ومدرسة الاميركان في بيروت
حتى نشوب الحرب الكبرى سنة ١٩١٤ تلك الحرب التي نشبت
وشتت كيان الشعوب وكانت القاضية على عدد كبير من
المشاريع الخيرية المفيدة منها مشروعنا هذا وعند نهاية الحرب
ورجوع كل مهاجر الى وطنه وثبوت الحالة على ما كانت عليه
سابقا استأنفت الجمعية عملها المجيد واخذت الله بيدها وصارت
ترسل الفتيات المعوزات الى مدارس مختلفة ليتثقفن بالعلوم
والمعارف ويصبحن قادرات على الخوض في غمار هذه الحياة
وهن متنورات بنور العلم ومتسلحات بسلاح الفضيلة
الفضيلة وهكذا بقيت الجمعية مثابرة على عملها هذا حتى سنة ١٩٢٤
حيث فكرت بان نقوم بتأسيس هدفنا ومشروعنا الكبير وهو المدرسة
فقامت جمعيتنا بالاشتراك مع الجمعية الخيرية الارثوذكسية بيافا وطالبت
ببناية دير ارام التي كانت مدرسة كبيرة للصبيان قبل الحرب
اي حرب ١٩١٤ والتي كانت الحكومة الانكليزية استحلتها قد اتخذتها
مأوى للاولاد الايتام ابناء الاحتلال من صبيان وبنات الذين
ليس لهم من يعتني بهم فلم تقبل الحكومة تسليمنا هذه المدرسة
الا عندما اخذت جمعيتنا على عاتقها وعهدتها المحافظة على
هؤلاء الاولاد الايتام الذين لم يكن لهم عائل ولا معين وهكذا تم لنا
الفوز باستلام هذه المدرسة وجعلنا قسم منها مدرسة للصبيان
تحت رعاية الجمعية الخيرية وقسم لها مدرسة للبنات
تحت رعاية جمعيتنا وسميت هذه المدرسة بمدرسة الارثوذكسية

FIGURE 13. A page from Adele Azar's notebook, Jaffa, 1914. Azar Family Papers.

organizers who were engaged in institutional movements, including Ceza Nabrawi, Zuleikha Shihabi, and Adele Azar. Very few women, like Huda Sha'rawi and possibly Halide Edip (in her early educational career in Syria), combined both organizational work with women and a literary career spent writing about the emancipation of women.

The Great War engendered major population displacements among the civilian population, which significantly affected the world of women in both rural and urban areas of Palestine. The most noticeable effects were the absence of adult males in urban centers, the creation of war orphans, and the relocation of refugees from Anatolia in the Syrian provinces. Palestine also experienced wholesale evacuation of the civilian population of coastal cities, Gaza and Jaffa in particular, as the war progressed. The impact of these events on women, who were often left to fend for themselves in the absence of adult males, has been recorded in documents dealing with the famine, the locust attack, and the medical emergencies countered by the civilian population. Edith Madeira, a nurse working with the Red Cross and Red Crescent in wartime Palestine, produced a detailed report on the health of the urban population in those times.[9] Kulthum Odeh, the Nazarene writer who was a student in the Russian seminary in Beit Jala, captured her own predicament, and those of women in traditional Arab society, in that period:

> My arrival to this world was met with tears, for everyone knows how Arabs like ourselves feel when we are told about the birth of a female, especially if this unfortunate girl happens to be the fifth of her sisters, and the family has not been blessed by a boy. Such feelings of hatred accompanied me since an early age. I do not recall my father ever being compassionate with me. The thing that increased my parents' hatred to me was the fact that they thought that I was ugly. This is why I grew up to avoid talking, evading meeting people, and focusing only on my education.[10]

Like many young women of her era, Odeh saw her freedom as an outcome of receiving an education—often against the will of her family, a phenomenon that Azar frequently witnessed for her generation. But the period also saw the entry of urban women into the public sphere and, as a result, enhanced education for girls and the creation of the earliest women's associations. Many of the latter took the form of charitable enterprises aimed at caring for war refugees and orphans.[11]

Much of the writing on the genealogy of the women's movement in Palestine and the Arab world posits a periodization that presents a progressive

FIGURE 14. The staff at the Jerusalem Mouristan Hospital, 1916. Photographic collection of Mona Halaby.

evolution from women's involvement in philanthropy and charity to increased politicization in the struggles of the Mandate period and beyond.[12] Islah Jad, in the often cited "From Salons to the Popular Committees: Palestinian Women, 1919–1989," suggests a dichotomy in which upper- and middle-class women's involvement in charity and patronage of the poor is contrasted with the later radicalization of religious and nationalist women in a feminist movements with social agendas.[13] Similarly, Stéphanie Abdallah and Valérie Pouzol (2013) suggest a three-pronged periodization of the movement: the predominance of identity issues and anticolonial struggles in the 1920s, struggles for voting and citizenship in the 1960s, and the emergence of struggles for social legislation, equality, and Islamic feminism in the 1990s. In all of this literature, the early years of the war are either ignored or subsumed under the rhetoric of the single issue of *sufur* (unveiling) movements. The earliest memoirs and biographical narratives, such as those of May Ziadeh, Kulthum Odeh, Anbara Salam, and Halide Edip, provide a rich alternative to this absence. They all expose the significance of war and the preceding constitutional revolution of 1908 as pivotal moments for new women's sensibilities.

Another way that the work of these charitable movements in the history of early feminism has been depreciated is the presumption that these pioneers were elitist and bourgeois. In most cases the elitism is seen as a derivative of the class privileges enjoyed by women like Halide Edip, Anbara Salam, and Huda Sha'rawi. Yet many of those activists, including Sha'rawi, saw their upper-class status as a chain on their emancipation, since it restricted their freedom of movement under the guise of "protecting the family name." Some flaunted their bourgeois placement as a marker of modernism setting them apart from veiled and domestically confined women in the lower classes. Alexandra Zarifeh's wedding photograph, taken in 1919, shows her wearing one of the latest Paris fashions and performing a coquettish gesture. Few writers have pointed out that it was precisely their middle-class status, and their ability to have domestic servants, that freed these women from the burdens of domesticity in order to undertake charitable work.[14] In the case of Azar and Katherine Siksik (the leader of the Orthodox Society for the Destitute in Jerusalem), charitable work was aimed at uplifting the poor while patronizing them. In any case this type of criticism is vacuous. In Syria and Palestine during and after the war, unlike the situation in western Europe, there did not exist a popular movement of working women that one can contrast with the work of these charitable societies.

In her history of the early women's movement in Palestine, Ellen Fleischmann lists the Rumi Orthodox women's association—of which Azar was one of the early founders—as the earliest existing native women's association.[15] Others include the Orthodox Aid Society for the Poor in Akka (1903), the Jaffa Orthodox Ladies Society (1910), the Haifa Orthodox Ladies Society (1908), and the Orthodox Society for the Destitute in Jerusalem (1919) run by Katherine Siksik.[16] In her history of the Women's movement, Matiel Moghanam mentions one Muslim group only, the Mohammadan Ladies Society from the World War I period in Jerusalem—apparently a reference to the Arab Ladies Association headed by Ni'mati al-Alami, daughter of the Musa Faidi al-Alami, the former mayor of Ottoman Jerusalem, established in 1919.[17] Another Muslim group was the Society of Arab Women's Union in Nablus, established in 1921. Those groups were the confessional precursors of the Arab Women's Associations that emerged in 1929 within the ranks of the nationalist movement. The early groups were confessional, meaning they served the charitable needs of their religious community but were not sectarian, in the sense that they targeted and served the destitute of all religious communities. Men's nationalist activities were conducted in parallel with women's charitable associations, in a process that Fleischmann identifies as "the feminization of benevolence." This created a niche within the nationalist movement, often initiated by women, which gave religious associations the freedom to maneuver independently of men's control but within the parameters of legitimacy and "respectability."

Azar became aware for the need to alleviate the conditions of poor women before the war by providing schooling for girls who had no access to mission schools. In 1910 most girls were unable to enter those schools owing to the economic crisis at the time. In her notebook, Azar wrote, "At my initiative a number of Jaffa Orthodox women sought to establish a national women's association to educate orphan and needy girls. This association was the first national women's group in Palestine. It was established on the 15th of February, 1910, with the objective of launching schools for the teaching of girls. We called our society the Orthodox Women's Association for the Support of Orphans in Jaffa [Jam'iyyat al-Sayidat al-al-urthodoxiyya li 'Addad al-Yatimat bi-Yafa]."

In *Preparing the Mothers of Tomorrow*, Ela Greenberg discusses the impact of the constitutional revolution of 1908 on the establishment of public schools in Palestine by the Ottoman administration (*nizamiyyah* schools), as well as by native educators, as a counterweight to missionary educational activities. Of the latter, the al-Dusturiyyeh College by Khalil Sakakini, and Dar al-Ma'aref College, headed by Muhammad al-Salih, were the most noteworthy. However, neither of these establishments included girls' schools, although they did recruit women teachers. The Ottoman administration established a number of primary (*ibtidai*) school for girls in major towns (Jaffa, Haifa, Nablus, and Jerusalem). Thus the field for girls' education continued to be dominated by Catholic, Protestant, and Jewish (Alliance) foreign schools. This monopoly affected urban society as a whole, since Muslim upper- and middle-class girls were compelled to attend these European and Europeanizing schools. The significance of the Rumi Orthodox movement thus lay in its attempt to break the hegemony of foreign missionaries over the control of girls' education. Adele Azar's deputy in the Orthodox Women's Association was Alexandra Kassab Zarifeh, an activist for women's rights. Born in 1897 in Jaffa, she was the daughter of Jurgi Bey Kassab, a Damascene Ottoman civil servant who moved to Jaffa and became engaged in commercial activities. In her early youth she was active in both the Red Crescent and Red Cross societies, in addition to her charity work in the Orthodox Women's Association. In the British Mandate years, she led women's demonstrations in Jaffa against British policies during the 1936 rebellion. She was particularly opposed to Haj Amin's call for ending the rebellion in 1938. During the 1947 military engagements with the Zionists, the *Filastin* newspaper published a satirical list of Christmas gifts for Jaffa figures, in which Zarifeh was given a tank to take her to the front.[18] Unlike Azar, Zarifeh began her early schooling in the Zahrat al-Ihsan (Flower of Charity) Orthodox school in 1903.

The Flower of Charity was established in 1880 by Labibeh Ibrahim Jahshan, a women's group in Jumaizeh (Beirut) whose objective was to secure a "modern, scientific" education for females in the Orthodox community.[19] The school was inaugurated on August 13, 1881, and headed by Labibeh Jahshan and Zarifeh Sursuq. The school consciously saw itself as an indigenous answer to missionary activities in female education.

> The success of our project was rooted in its response to a burning need within the Orthodox community to meet [the missionary] challenge. Beirut was, in the second half of the nineteenth century, experiencing a sudden and speedy growth as a result of becoming the capital of a large Ottoman province which included Mount Lebanon [and northern Palestine]. Within the Rumi Orthodox community emerged a rich and extended bourgeois class which sought education and scientific knowledge to enter the modern world. The challenge came from the Catholic and Protestant missions that were heavily engaged in recruiting and mobilizing orthodox young men and women in their educational establishments. The attraction posed by these missions became a major concern and provocation for Orthodox clerical and lay circles—especially within the middle classes. They rallied to establish modern educational facilities to teach science, technology, and modern languages to their members. Zahrat al-Ihsan was thus established to be the first institute for Orthodox females in Lebanon at the turn of the century. It prided itself in teaching Arabic, French, and English—in addition to the principles of Greek and Russian.[20]

Zahrat al-Ihsan was a magnet not only for female students in Lebanon but also for young women, like Alexandra Kassab Zarifeh, from the Syrian and Palestinian communities, and the school became a model for similar educational groups in Jaffa, Akka, Tripoli, and Jerusalem. Azar narrates how the Orthodox Women's Association combined their charitable orphanage work with schooling. It was in those years that Adele Azar became known as the "mother of the poor" for her charitable activities. Later, when the school was well established, she became known as "the boss" (al-Za'eema). Together with her compatriots, she continued to send girls to Miss Arnot's Mission School in Jaffa and to the Flower of Charity in Beirut. To confront a society that was still hesitant to accept the education of females, "we continued to arm these needy girls with the weapons of science and virtue to face life and find work."[21] The war years disrupted much of their educational effort, since travel became hazardous and resources scarce. Immediately after the termination of hostilities, the women's association shifted their main focus from relief work for the poor to the establishment of their own school for girls.

After the war, the British occupation authorities had requisitioned the boys' school to serve as a center for war orphans. Azar found herself negotiating the fate of those orphans with army officers:

> The Government would not give us this school unless we gave assurances that we would continue to care for those orphans who had no place to go to. Thus we took over the school building. We transferred the school for boys under the tutelage of the Orthodox Charitable Society, while we established a separate section for girls under the control of the Women's Association. We called the school the Orthodox National School for Girls in Jaffa. At its inauguration in 1924 it contained one hundred local Christian and Muslim girls. They were taught by Najla Musa, Suriya Battikha, and Lisa Tannous. In the next few years the number of students increased to 12 teachers and 250 students.

The curriculum of the school was vocational in order to prepare the students for employment. The languages taught were Arabic and English—in contrast to French and German, which prevailed in girls' missionary schools. The school included a workshop for tailoring and dressmaking and had its own girl scout unit. The main source of funding for the school and the workshops was Orthodox endowments—mainly the revenue of Rumi waqf estates belonging to the Church of St. George (known popularly as al-Khader) and private family endowments from the estates of wealthy Orthodox families.[22]

Virtually all the women's associations in the postwar years were engaged in an activism defined in terms of charity, whether it involved alleviating poverty, working with orphans, or teaching destitute girls. Both Alexandra Zarifeh and Adele Azar use terms like *adadd* (support), *ihsan* (charity), and *irtiqa'* (elevation [of the poor]), to describe their activities. Zahrat al-Ihsan, the most prominent women's organization from the 1880s, took charity as its motto and raison d'être. But this was not the charity of endowments—of soup kitchens and *takaya*—that continued to follow the tradition of Haski Sultan. Using the language of Christian Orthodox benevolence, it was institutional

FIGURE 15. Miss Arnot's Mission School for girls, Jaffa, 1900. Despite her opposition to missionary schools, Adele Azar had the highest regard for Arnot's school, which she had attended herself. Matson Collection, Library of Congress.

work of middle-class women aiming at delivering destitute women from poverty, through the education of girls and their gainful employment on the road to independence and elevation. One of their (mainly) unstated objectives was to save these girls from missionary groups. With few exceptions, their work in the aftermath of World War I maintained a distance from authority and from political confrontations, but they were at the same time keenly aware of the political implications of their work. Fleischmann notes that "distinctions among [the categories of] political, charitable, and social in Palestinian society, [were] fluid. . . . A major dichotomy in the early women's charitable organizations existed in their maintaining gender subordination though support of the tradition of women's work in a 'separate sphere' while simultaneously creating power for themselves though collective action that ultimately had social and political implications extending beyond 'helping the poor.'"[23] Charitable work did not cease with the transition of the women's associations into direct political activism during the 1930s, but the main focus of their activity began to include the adoption of objectives and slogans that subordinated their work to the national movement.

THE "MOTHER OF THE POOR" BECOMES AL-ZA'EEMA

The main problem facing the women's association after they established the girls' school was the securing of work opportunities for their graduates. Except for traditional involvement of rural women in agriculture, where men and women worked jointly in the fields, the problem was coming from social pressures against the engagement of urban women in public employment, except in "acceptable" arenas such as teaching and domestic tailoring.

> It was objectionable in the public mind when our school opened for young women to engage in public employment. . . . [E]ven needy families who were desperate for income resisted permitting work to their female relatives. I spent extensive efforts in convincing [those families] that there is no shame in their women seeking gainful employment, as we can witness by then in the neighboring countries of Egypt, Syria, and Lebanon. Eventually I was able to secure employment for these graduates in the departments of Postal Services, telephone exchanges, and in government civil service. I was able also to find work in commercial establishments and in hospitals as nurses. For this work I became known as the Boss, al-Za'eema.[24]

Azar's work with the destitute was an unarticulated emancipatory discourse, which is also how she saw the work of her contemporary champions of women's rights, such as Ceza Nabrawi and Qasim Amin in Egypt, and Sadhej Nassar in Palestine. This was expressed in her reference to the need for "catching up" with the situation in Egypt and Syria, rather than in terms of the struggle for *sufur* (unveiling), which is recurrent theme in the work of Anbara Salam and Huda Sha'rawi.[25] This was partly due to early involvement with the Jaffa Orthodox community, where veiling was not an issue, and possibly to the absence of a social agenda in her struggle for women's rights. In her mind, working with girls' education and employment was an essential component of her work in charity (*'amal al-ihsan*) for the poor and destitute.[26] During the thirties she began to appear in public circles as a speaker on behalf of the women's and national movements. She also held a salon for literary figures at her home—but she relates this in passing, and we know very little about the nature of this salon and the people who frequented it.[27]

Azar's activity in the national movement evolved from her leadership of the Orthodox Women's Association and its linkages during the 1930s with nationalist agitation. In 1931 she was elected chairwomen of the Palestinian Women's Congress, held in Jaffa. During the meeting she issued a call: "Women of Palestine, help your nation by giving your jewelry" (Ya nisa' Falasteen, qadimina hileekunna wa sa'idna ummatikunna).[28] During the Arab rebellion of 1936 to 1939 the Jaffa branch of the Arab women's movement was established in Jaffa. The organizing meeting was held at her home. She was elected as deputy head of the association, whose executive committee by then was evenly divided between Muslim and Christian (mostly Orthodox) members.[29]

The association was particularly active in Jaffa in support of the rebellion. Azar and Zarifeh, both members of the executive committee, used their experience with the Orthodox Women's Association to establish workshops for the Arab Women's Union in order to train young "destitute women" in crafts and tailoring. We are not told what crafts these were, but the women's group targeted the "daughters of this suffering humanity."[30] During the winters of the years 1936 to 1939 the society began a campaign in support of the militants. "We delivered packages of winter clothing—coats, shirts, and woolen pullovers—to the mujahideen in their trenches and in mountain areas. We also sent food packages cooked in our kitchens to the fighters and to their families."[31]

The women's association had a mixed and problematic relationship with the British colonial authority. Initially, Sa'da Tamari, the first president of the association, and Adele Azar had to negotiate with the British the terms for using the orphanage and the teaching facilities. Azar explains that the terms imposed by the military government were acceptable to their movement, since it involved accommodating the large number of war orphans that the government was unable to take care of.[32] During the twenties Adele entertained public officials, including the high commissioner, at her "literary" salon (an exaggerated term, since she seems to have had limited literary talents).[33] The years of the rebellion changed this relationship. The leadership of the Orthodox association supported the strike and sent material aid to the mujahideen.

Several members of the executive committee objected to the Nashashibi leadership (who headed the Defense Party) and its call for the strike in Jaffa Port, since—in their view—it resulted in moving commercial activities from Jaffa to the newly established port facilities in Tel Aviv.[34] They also distanced themselves from the Husseini leadership. At least, Alexandra Zarifeh

FIGURE 16. Adele Azar, "the Boss" (*second from right*) in a public ceremony in Jaffa with Yusif Haikal (*third from right*), the last Arab mayor of Jaffa, and Habib Homsi (*fourth from right*), Jaffa, 1947. Azar Family Collection.

objected to Husseini's call for ending the rebellion in 1939, feeling, as she put it, "that he was working at the behest of the British."

A turning point in Azar's career took place in 1944, when she was invited to Cairo to attend the Arab Women's Congress headed by Huda Sha'rawi, on December 7, 1944. Six years earlier Sha'rawi had organized the Women of the East Congress in support of Palestine in Cairo. Although Tarab Abdulhadi had been the official head of the delegation, Sadhej Nassar had stolen her thunder with a long speech on the dangers of Zionism for not only Palestine but also Syria and Egypt. She made headlines in the Egyptian press as an articulate and militant defender of the cause of Palestine.[35] But there was very little on women's rights in her speech. Like that of all her colleagues from Palestine, her intervention was political and aimed at mobilizing women from the Arab world, Turkey, and Iran in support of Palestine.

At the Arab Women's Congress, Palestine was represented by Tarab Abdulhadi (from Nablus), Zuleikha (Zlikha) Shihabi (from Jerusalem), Asma Toubi (from Nazareth), and Sadhej Nassar (from Haifa). Jaffa was not represented, for unknown reasons, but Adele Azar sent a telegram in support of the conference in her capacity as vice president of the Arab Women's Union, and president of the Orthodox Women's Association. In 1944, however, Adele was officially invited to the Arab Women's Congress as a leading representative of Palestinian women. This meeting would have an agenda in which the social conditions were highlighted next to the usual political platforms. She saw this as a crowning moment in her feminist career.[36] "I went to Cairo in my combined role as the head of the Orthodox Women's Association and the deputy head of the Arab Women's Union in Jaffa. In my speech to the congress I focused on the call to strengthen Arab Unity and reinforce Arabic as the language of education. I also stressed the need for the education of rural and peasant women."[37]

The delegation used their visit in Cairo to meet with the press, with members of Egyptian and Arab women's groups, and with political figures, including Prime Minister Ahmad Maher Pasha. They visited Abdeen Palace and were hosted by Queen Faridah and Princess Shweikar. King Farouk also invited them for a trip on the royal train to Anshas. Azar was in her element with royalty. In her diary, she dwelled at length on her reception and the public entertainment organized for them by Sha'rawi, including musical concerts with Um Kalthum and the cabaret performances by Bad'ia Masabni, the "queen of dance." Masabni was well known to the Palestinians, as she had held several summer concerts in Jaffa and Jerusalem.[38]

During the war of 1948, the Orthodox Women's Association maintained their charitable activities in protecting destitute girls and worked with the residual inhabitants of a deserted Jaffa, who remained in the city after the expulsion of most of its population. Alexandra Zarifeh took over as the principal of the girls school run by the Orthodox Women's Association and maintained the semblance of teaching, but only for a short period.[39] Most of the members of the association became refugees in Jordan and Lebanon and reconstituted themselves as the Society of Palestinian Women in 1949. Their main work was with refugee children, for whom they established Dar Is'ad al-Tufulah (Institute for Elevating Childhood) in Suq al-Gharb. During the later years of Palestinian resistance in Lebanon, the institute received the children of Palestinian martyrs at the request of the PLO. Adele Azar died in 1965. Zarifeh died in 1969 and was eulogized by Yasir Arafat and Shafiq al-Hout.

CONCLUSION: A MISSING LINK?

The prevailing view in the literature on the women's movement in Palestine before 1929 is that it was either nonexistent or dominated by charitable associations and upper-class "ladies' societies." In the words of Hamida Kazi, "the participation of women was passive, inarticulate and unorganized. Under a strict social order, freedom of movement for women was almost non-existent."[40] This perspective is, as demonstrated in this chapter, factually inaccurate and misconceives the feminist content of early charitable associations, especially those operating during and after World War I, when charity was linked with the education of girls and preparing them for employment.

The link between religious endowments and charitable associations for orphans and the destitute is very old. In Ottoman Syria these endowments were often patronized by princely families and upper-class women, beginning in the sixteenth century. Both public and private (*dhirri*) waqf were often allocated by propertied women for supporting the education of poor girls. At the turn of the century, education for girls was mainly limited to foreign mission schools (Catholic and Protestant). Public schooling for Muslim girls was limited to *kuttab* schools and to the few primary schools for girls launched as part of the Ottoman *nizamiyyah* schools in the second half of the nineteenth century. During World War I, native Arab women were involved in charitable work for the relief of famine victims, war orphans, and war refugees. Nursing was one of few arenas open to urban women in public employment. The work of the Ottoman Red Crescent Society allowed for a number of women (and men) to serve war victims while ostensibly performing a national duty.

The most important feature of Azar's modest diary is that it provides a missing link demonstrating the process in which local indigenous women's associations provided a base for a wider national women's movement. Adele Azar's notebook highlights the significant role of Orthodox women's associations in initiating schooling for destitute girls and, later, vocational training for employment in the public sphere. The objective of those associations was to "rescue" the girls from missionary education and to ground them in a "national" Arabic curriculum—even though many of those activists, including Azar and Zarifeh, had themselves been the beneficiaries of mission schools. The Orthodox associations were among the first—if not *the* first in Palestine—indigenous women's groups devoted to the teaching of girls. During the 1930s many of these groups adopted nationalist agendas against Zionism and for nativist cultural education. A major factor reinforcing this nationalist turn was the internal struggle of the Christian Orthodox community against the Greek ecclesiastical hierarchy for the control of the vast resources of the church. This internal struggle was peculiar to Palestine, since in Syria and Mount Lebanon the Arabization of the church and control over its resources was resolved earlier without a conflict with the ruling authorities. This brought the Rumi Orthodox leadership, including the leadership of women's associations, into a position against the Ottoman administration and, later, the colonial Mandate government. Azar's memoirs also demonstrate the manner in which Orthodox groups were precursors to Arab women's associations, involving joint Christian and Muslim women activists in the national struggle.

Those early associations are often dismissed or marginalized in the history of the women's movement, described as resting on the preoccupations of "salon ladies"—upper-class or bourgeois women divorced from the fate of the working poor. Malek Hassan Abisaab, in his essay "Unruly Factory Women," for example, questions the feminist credentials of these upper-class women. He highlights the manner in which many of them, including Anbara Salam, allied themselves with their patrician families and with traditional nationalist groups against the working poor, including aiding state repression of labor demands by working women.[41]

The problem with this critique is that it conflates class struggles belonging to a later period of the Mandate, beginning with the 1940s, with those of an earlier period, at the turn of the century, when the focus of struggle for women's rights was either embryonic or nonexistent. It also assumes a nonexistent dichotomy—derived from the history of European women's struggles—in characterizing early Arab feminism, one that posits a radical women's trade union and social struggles pitted against middle-class institutional demands. During the constitutional revolution of 1908–1909 and World War I, the only movement for women's rights was indeed a "bourgeois movement," and the struggles of many of groups were led by aristocratic ladies like Huda Sha'rawi, Halide Edip, and Anbara Salam. The objectives of these women were limited to the struggle for unveiling (*sufur*), the expansion of public education for women, and the expansion of public employment—mostly in "appropriate" fields. Women who belonged to what later became identified as a feminist genre were intellectuals who lamented the social conditions of women in the Arab East and aimed at catching up with a European modernity, or an Islamic adaptation of a women's modernity. Those were writers such as May Ziadeh, Kulthum Odeh, Malak Hafni, and Ceza Nabrawi, all of whom—with very few exceptions—did not belong to those associations.

Adele Azar in this context acquired a feminist consciousness before the term was utilized. Her path was that of charity and the utilization of religious endowments for the elevation of the conditions of poor women. There is a distinct difference, however, between the charitable work of Haski Sultan on behalf of the urban destitute, one in which upper-class women immortalized their names through good deeds, and the charitable associations of Azar's generation. The work of the latter was consciously targeted to females whose fate was sealed in the domestic sphere and in the poorhouse (orphanages). The movement Azar established was forged while women tried to launch educational facilities as alternatives to mission schools, and it developed in the context of the nationalist struggle against Zionism and colonialism. But it had one major focus that constituted its feminist core: the training and teaching of girls to become independent human beings.

One should be cautious, though, about extrapolating too much from the fragmentary diaries of Adele Azar. The terms *feminist consciousness, national movement, indigenous,* and *sectarianism* are used here retrospectively to describe groups and processes that began to appear during and after the Great War. All the women's associations that are described were highly localized affairs. They emerged concurrently but separately in cities like Acre, Jerusalem, Haifa, Nablus, and Jaffa, where the devastation of war produced a crisis in the traditional social fabric of society. Charitable work that previously had involved the work of upper-class women and benevolent endowments (waqf), *sadaqat* (alms), and Christian Orthodox charities (soup kitchens and bread distribution) suddenly was transformed and energized by middle-class women who initiated a movement to help the poor through education and the creation of employment possibilities. While using the same vocabulary of benevolence, these women consciously, and sometimes unconsciously, set up radically new forms of women's organizations that had not existed previously.

EIGHT

Ottoman Modernity and the Biblical Gaze

THE WAR PHOTOGRAPHY of Khalil Raad is significant for two reasons: It sheds new light on a little-known aspect of his work and challenges his assessment as predominantly a portrait and landscape photographer. It also modifies a dominant perception of Raad as a biblical and a nativist photographer who adopted and internalized the "orientalist" image of the Holy Land. Annalies Moors, for example, suggests that "Raad's presentation of Palestinian Arabs often used biblical connotations that conscribed their lives as static."[1] In his images of the military and scenes of warfare, which I discuss here, he is clinical, "realistic," and considerably engaged in the Ottoman political agenda in Syria and Palestine. Yet in the most comprehensive compendium of Raad's work, published in 2010 by Rona Sela, there is not a single image of his war photography.[2] In two other photographic compendiums using Raad's work, those by Walid Khalidi (*Before Their Diaspora*) and Elias Sanbar (*Les Palestiniens: La photographie d'une terre et de son peuple de 1839 à nos jours*), there are a few references to public protest images, as well as portraits of Turkish military commanders such as Enver Pasha and Cemal Pasha—but these photographs are marginalized by the focus on Raad as a landscape photographer and studio artist.[3]

RAAD'S CAREER AS A PROPAGANDIST

On the evening of Monday, March 29, 1915, Khalil Raad was summoned by Nihad Bey, deputy commander of the Jerusalem garrison, to the headquarters of the Manzil—the commissariat of the Fourth Imperial Army in the sequestered Notre Dame building near the New Gate. Amiralai Ali Roshen

FIGURE 17. Motorboat on the road to Jericho, in Jerusalem, 1915. Raad Collection, Institute for Palestine Studies, Beirut.

Beyk, the head of the Manzil, had organized at the behest of Cemal Pasha a "cinematographic" record of Ottoman army preparations in Palestine, and particularly in the Jerusalem areas of Nabi Samuel and Baq'a.[4] The event scheduled for March 31, 1915, was the public launching of the motorized boats of the Ottoman navy in the Dead Sea, aimed at transporting grain supplies from Transjordan to the Beersheba-Sinai battlefields of the Sinai Front.

For that particular event, Raad was chosen to provide the still photography, while Lars Larsson, from the American Colony team, was charged with making a film of the event. Raad captured a historical shot of the commander and staff of the Notre Dame Commissariat as they were loading the boat onto the wooden mobile float that was to transfer the equipment to Jericho and the Dead Sea. That event would take Raad on a long journey of collaboration with Cemal Pasha and the Ottoman army to Beersheba, Gaza, al-Arish, Hafir, and the breadth of the Sinai Front.

Raad's involvement with public photography, as opposed to his work in studio portraits and staged "biblical" scenes, began at a juncture in his professional career, in 1913, when his niece Najla married John, the son of his mentor and later fierce competitor on Jaffa Road, the photographer Garabed Krikorian. The marriage both sealed a partnership and ended the long-

FIGURE 18. Khalil Sakakini, Jerusalem, 1906. Signed portrait by Khalil Raad, Institute for Palestine Studies Photo Archives, Ramallah.

standing and fierce competition between Raad and Krikorian, his former benefactor and teacher. Their deal involved a division of labor whereby the Krikorian Studio would specialize in portraiture, while Khalil would devote himself to public events and street life.[5] Among his earliest works from this period are a number of shots he took of public hangings, by the Fourth Army, of soldiers accused of collaboration, presumably with the British. These were taken at the Damascus Gate in mid-1915 and preceded the famous public execution of Arab nationalist figures from Beirut and Damascus. But Raad continued to do studio portraits during the war. He had already established

FIGURE 19. Khalidi brothers Hasan-Shukri and Hussein-Fakhri in Ottoman Army Medical Corps uniforms, Jerusalem, 1915. Portrait by Khalil Raad. Raad Photographic Collection, IPS, Beirut.

himself as a master in the field while working with Krikorian. One can get a glimpse of the exceptional quality of his portraiture in the iconic photo of Khalil Sakakini, which the writer had commissioned Raad to do as a memento for his fiancée, Sultaneh Abdo, before his fateful trip to America. Sakakini's reflective gaze and naturalness became a famous reference point for the freethinking group that constituted the literary Party of Vagabonds after the war.

During the war it became customary for local middle-class conscripts to have their portraits taken while dressed in army uniforms with guns, swords, and other military paraphernalia provided by the studio against an idyllic natural (mostly European) background. For some reason many of these backdrops were forest surroundings or country roads lined with trees. The portraits were standardized heroic postures meant as souvenirs for the family, fiancées, and friends before the men were shipped to the front or other military locations. These portraits were standardized issues, and Raad's portraits were basically similar to those taken by Krikorian, Savidies, Sawabinji, and other native studio photographers, many of them Armenians. Raad, however, during the war, and possibly because of his direct involvement with the military, began to capture soldiers in more engaged and animated postures that diverged from the conventional soldiers' portraiture. We see this diversity in the portraits of the two Khalidi brothers, young Jerusalem doctors who were conscripted in early 1915 just as they graduated from medical college in Beirut. Hasan-Shukri and Hussein-Fakhri al-Khalidi were pictured facing each other and looking beyond the camera, with a certain apprehension regarding the events about to descend upon them. Hasan was soon transferred to Janaq Qal'a (Gallipoli), where he was severely wounded. Hussein managed to stay close to the home front and went on to become the mayor of Jerusalem.

At the beginning of the war, Raad was able to gain special access to Ottoman official circles and to military installations—an access that was probably enhanced by his father's personal friendship with Cemal Pasha.[6] According to Badr al-Hajj, Cemal commissioned Raad to take a series of publicity photos of Ottoman army installations and activities, which were "clearly ... intended for use as propaganda by the Ottoman forces."[7] Ruth Raad, Khalil's daughter, remembers that Ahmad Cemal gave full access to Raad to visit the Egypt-Palestine front to undertake this task.[8] Except for the collection preserved in the Archival Collection at St. Antony's College (Oxford University), reference to this collection has all but disappeared. It is most likely that Raad suppressed these photographs because they could have compromised him with the British military government and exposed him to charges of collaboration with the enemy. They certainly do not appear in his 1933 catalogue inventory. The British had already punished a number of Palestinian public figures, including Abdul Qadir al-Musaghar and Sheikh As'ad al-Shuqairi, the mufti of the Fourth Army, for their work on behalf of Cemal Pasha's administration.

The subjects of Raad's war photography can be grouped in five categories:

a. Portraits of the Ottoman (and German) commanders taken between 1915 and 1918, in addition to a huge number of standardized pictures of army conscripts and officers for the same period.

b. Military installations, battle preparations, and battle scenes from the Ottoman front (1915–1918). Many of those were commissioned propaganda stills taken at the behest of Ahmad Cemal Pasha.

c. Entry of the British army into Palestine and the occupation of the southern sector on December 1917.

d. Scenes of the 1928–1929 demonstrations and the 1936–1939 rebellion—mostly showing deserted streets under curfew, army check-posts, searches of the civilian population, and street scenes of urban strikes. No pictures of rebels are available from Raad, except for the reference to his presumed portrait of Qassam, below)

e. British military presence in the 1940s.

Raad's commissioned work for the Ottoman forces ranges from official portraits of military commanders (Ali Fuad Pasha, Enver, Ahmad Fuad, General von Falkenhayn, and Ali Roshen Bey); army installations (antiaircraft guns, signaling units, trenches, engineering workshops, army hospitals, and field kitchens); army maneuvers in Jerusalem, Beersheba, and Sinai; telegraph and railroad lines; and political events (celebrations of the sultan's birthday at the Manzil, reviews of troops before going to battle, parliamentary delegates from Istanbul visiting the front, Jerusalem notables entertaining German officers, etc.).[9]

Many of the photographs in the Ottoman collection can be found in other historical archives (e.g., the Matson Collection at the Library of Congress and the Yildiz Collection),[10] especially those that involved visiting dignitaries. However, a few of the photos were of a sensitive military character, taken in out-of-bounds zones or at the battle front. The fact that they were printed as postcards, thus ensuring wider circulation, must have been intended to impress a wider European public (and possibly enemy intelligence) or to raise public morale at the home front. Of significance here are shots of antiaircraft guns, taken at a time when enemy aircraft was threatening advanced Ottoman positions in Suez and Beersheba.[11] Another picture (item number 5/1/10, Saunders Collection) shows soldiers of the signaling units on Nebi Samuel. Almost all of those pictures are either posed or show soldiers in regular training exercises. They are obviously intended to signify discipline, preparedness, and command of the latest in military technology (telegraph lines, field telephones, high-powered antiaircraft guns, and so on). One of the most interesting stills of military installations shows underground technicians putting out the newspaper *Shul,* the organ of the Ottoman army in Beersheba.[12]

The portraits of Ahmad Cemal Pasha (military ruler of Syria and Palestine), Mersinli Cemal Pasha (commander of the Fifth Army Corps in Palestine), and Friedrich Kress von Kressenstein (1870–1948, commander of the Eighth Army Corps in Defense of Gaza), and Miralai Ali Fuad Pasha (commander of the Twentieth Army Corps and the last defender of Jerusalem), and many others, show a degree of intimacy and familiarity with the subjects that contrasts with other formal portraits of officials taken by Raad. This is particularly noticeable in the series taken of Mersinli Cemal Pasha on horseback at the St. George compound, and those with his assistant and two children playfully engaged with the photographer. A close-up portrait of Ahmad Cemal, then minister of the navy and the fearful dictator of Syria and Palestine, as well as a second portrait of the same Cemal Pasha having afternoon tea with the children and ladies of the American Colony (attributed to Raad), suggest that Raad was consciously involved in providing a "human face" for the Ottoman leadership, which was becoming increasingly alienated from the civilian population.

Cemal Pasha, very conscious of his image and the need to publicize his military achievements in Palestine, commissioned Raad to do a series of forty propaganda images of army maneuvers, battle preparations, and battle scenes. Those began with the cinematographic project of the Ottoman forces in Jericho and the Dead Sea mentioned earlier, and continued in Gaza, Beersheba, Sinai, and the Suez Front.

Raad also accompanied, and took a number of stills of, the military leadership while on missions—the most famous of which is one of General Kress von Kressenstein in a Jeep with General Falkenhayn and Prince Hohenlocke, taken on Jaffa Road on the eve of the Suez Campaign.[13]

However, it would be a mistake to assume that Raad's work on the Ottoman army was only publicity or of publicity quality. At least on two occasions Raad's work reflected astutely on the cruelties of war and could have been used as damming evidence of Cemal's cruel behavior toward the civilian population. The first image, *Traitor Hanging in Damascus Gate* (Khalil Raad Photographic Collection: R-55, IPS, Beirut), shows a gruesome figure of a hanged man, with a large billboard in Turkish and Arabic listing his presumed crime ("collaboration with the enemy"). A second image, of one of the Ottoman volunteer labor battalions (*tawabeer al-amaleh*), shows a number of old and helpless men doing backbreaking work, carrying rocks by hand to build the southern military road to Beersheba (Khalil Raad Photographic Collection: R-516, IPS, Beirut).[14] Both the hanging and the forced labor were major issues of contention among the civilian population, as were forced relocation of civilians and exile of "suspect" groups. That Raad chose to take these pictures, and later display them, qualifies his role as an instrument of propaganda for the authorities.

RAAD'S PUBLIC PHOTOGRAPHY
DURING THE MANDATE

In contrast to Raad's work during the Ottoman period, his work during the Mandate was more reflective of public sensitivity to the presence of an occupation army. Except for his work during the initial period of British military government (1918–1920), which showed the triumphal entry of General Allenby and Allied soldiers into Jerusalem, the images from the 1920s and 1930s contain numerous scenes of city streets under curfew, police action against demonstrations, frisking of civilians by Indian and British soldiers, and the presence of military vehicles and armed soldiers in the streets.

There is a noticeable absence of rebels and rebellious activities in Raad's work, even though Badr al-Hajj claims that Raad took the only known photograph of resistance leader Izz Eddin al-Qassam. This is unlikely, and there is no evidence that the photograph was taken by him. Raad's pictures during the late 1920s and 1930s of urban clashes with the police and rural resistance show neither romanticism nor images of heroism such as we have seen in his photographs of Ottoman troops, nor the intimacy of the portraits of Turkish and other public officials that he took during the Great War, of Cemal, Ali Fuad, Mersinli, Roshen Beyk, and General von Kressenstein.

Khalil Raad continued his monitoring of public events during the Mandate. His main war-related photos include: the entry of General Allenby into the city from Jaffa Road; police action against anti-Balfour-Declaration demonstrations in November 1929; British army installations outside Jerusalem; Indian and British soldiers on guard duty in public spaces; riot police controlling demonstrations (no dates provided); curfews and strikes during the 1936 rebellion in Jaffa and Jerusalem; and British mechanized divisions moving into urban areas (Khalil Raad Photographic Collection: R-1289, 1291, 1296, 1290, IPS, Beirut). There are numerous photos showing Indian and British troops and police frisking and searching civilians in the street (Khalil Raad Photographic Collection: R-1318–1337, IPS, Beirut). Those include Arabs, Jews, and several Muslim and Christian religious

FIGURE 20. *Shul* newspaper, underground printing press, Beersheba, 1916. Photo by Khalil Raad. Raad Photographic Collection, IPS, Beirut.

figures. Those are the only images where women also appear in the setting, as bystanders, onlookers, and companions of the searched males. Otherwise, Raad's war photography is an exclusively male domain.

One feature that separates Ottoman military figures (Turks, Albanians, and Arabs) from the British in Raad's work is the degree of intimacy and familiarity he engaged in with the former, and the distance he maintained from the latter. This is no doubt the result of his working closely with the Ottoman military commanders in Jerusalem, even during times of hardship and disintegration of the war front. With the British, one gets the impression that he saw them as an army of occupation dealing with population control and suppressing rebellion. Whether this distinction betrays the photographer's political views toward Turkish and British rule is hard to establish. What we can say, however, is that Khalil Raad, as a photographic artist and craftsman, remained a product of the Ottoman era. His frame of mind was shaped by the communitarian structure of Jerusalem. His intellectual development was clearly influenced by the city and the country as a product of the biblical imagination—which influenced him as a commercial photographer of tourists and pilgrims. His portraiture was shaped by his training under Ottoman-Armenian traditions of photography (by Krikorian and the

Abdallah brothers). But the Great War ruptured these traditions and compelled Raad to think of Palestinian modernity in new terms dictated by military machines, airplanes, railroads, telegraphic signals, and the thousands of men who operated this technology. In the crucial years of the war, he provided us with a record of these events that is free from the orientalist gaze and biblical reconstructions.

NOTES

INTRODUCTION

1. Tamimi and Behçet 1916, 1:4, 2:6. Also see a later reprint, [Muḥammad] Rafiq Tamimi, *Wilayat Bairūt,* vols. 1 and 2 (Beirut: Dār Lahad Khatir, 1979). All translations are mine unless otherwise noted.

2. Tamimi 1979, 1:84–125.

3. See for example the section on Nabulsi traditions in Tamimi 1979, 1:121–138.

4. Tamimi 1979, 2:4.

5. Tamimi and Behçet 1916, 1:83–86.

6. For example, see Tamimi and Behçet 1916, 1:412–415.

7. Melhim 2002.

8. Al-Odat 1992a, 81.

9. Ahmad 2015; see also Strohmeier 2001, 57–62; Strohmeier 1991.

10. Al-Odat 1992a, 80–83.

11. Kazziha 1972.

12. Abu-Manneh 1998.

13. Kayali 1997.

14. Kayali 1997, 301–304; Johan Straus, "The Disintegration of Ottoman Rule in the Syrian Territories as Viewed by German Observers," in Philipp and Schäbler 1998, 307–329.

15. St. Laurent and Taskomur 2013.

16. Ḥakīm 1964, 202–213. Later Hakim becomes much more critical when he discusses Jamal Pasha's *Idahat* (Explanations), the addendum to Jamal's memoirs explaining his reasoning for the trial and execution of the Arab nationalists in 1915–1916. See 241–242.

17. Khālidī 2010.

18. Abu-Manneh 1980.

19. Campos 2011.

20. Hanssen 2011.

21. The *millet* system was that by which, in the Ottoman sultanate and other Islamic caliphates, Jews and Christians were allowed to administer their civic affairs autonomously in return for paying a *jizya,* or poll tax.

22. Makdisi 2002.

23. See maps in *Filistin Risalesi,* discussed in chapter 2.

2. ARABS, TURKS, AND MONKEYS

Cited in Darwazeh and Darwazeh 1971, 278.

1. Darwazeh and Darwazeh 1971, 296.

2. Darwazeh and Darwazeh 1971, 295.

3. Brummett 2000.

4. Qadrī 1993, 8–9.

5. Qadrī 1993, 6; Darwazeh and Darwazeh (1971, 300–304) discuss the progression of the Turkification campaign and the accompanying anti-Arab pronouncements within CUP circles.

6. Qadrī 1993, pp. a-b.

7. Darwazeh and Darwazeh 1971, 295–296.

8. This biographic section is derived from Altay Atli's "Cemal Pasha," in Atli 2016.

9. Atli 2016.

10. Qadrī 1993, 39.

11. Qadrī 1993, 39–52. Qadrī claims that these secessionist positions were the product of a small faction of the Decentralization Party led by Haqqi al-AlAdhm and did not reflect the position of the Decentralization Party, which remained loyal (see 43).

12. Qadrī 1993, 47.

13. Lüdke 2005, 75.

14. Lüdke 2005, 76.

15. Darwazeh 1993, 242.

16. Lüdke 2005, 55–83.

17. Lüdke 2005, 55–83.

18. Aziz Bek 1933.

19. Darwazeh 1993, 241.

20. Kayali 1997, 193–194.

21. Kayali 1997, 195.

22. *A Handbook of Syria: Including Palestine,* 1920.

23. Luke, Keith-Roach, Wauchope, and Samuel 1922.

24. Bosworth 1986, 39.

25. Jaussen 1908. I thank Edhem Eldem for bringing Jaussen's book to my attention.

26. Cited in Salih 2005.

27. Salih 2005, 63–64.

28. Kolordu 1915.

29. Kolordu 1915, 13–14.

30. Kolordu 1915, 28.

31. Kolordu 1915, 29.

32. Kolordu 1915, 38.

33. Kolordu 1915, 37.

34. Kolordu 1915, 30.

35. Kolordu 1915, 34.

36. Kolordu 1915, 32.

37. Salih 2005, 52–54.

38. Salih 2005, 52.

39. Salih 2005, 52–53.

40. Salih 2005, 54.

41. Nimr 1961, 3:66, my emphasis; Salih 2005, 57.

42. Rafinq Tamilmin and Muḥammad Bahjat, *Wilāyat Bayrūt* (Beirut: Maṭba'at al-Iqball, 1914). Published simultaneously in Arabic and Turkish.

43. Salih 2005; see also Darwazeh 1993, 1:280.

44. Sakakini 2003, 2:24.

45. Sakakini 2003, 2:264.

46. Sakakini 2003, 2:264.

47. Von Sanders 1928, 214.

48. 'Awdāt 1992.

49. Sakakini 2003, 2:157, 221, 223, 224, 225, 226, 245, 264, 305, 313.

50. Atli 2016.

51. See especially Kharita Da'iratsi Matbaasinda Tabaa Idilishder 1328/1912; Tekin and Bas 2001, 12–13.

52. Kolordu 1915, 1–2.

53. Anameriç 2008, 4.

54. Çelebi 2008.

55. Bekir and Kacar 2010, 37.

56. Celebi, quoted in Bekir and Kacar 2010, 41.

57. *Cedid Atlas,* 1803.

58. *Cedid Atlas,* 1803, 18, 24.

59. Lutfi Beyk 1891.

60. *Kudus Sancagi Haritasi* (1904), available in Sarınay 2009, 73.

61. *Kudus and Nablus* 1328/1912.

62. Salhi 2008, 28–29.

63. Scholch 2006.

64. Scholch 2006, 13. See also Abu-Manneh 1978, 23.

65. Scholch 2006, 13–14.

66. Scholch 2006, 14.

67. Scholch 2006, 14.

68. Abu-Manneh 1978, 24–26.

69. Tekin and Bas 2001.

70. This is close to the number arrived at by Justin McCarthy in his *Population of Palestine*. This is the number of Ottoman nationals, which excludes foreigners residing in the Holy Land at the time. See McCarthy 1990, 38–41.

71. See for example the diary of Ihsan al-Turjman, a soldier in the Fourth Army, in Salim Tamari, *'Am al-jarad: Al-Harb al-'Uzmá wa-mahw al-madi al-'Uthmani min Filastin* (Beirut: Mu'assasat al-Dirasat al-Filastiniyah, 2008). This was published in English as Salim Tamari, *Year of the Locust: A Soldier's Diary and the Erasure of Palestine's Ottoman Past* (Berkeley: University of California Press, 2011).

72. Brummett 2000, 69, 322.

73. Brummett 2000, 70, 322–332.

74. See for example Atay 1918; Cemal Pasha (1922) 2000.

75. Brummett 2000, 323.

76. Hanioglu 2008, 144.

77. Brummett 2000, 324–325.

3. THE SWEET AROMA OF HOLY SEWAGE

1. Hanssen, Philipp, and Weber 2002, 43.

2. Makdisi 2002.

3. Çelik 2008, 80–81.

4. Çelik 2008, 80–115; Makdisi 2002, 36–39.

5. Hanssen, Philipp, and Weber 2002, 19.

6. Qafisheh 2010.

7. Kendall 1948, 8–10.

8. Kendall 1948, 4–5.

9. Kendall 1948, 4–5.

10. On the perception of Ottoman urban neglect of the Arab province, see Eldem, Goffman, and Masters 1999, 204, 209. For an earlier view of Palestine, see Obenzinger 1999, 244–245.

11. Hysler-Rubin 2011, 240–241.

12. See for example Kendall 1948, 4. See also Ayalon 2004, 3. The latter work refers to "building from scratch" by the Mandate authorities, in reference to educational institutions.

13. Lemire 2000, 13–14.

14. Raymond 2002. See especially "The Ottoman Conquest and the Development of the Great Arab Towns" (17–34) and "Islamic City, Arab City: Orientalist Myths and Recent Views" (1–16). Also see Çelik 2008.

15. See Mazza 2009, 23–24; Hala Fattah, "Planning, Building and Populating Jerusalem in the Ottoman Period," 1999, Jerusalemites, http://jerusalemites.org/old/jerusalem/ottoman/7.htm.

16. Kol Ordu 1915. For the Ottoman boundaries of "Palestine," see Scholch 1993, 9–17; for Palestine in Ottoman postal history, see Koleksiyonu and Giray 2004; for the shifting Ottoman cartography of Palestine, see Tamari 2011b.

17. Kol Ordu 1915, appendix, topographic map of Palestine.
18. Hanssen, Philipp, and Weber 2002, 17.
19. Çelik 2008, plans can be found following p. 23.
20. Çelik 2008, 163–169.
21. Tamari 2011a.
22. Tamari 2011b, 10–13.
23. Hanssen 2002, 204–205; and Celik 2008, 138–141.
24. Ergut 2007.
25. Ergut 2007, 175.
26. Ergut 2007, 185.
27. Khoury 1993, 155–158.
28. Ergut 2007, 178.
29. Kana'an 2001.
30. Mark Levine, in Monterescu and Rabinowitz 2007, 283.
31. Kana'an 2001, 132.
32. Al-Miliji 1949, 10.
33. Al-Miliji 1949, 11.
34. Al-Miliji 1949, 11–12.
35. Ḥakīm 1966, 202–203.
36. Ḥakīm 1966, 211–213.
37. Al-Miliji 1949, 9.
38. LeVine 2007.
39. Al-Miliji 1949, 13.
40. Khalidi 1984, 43.
41. Campos 2011, 27.
42. Kushner 1996.
43. Kushner 1996, 351–352.
44. Kushner 2005, 193–198.
45. The original Jawhariyyeh photo appears in Khalidi 1984, 43 (Arabic edition).
46. The two Jawhariyyeh photos are cited in Campos 2011, 29 and 32. Campos provides a third photo (p. 30), however, from the collection of the Arab Studis, showing men and women gathered outside Jaffa Gate and raising the Ottoman banner in celebration of the new constitution.
47. For a discussion of the significance of the festival of Nebi Rubeen, see Tamari 2009, 27–31.
48. Scholch 1993.
49. Tamari 2009, 22–35.
50. Misselwitz and Rieniets 2006, 306–307.
51. Nashāshībī 1990, 14–15. See also the entry for Raghib Bey Nashashibi in 'Abd al-Hādī 2006.
52. Khoury 1987.
53. Lemire 2000, 12.
54. Lemire 2000, 18; Nashāshībī 1990, 23.
55. Nashāshībī 1990, 22–30.

56. For a discussion of gerrymandering as an instrument of contestation of urban space in Jerusalem's recent history, see Dumper 1997, 63–64.

57. Kushner 2005, 224–225.

58. Keith-Roach and Eedle 1994, following page 108.

59. Keith-Roach and Eedle 1994, 147–151.

60. Located in the Institute for Palestine Studies, Beirut. Extensive segments of this collection were published in Khalidi 1984 and Sanbar 2004.

61. Jawharīyah, Tamārī, and Nassar 2003.

62. Jawharīyah, Tamārī, and Nassar 2003, 54–55.

63. Jawharīyah, Tamārī, and Nassar 2003, 55.

64. Jawharīyah, Tamārī, and Nassar 2003, 55–56.

65. Jawharīyah, Tamārī, and Nassar 2003, 56.

66. Jawharīyah, Tamārī, and Nassar 2003, 74.

67. Jawharīyah, Tamārī, and Nassar 2003, 75.

68. Jawharīyah, Tamārī, and Nassar 2003, 75–76.

69. For a discussion of the *odah* as an urban space see, Tamari 2009, 90–92.

70. Barghūtī, Totah, and Muḥammad Zaynahum Muḥammad 'Azab 2001. The book was published originally in Jerusalem in 1920, but references to technological innovations of the Ottoman state are written in the present tense, suggesting that it was authored during the Ottoman administration of Jerusalem.

71. Barghūtī, Totah, and Muḥammad Zaynahum Muḥammad 'Azab 2001, 248–252.

72. For a discussion of Amman as an Ottoman Circassian frontier town, see Rogan 1999.

73. Avci 2009, 974.

74. Çelik 2008, 113–114.

75. Avci 2009, 972–973.

76. Çelik 2008, 114.

77. Avci 2009, 973.

78. Avci 2009, 973.

79. Avci 2009, 973–974.

80. Gradus 1977, 178–179; Luz 2005, 197.

81. Luz 2005, 197, 200.

82. Avci 2009, 981.

83. Luz 2005, 199.

84. Kushner 2005, 195.

85. Kushner 1996, 356.

86. Çelik 2008, 115.

87. Luz 2005, 197; Gradus 1977, 202.

88. In his biography of Ali Ekrem Bey, David Kushner (2005, 138–139) relates how, despite Ekrem Bey's ideological predisposition as a democrat and liberal, and later as a defender of the constitutional revolution, he controlled a network of spies to monitor and report on Arab nationalist activity. He also wrote to the High Porte

on several occasions recommending the appointment of Turks over Arab candidates to administrative posts in Palestine and Syria.

4. A "SCIENTIFIC EXPEDITION" TO GALLIPOLI

1. Al-Baqir, Kurd Ali, and al-Habbal 1334/1916, 6, 21. Kurd Ali was the chief author of the companion report to this volume of the expedition to the Hijaz; see Kurd 'Alī 1916.
2. Fischbach 2006, 448–449.
3. Khuri-Makdisi 2010.
4. Fakher Eldin 2008, 70–82.
5. Kurd 'Alī 1916, 219.
6. Al-Baqir, Kurd Ali, and al-Habbal 1334/1916, 8–9.
7. See for example Al-Baqir, Kurd Ali, and al-Habbal 1334/1916, 63–64.
8. Al-Baqir, Kurd Ali, and al-Habbal 1334/1916, 150–151.
9. Al-Odat 1992b, 221–222.
10. Yehôšua' 1974, 74.
11. Ali al-Rimawi, *Al-Najah,* no. 50, quoted in Yehoshua 1981, 74–75.
12. Yehoshua 1981, 75.
13. *HaHerut,* April 8, 1913, quoted in Yehoshua 1981, 76.
14. For Rimawi's hagiographic poetry, see al-Baqir, Kurd Ali, and al-Habbal 1334/1916, 67–68, 196–197, 208–211, 283–284. His odes to the Ottoman armed forces and to Enver appear in *ArRihla al-Anwariyyeh,* 229–233, 250–252.
15. *Palestine Gazette,* suppl. 38a, December 26, 1918, cited in Yehoshua 1981, 76.
16. Tamīmī 1991, 73.
17. Tamīmī 1991, 2.
18. 'Awdāt 1987, 272.
19. 'Awdāt 1987, 273.
20. 'Awdāt 1987, 273–274.
21. Al-Baqir, Kurd Ali, and al-Habbal 1334/1916, 198.
22. *ArRihla al-Anwariyyeh,* 234–236.
23. 'Awdāt 1987, 673–674; Tamīmī 1991, 14–15.
24. Tamīmī 1991, 19–20.
25. Al-Baqir, Kurd Ali, and al-Habbal 1334/1916, 90.
26. Al-Baqir, Kurd Ali, and al-Habbal 1334/1916, 91.
27. Al-Baqir, Kurd Ali, and al-Habbal 1334/1916, 92.
28. Al-Baqir, Kurd Ali, and al-Habbal 1334/1916, 93. For Cemal Pasha's public works schemes and infrastructural investments in Syria and Palestine, see Kayali 1998.
29. Al-Ghazi 2013.
30. Seikaly 1981. The Arabic edition is included in Roger Owen and Marwan R. Buheiry, *Al-Ḥayāh al-fikrīyah fī al-Mashriq al-'Arabī, 1890–1939* (Beirut: Markaz Dirāsāt al-Waḥdah al-'Arabīya, 1983).

31. Seikaly 1981, 126–127.

32. Seikaly 1981, 137.

33. Seikaly 1981, 131, quoting Muhammad Kurd Ali, "Al-Arabiyya wal Turkiyya," *Al-Muqtabas* 4, no. 2 (1909): 109–112.

34. Al-Baqir, Kurd Ali, and al-Habbal 1334/1916, 138.

35. Al-Baqir, Kurd Ali, and al-Habbal 1334/1916, 143.

36. See especially "Reflections on Urbanism in the Sultanate" and "A Descriptive Note on Anatolia" in Al-Baqir, Kurd Ali, and al-Habbal 1334/1916, 222–234.

37. See Tamari 2011a.

38. Al-Baqir, Kurd Ali, and al-Habbal 1334/1916, 213.

39. Al-Baqir, Kurd Ali, and al-Habbal 1334/1916, 214.

40. Al-Baqir, Kurd Ali, and al-Habbal 1334/1916, 215.

41. Al-Baqir, Kurd Ali, and al-Habbal 1334/1916, 216.

42. Al-Baqir, Kurd Ali, and al-Habbal 1334/1916, 218.

43. Al-Baqir, Kurd Ali, and al-Habbal 1334/1916, 219.

44. Al-Baqir, Kurd Ali, and al-Habbal 1334/1916, 231.

45. Al-Baqir, Kurd Ali, and al-Habbal 1334/1916, 233.

46. Al-Baqir, Kurd Ali, and al-Habbal 1334/1916, 233.

47. Al-Baqir, Kurd Ali, and al-Habbal 1334/1916, 247.

48. Al-Baqir, Kurd Ali, and al-Habbal 1334/1916, 247–248.

49. Al-Baqir, Kurd Ali, and al-Habbal 1334/1916, 248.

50. Al-Baqir, Kurd Ali, and al-Habbal 1334/1916, 248.

51. Al-Baqir, Kurd Ali, and al-Habbal 1334/1916, 249.

52. Al-Baqir, Kurd Ali, and al-Habbal 1334/1916, 266.

53. Al-Baqir, Kurd Ali, and al-Habbal 1334/1916, 268–270.

54. Al-Baqir, Kurd Ali, and al-Habbal 1334/1916, 270.

55. Al-Baqir, Kurd Ali, and al-Habbal 1334/1916, 278.

56. Zurcher 2016.

57. Al-Baqir, Kurd Ali, and al-Habbal 1334/1916, 279.

58. Al-Baqir, Kurd Ali, and al-Habbal 1334/1916, 278.

59. Al-Baqir, Kurd Ali, and al-Habbal 1334/1916, 78.

60. Al-Baqir, Kurd Ali, and al-Habbal 1334/1916, 79.

61. Cicek 2013, 68–69.

62. Cicek 2013, 69.

63. Cicek 2013, 69–70.

64. Cicek 2013, 70.

65. Kurd 'Alī 1916.

66. Al-Ghazi 2013.

67. Kurd 'Alī 1916, 233.

68. Kurd 'Alī 1916, 101.

69. Kurd 'Alī 1916, 96, 116.

70. Kurd 'Alī 1916, 124.

71. Kurd 'Alī 1916, 126.

72. Kurd 'Alī 1916, 219.

73. Kurd ʿAlī 1916, 221–222.

74. Kurd ʿAlī 1916, 221.

75. Kurd ʿAlī 1916, 224.

76. Kurd ʿAlī 1916, 228.

77. Kurd ʿAlī 1916, 254.

78. Kurd ʿAlī 1916, 253.

79. Kurd ʿAlī 1916, 255.

80. Kurd ʿAlī 1916, 259.

81. Kurd ʿAlī 1916, 259.

82. Kurd ʿAlī 1916, 266–270.

83. Sherif Hussein, the prince of Mecca, sent a note to Enver apologizing for his inability to come to Medina, and he sent two jeweled swords to the two commanders (Kurd ʿAlī 1916, 269).

84. "Sharif Hussein's Proclamation of Independence from Turkey, 27 June 1916," posted August 22, 2009, FirstWorldWar.com, www.firstworldwar.com/source/arabindependence_hussein.htm.

85. See Al-Salih 2005, 64–65.

86. Al-Baqir, Kurd Ali, and al-Habbal 1334/1916, 219.

87. See Abu-Manneh 2011, 145–165.

88. Nimr 1961, 3:99–126.

5. TWO FACES OF PALESTINIAN ORTHODOXY

1. Issa, n.d., "Mudhakarat, 1903–1948: Min Dhikrayat al-Madi," 13–14.

2. Issa, n.d., "Mudhakarat," 14.

3. Abu-Manneh 1980.

4. Abu-Manneh 1980, 296.

5. Hanioglu 2008, 106–107.

6. Hanioglu 2008, 107.

7. Hanioglu 2008, 107; Kayali 1997.

8. Hanioglu 2008, 108.

9. See Hanioglu 2008, 142–145.

10. Masters 2013, 136–138.

11. Khater 2010.

12. Khuri-Makdisi 2010.

13. Makdisi 2000.

14. Ḥakīm 1966, 23–26.

15. Ḥakīm 1966, 202.

16. Ḥakīm 1966, 202–203.

17. See the discussion of the status of the Antiochian Church in Ḥakīm 1966, 129–145.

18. See the discussion by Michael Bracy (2011, 19–21) on the affinities of the Christian communities in the Middle East with their "Eastern" and Islamic roots.

19. Material on Hakim's childhood and early relation with the Orthodox Church is derived from Ḥakīm 1966, 104–117.

20. Ḥakīm 1966, 106.

21. Ḥakīm 1966, 106.

22. See Jawharīyah, Tamārī, Nassar, and Elzeer 2014, 10.

23. Jawharīyah, Tamārī, Nassar, and Elzeer 2014, 10.

24. Ḥakīm 1966, 130.

25. Ḥakīm 1966, 130–131.

26. Abū Ḥannā 2005, 132–133.

27. Khalidi 2006, 95, 247; Issa, n.d., "Mudhakarat, 1903–1948: Min Dhikrayat al-Madi," unpublished manuscript.

28. Issa, n.d., "Mudhakarat," 16.

29. Issa, n.d., "Mudhakarat."

30. Barghouti 1928, 9.

31. Barghouti 1928.

32. The main papers were *Al-Quds, Al-Karmil,* and *Filastin.* But several minor newspapers and weeklies also were launched by Orthodox writers after the constitutional revolution: *Al-Insaf* (founded 1908), *Al-Ahlam* (Dreams; founded 1908), *Al-Nasik* (founded 1908), *Al-Bulbul al-Ta'ir* (founded 1908*), Al-Dik al-Sayyah* (founded 1908), *Abu Shaduf* (founded 1912), and *Munabbih al-Amwat* (founded 1908). See Musallam 2013.

33. The main source for this is Yehoshua 1981. See also Musallam 2013.

34. Sakakini 2004.

35. For a statistical source on the magnitude of these endowments see Fakhri Ed-Din and Tamari, forthcoming 2017.

36. Ḥakīm 1966, 195–196.

37. See *Birzeit: Histoire d'une localite et de sa mission latine dans las Montagne d'Ephraim* 2008.

38. *Birzeit: Histoire d'une localite et de sa mission latine dans las Montagne d'Ephraim* 2008, 38.

39. Ibn Nāṣir 1998, 102–103.

40. Ibn Nāṣir 1998, 105.

41. Ibn Nāṣir 1998, 104, 109.

42. Robson 2011a, 47–51.

43. Robson 2011b, 6–23.

44. Robson 2011a, 78–79.

45. Cited by Robson 2011b, 8.

46. Ḥakīm 1966, 196.

47. 'Ārif 1951, 35; Yehôšua' 1974, 8.

48. Yehôšua' 1974, 51–52.

49. Yehôšua' 1974, 53.

50. Yehôšua' 1974, 10–11.

51. At least this is the claim made by the family. See Yehôšua' 1974, 47.

52. "Sheikh Ali al-Rimawi," Falestinona, October 31, 2012, www.falestinona.com/OurPalWebSite/ArticleDetails.aspx?ArticleId=4531#.UYwUsSvF30A.

53. Yehôšuaʿ 1974, 54–55.

54. For the history of *Al-Quds* and a biography of Jurgi Hanania, see Hanania 2007.

55. Ḥakīm 1966, 195.

56. Ḥakīm 1966, 195–196.

57. Bedross Der Matossian, "The Young Turk Revolution: Its Impact on Religious Politics of Jerusalem (1908–1912)," 2009, paper 126, University of Nebraska, Lincoln, http://digitalcommons.unl.edu/historyfacpub/126.

58. Ḥakīm 1966, 196–197.

59. Papastathis and Kark 2014, 42.

60. Papastathis and Kark 2014, 42.

61. Ḥakīm 1966, 195.

62. Hanania 2007.

63. Yehôšuaʿ 1974, 69–72.

64. Yehôšuaʿ 1974, 71.

65. Ḥakīm 1966, 195–196.

66. Ḥakīm 1966, 195–196.

67. Dr. Dahesh was the pen name of Salim Musa al-Ashi (1908–1984), a Palestinian-Lebanese spiritualist and founder of the Daheshist movement, which believed in reincarnation. See "About Dr. Dahesh," n.d., Dahesh Heritage, accessed December 1, 2012, http://daheshheritage.org/index.php/en/about/about-dr-dahesh.html.

68. Issa, n.d., "Mudhakarat," 9.

69. Issa, n.d., "Mudhakarat," 9.

70. Jacobson 2011, 78.

71. Issa, n.d., "Mudhakarat," 11.

72. Issa, n.d., "Mudhakarat," 10.

73. Khalidi 2006, 93.

74. Khalidi 2006, 93.

75. Bilu was an early wave of Jewish Zionist migration to Palestine in the 1880s, often referred to as the first Aliyah.

76. Abu Ibrahim [Menashe Meirovitz], "Rasa'il al-Fallah," *Filastin,* no. 151 (June 23, 1912): 1, quoted in Dolbee and Hazkani 2015.

77. Abu Ibrahim 1912, quoted in Dolbee and Hazkani 2015.

78. Thanks to Shay Hazkani, who brought my attention to Abu Ibrahim's columns in *Filastin,* and who pointed out the correspondence between Issa al-Issa and Menashe Meirovitz.

79. Sakakini 2004, 1:348–352.

80. Issa, n.d., "Mudhakarat," 11–12.

81. Issa, n.d., "Mudhakarat," 12.

82. Issa, n.d., "Mudhakarat," 13.

83. Issa, n.d., "Mudhakarat," 14–15.

84. Mandel 1976, 65, 75, 78, 100, 121, 182.

85. As'ad 2017.

86. He was later tried for treason by Jamal Pasha's military tribunal and sentenced to death. His sentence was commuted, but he died in jail in Aley one year later, in 1916, according to Hafiz Bey al-Said, quoted in Manaa 1990, 207–208.

87. Ḥakīm 1966, 211–212

88. Ḥakīm 1966, 212.

89. Ḥakīm 1966, 212–213.

90. Ḥakīm 1966, 203.

91. Ḥakīm 1966, 205–207.

92. Ḥakīm 1966, 208.

93. Ḥakīm 1966, 209.

94. Ḥakīm 1966, 211.

95. Ḥakīm 1966, 210.

96. Hanna al-Issa in Manaa 1990, 305.

97. Campos 2011, 163–165.

98. Jacobson 2011, 73–79.

99. Issa, n.d., "Mudhakarat," 13.

100. Issa, n.d., "Mudhakarat," 13.

101. Campos 2011, 201–202.

102. Cleveland 1971, 125.

103. Bracy 2011, 20.

104. Odat 1992b, 477.

105. Bracy 2011, 19.

106. Issa, n.d., "Mudhakarat," 4–6.

6. A FARCICAL MOMENT

1. A leading Nabulsi political satirist muses on the theme of revolutionary Nablus: "During the 1936 revolution, Nablus had been given the name 'Mountain of Fire,' though it is not fiery. It is, rather, a mild baby sleeping on the breasts of his mother. Some anthropologists have indicated that mountain inhabitants have rough and coarse behaviour unlike the easy-going and peaceful valley dwellers; but the behaviour of Nablus people has always been genial. In 1936, it was the countryside of Nablus that was untamed, and the city was contented with taking off the fez and wearing the *kaffiah* to bluff the British forces and distract them from the movements of the revolutionaries." Aref Hijjawi, "Nablus: The City of Strong Women," *This Week in Palestine,* no. 107 (March 2007).

2. Khalid Ziadeh, introduction to *Asbāb al-inqilāb al-'Uthmānī wa-Turkiyā al-fatāh,* by Muḥammad Rawḥī Khālidī and Khalid Ziadeh ('Ābdīn, al-Qāhirah: Ru'yah lil-Nashr wa-al-Tawzī', 2011), 1–28.

3. Muḥammad Rawḥī Khālidī and Khalid Ziadeh, *Asbāb al-inqilāb al-'Uthmānī wa-Turkiyā al-fatāh* ('Ābdīn, al-Qāhirah: Ru'yah lil-Nashr wa-al-Tawzī', 2011), 134.

4. Mannā' 1999, 242–243.

5. Na'imeh Ziad, "Ihsan al Nimer, Da'irat al Ma'arif al Filastiniya," Najah University website, 2012, http://ency.najah.edu/node/23.

6. Ziad 2012.

7. Ziad 2012.

8. 'Awdāt 1987, 637.

9. 'Awdāt 1987, 636.

10. Nimr 1938, 3:95.

11. Nimr 1938, 3:95.

12. Doumani 1998, 57–65.

13. Nimr 1938, 3:106.

14. Ihsan Nimr uses the term *al-haraka al-raj'iyya,* which in the 1960s came to be used in reference to "reactionary" movements. But after it was published in 1938, the term referred to the act of restoration, both in its derivation (from *istirja'*) and in the context of his analysis.

15. The Mohammadan Sharia Society was established by Kamil (Kiamil) Pasha, the grand vizier, in order to mobilize Islamic support for the restoration.

16. Nimr 1938, 3:107.

17. Nimr 1938, 3:108.

18. Nimr 1938, 3:109.

19. Nimr 1938, 3:110.

20. Nimr 1938, 2:520–533.

21. Nimr 1938, 2:497–506.

22. Nimr 1938, 2:507–516.

23. Nimr 1938, 2:520–549.

24. Nimr 1938, 2:288–292.

25. Doumani 1995, 111–114, 177–178, 241–242.

26. Doumani 1995, 241.

27. Nimr 1938, 2:540–548; Doumani 1995, 241–242.

28. See Nimr 1938, 540–553, and 540n1; Doumani 1995.

29. Darwazeh 1993, 1:122.

30. Mannā' 1995, 133–134.

31. Darwazeh 1993, 127–128.

32. Darwazeh 1993, 126.

33. Darwazeh 1993, 123–124.

34. Darwazeh 1993, 124–125.

35. Darwazeh 1993, 174.

36. Darwazeh 1993, 176.

37. Darwazeh 1993, 181.

38. Darwazeh 1993, 182.

39. Darwazeh 1993, 187.

40. Darwazeh 1993, 197.

41. "1909: Dervish Vahdeti, for the 31 March Incident," Executedtoday.com, July 19, 2013, www.executedtoday.com/2013/07/19/1909-dervish-vahdeti-for-the-31-march-incident/.

42. Darwazeh 1993, 187.

43. Darwazeh 1993, 188.

44. Darwazeh 1993, 188.

45. Darwazeh 1993, 188–189.

46. Nimr 1938, 3:49.

47. Nimr 1938, 3:47–48.

48. Nimr 1938, 3:50.

49. Tamimi and Yazar 1916, 1:105.

50. Nimr 1938, 3:48–49. See also Aql 2005, 312–313.

51. Nimr 1938, 3:49.

52. Nimr 1938, 3:143.

53. Nimr 1938, 3:143–144.

54. Nimr 1938, 3:144.

55. Nimr 1938, 3:144–145.

56. Ya'coub 2014.

7. ADELE AZAR'S NOTEBOOK

1. Azar 1911–1948, 2.

2. Issa 1997; Daraghmeh 1991.

3. 'Abd al-Hādī 2005, 2006.

4. Greenberg 2010.

5. Şālih 2011.

6. Fleischmann 2003, 104–105.

7. See Abdallah and Pouzol 2013; see also Fleischmann 2000.

8. I am grateful to Dr. Efteem Azar, Adele's grandson, who gave me her note-book and a number of photographs from the family collection in Amman on December 20, 2014. For published references, see, for example, Women of the East Congress, Cairo 1938.

9. Edith Madeira, "Report for Nursing Service, 1917–1918," in the Edith Madeira Papers. According to the Discover website, "Edith Madeira (1865–1951) served as the chief nurse for the American Red Cross Commission to Palestine from June 1918 to January 1919. The Commission was formed 'to look after the sickness and starvation of the civilian population in the occupied area of Palestine.' . . . [H]er 'Report for Nursing Service' detailing the Commission's work in Palestine" examined the medical and hospitalization conditions in Palestine during World War I. Her report and diary are available from the Pennsylvania Historical Society at http://discover.hsp.org/Record/ead-2053/Description#tabnav.

10. Quoted from Iqbal Tamimi, "Remembering Professor Kulthum Odeh (1892–1965)," *London Progressive Journal,* October 17, 2008, http://london

progressivejournal.com/article/284/remembering-professor-kulthum-odeh. The original quote is more poignant in Arabic and comes from Mahamid 2004, 39.

11. See Greenberg 2010.

12. 'Abd al-Hādī 2015, 11–14.

13. Jad 1990.

14. Fleischmann 2003, 101.

15. I use the term *Rumi Orthodox* here, rather than the usual *Greek Orthodox,* as a more appropriate reference to the Christian orthodox community in the Arab East, where the term *Greek* refers to the ethnic composition of the patriarchate and its ecclesiastic hierarchy. In Arabic this duality of terms does not exist, since the standard term for the church is *Rum Orthodox.*

16. Fleischmann 2003, 104–109.

17. Moghanam 1976.

18. Zarifeh 2014.

19. Kusti 1996, 236. For information about the Flower of Charity School, see Orthodox Wiki, http://ar.orthodoxwiki.org.

20. Kusti 1996, 241.

21. Azar 1911–1948, 3.

22. Azar 1911–1948, 4–5. Among the family endowments cited by Azar was the religious waqf established by Urjwan al Far, which came from the revenue of commercial stores in Ajami.

23. Fleischmann 2003, 103.

24. Azar 1911–1948, 17.

25. Azar 1911–1948, 10.

26. Azar 1911–1948, 4–5.

27. Azar 1911–1948, 10–11.

28. Malak 1996. Malak devotes a whole page to the life of Adele Azar. In her notebook Azar does not mention this episode of her work.

29. Azar 1911–1948, 11. Azar lists the executive members as follows: Wajiha Abu S'uud, president; Adele Azar, vice president; Alexandra Zarifeh, secretary; Fatmeh Abu Laban, treasurer; Jamileh Qunbargi, member; Fortuneh Sukkar (Rock), member.

30. Azar 1911–1948, 11–12.

31. Azar 1911–1948, 12.

32. Azar 1911–1948, 3.

33. Azar 1911–1948, 10.

34. Zarifeh 2014. Zarifeh writes, "Fakhri Nashashibi initiated the movement to extend the strike to Jaffa port. He was on close social terms with the Zarifeh family, as was his brother Azmi, the Qaimmaqam of Jaffa. Alexandra warned him that the Jews will establish [an alternative] port in Tel Aviv, which happened shortly thereafter. He was exposed after the rebellion and was pursued by a young man from the well-known Madhoun family, [who were] Jaffa seamen. He followed him to Baghdad and emptied several bullets in [Fakhri Nashashibi's] head" (2).

35. Women of the East Congress, Cairo 1938, 188–193.

36. Azar 1911–1948, 13.

37. Azar 1911–1948, 12–13.

38. Azar 1911–1948, 13–14.

39. Zarifeh 2014, 4.

40. Hamida Kazi, "Palestinian Women and the National Liberation Movement: A Social Perspective," *Khamsin,* November 13, 2013, https://libcom.org/library/palestinian-women-national-liberation-movement-social-perspective-hamida-kazi.

41. Abisaab 2004, 55–82. See also Abisaab 2010.

8. OTTOMAN MODERNITY AND THE BIBLICAL GAZE

1. Annalies Moors quoted in Semmerling 2004, 6. See also Moors and Machlin 1987, 61–77. This latter work displays one certified photograph by Raad (*Bethlehem Girls,* 64), but it is misattributed to Bonfils. I believe the two authors also overinterpret "the assumed sensuality of the female figures, the presentations of Bethlehem women by the photographer as 'models of virtue.'" There is no question that Raad had internalized biblical and orientalist motifs in his work, but not consistently. The fact that the picture was (mis)judged to be the work of Bonfils may have helped in finding orientalizing features in it. Raad may have simply found Bethlehem girls more accessible through his personal and family connections. The picture in question is very playful: the eyes of the two women are engaged in a flirtatious dialogue with the camera, and it exhibits hardly any exoticizing features.

2. Sela 2010. Sela includes the very useful 1933 catalogue of Raad's work in her book. It is revealing that under "Turkish War Pictures" she excludes the forty images that he produced as publicity for the Ottoman army—with the possible exception of two or three images. Only nine pictures are listed from his catalogue for that period. It is also striking that Raad uses the term *British Occupation* for the Mandate period, a term he does not use for the period of Ottoman rule (cf. Ra'ad and Sela 2010, 244–245).

3. Khalidi 1984; Sanbar 2004.

4. This event is reconstructed from the diary of Ihsan Hasan al-Turjman, who was an eyewitness to the cinematography. See Tamari 2008. The diary entry is for March 31, 1915.

5. Hajj 2001, 37–38.

6. Hajj 2001, 38.

7. Hajj 2001, 38–39.

8. Cited by Hajj 2001, 41.

9. Khalil Raad, Saunders Photographic Collection, Middle East Centre Archives, St. Antony's College, Oxford University.

10. For the Yildiz Collection, see Balci 2009. For the Library of Congress collection see www.loc.gov/pictures/item/2005676184/. Raad's name does not appear in Yildiz Collection, and in only three or four photographs is he identified in the Library of Congress collection.

11. Col. Saunders Collection, item number 5/1/10, Raad Album, Middle East Centre Archives, St. Antony's College, Oxford University.

12. Col. Saunders Collection, item number 5/1/7, Raad Album, Middle East Centre Archives, St. Antony's College, Oxford University.

13. The reference to this photograph and Raad's authorship can be found in the Axis Forum, Tosun Sarai, December 9, 2007, http://forum.axishistory.com/view-topic.php?f=80&t=129705&start=30 accessed October 1, 2012.

14. I am referring here, and elsewhere, to the Raad catalogue numbers in the Raad Photographic Collection of the Institute for Palestine Studies in Beirut.

BIBLIOGRAPHY

UNPUBLISHED DIARIES AND MEMOIRS

Ahmad, Rowaida Fadel. 2015. "Al-Madrasa al-Salahiyya fil-Quds, 588–1336" (Al-Salahiyyah School, Jerusalem, 588–1336 AH/1192–1918 AD). Master's thesis, Najah National University.

Azar, Adele [Shamat]. 1911–1948. Notebook. Unpublished manuscript, Azar Family Papers, Amman, Jordan.

Ibn Nāṣir, Mūsá. 1903. "Tārīkh qaryat Bīr Zayt mundhu khurūj al-rajul al-awwal." Nasir Family Papers, Birzeit.

Issa, Issa al-. n.d. "Mudhakarat, 1903–1948: Min Dhikrayat al-Madi." Unpublished, handwritten memoir. Estate of Raja al-Issa, Amman, Jordan.

Zarifeh, Edward. 2014. "Alexandra Kassab: Sirat Mundadilah" (A biography of a militant woman). Unpublished essay.

PUBLISHED REFERENCES

'Abd al-Hādī, Fayḥā'. 2005. *Adwār al-mar'ah al-Filasṭīnīyah fī al-thalāthīnīyāt: Al-musāhamah al-siyāsīyah lil-mar'ah al-Filasṭīnīyah: Riwāyāt al-nisā', nuṣūṣ al-muqābalāt al-shafawīyah.* Al-Bīrah: Markaz al-Mar'ah al-Filasṭīnīyah lil-Abḥāth wa-al-Tawthīq.

———. 2006. *Adwār al-mar'a al-Filasṭīnīyah fī ǎl-arba'īniyyāt: 1940s: Al-musāhama as-siyāsiyya lil-mar'a al-Filasṭīnīyah: Riwāyāt an-nisā': Nuṣūṣ al-muqābalāt aš-šafawiyya.* Al-Bīra: Markaz al-Mar'a al-Filasṭīnīyah lil-Abḥāthwa-ǎl-Tawṭīq.

———. 2015. *The Role of Palestinian Women in the 1930s: The Political Participation of Palestinian Women; Women's Oral Narratives.* Ramallah, Palestine: Al-Nasher Publishing.

'Abd al-Hādī, Madhi. 2006. *Palestinian Personalities: A Biographic Dictionary.* Jerusalem: PASSIA.

Abdallah, Stéphanie Latte, and Valérie Pouzol. 2013. "Citizenship, Gender, and Feminism in the Contemporary Arab Muslim and Jewish Worlds." In *A History of Jewish-Muslim Relations,* edited by Abdelwahab Meddeb and Benjamin Stora. Princeton, NJ: Princeton University Press.

Abisaab, Malek Hassan. 2004. "'Unruly' Factory Women in Lebanon: Contesting French Colonialism and the National State, 1940–1946." *Journal of Women's History* 16, no. 3 (Fall).

———. 2010. *Militant Women of a Fragile Nation.* Syracuse, NY: Syracuse University Press.

Abū Ḥannā, Ḥannā. 2005. *Ṭalā'iʿ al-nahḍah fī Filasṭīn: Khirrijū al-madāris al-Rūsīyah, 1862–1914.* Beirut: Mu'assasat al-Dirāsāt al-Filasṭīnīyah.

Abu-Manneh, Butrus. 1978. "The Rise of the Sanjaq of Jerusalem." In *The Palestinians and the Middle East Conflict,* edited by Gabriel Ben-Dor. Ramat Gan, Israel: Turtledove Publishing.

———. 1980. "The Christians between Ottomanism and Syrian Nationalism: The Ideas of Butrus al-Bustani." *International Journal of Middle East Studies* 11, no. 3 (May): 287–304.

———. 1998. "The Genesis of Midhat Pasha's Governorship in Syria, 1878–1880." In *The Syrian Land: Processes of Integration and Fragmentation: Bilād al-Shām from the 18th to the 20th Century,* edited by Thomas Philipp and Birgit Schäbler. Stuttgart, Ger.: F. Steiner.

———. 2011. "Arab Ottomanists' Reactions to the Young Turk Revolution." In *Late Ottoman Palestine: The Period of Young Turk Rule,* edited by Y. Ben-Bassat and E. Ginio. London: I. B. Tauris.

Aql, Muḥammad. 2005. *Wathā'iq maḥallīyah min Filasṭīn al-ʿUthmānīyah wa-dirāsāt tawthīqīyah.* Ramallah, Palestine: Al-Nasher.

ʿĀrif, ʿĀrif. 1951. *Al-Masīḥīyah fī al-Quds.* Jerusalem, n.p.

As'ad, Abdul Rahman. 2017. "Hafiz al-Sa'eed: 1841–1915." *Encyclopedia Palestina.* Accessed March 17. www.palestinapedia.net/%D8%AD%D8%A7%D9%81%D8% B8-%D8%A7%D9%84%D8%B3%D8%B9%D9%8A%D8%AF.

Atay, Falih Rifki. 1918. *Ates ve günes.* [Istanbul]: Halk Kitaphanesi.

Atli, Altay. 2016. Turkey in the First World War website. Accessed August 4. www .turkeyswar.com.

Avci Y. 2009. "The Application of Tanzimat in the Desert: The Bedouins and the Creation of a New Town in Southern Palestine (1860–1914)." *Middle Eastern Studies* 45, no. 6: 974.

ʿAwdāt, Yaʿqūb. 1987. *Min aʿlām al-fikr wa-al-adab fī Filasṭīn* (Amman, Jordan: Wakālat al-Tawzīʿ al-Urdunīyah.

———. 1992. *Min aʿlām al-fikr wa-al-adab fī Filasṭīn.* Al-Quds: Dār al-Isra'.

Ayalon, Ami. 2004. *Reading Palestine: Printing and Literacy, 1900–1948.* Austin: University of Texas Press.

Aziz Bek. 1933. *Intelligence and Espionage in Lebanon, Syria and Palestine during World War I, 1913–1918* [in Arabic]. Beirut: n.p.

Balci, Kerim. 2009. *Al-Quds: Jerusalem in Historical Photographs*. Istanbul: IRCICA.

Baqir, Muhammad al-, Muhammad Kurd Ali, and Hussein al-Habbal. 1334/1916. *Al-Bi'thah al-'ilmīyah ilá dār al-khilāfah al-Islāmīyah*. Dar Sadir: Scientific Press.

Barghouti, Omar Salih al-. 1928. *Mir'at al-Sharq* (Jaffa), no. 542 (January 19).

Barghūtī, 'Umar al-Ṣāliḥ, Khalil Totah, and Muḥammad Zaynahum Muḥammad 'Azab. 2001. *Tārīkh Filasṭīn*. Cairo: Dār al-Ma'ārif.

Bekir, Karliga, and Mustafa Kacar. 2010. *Seventeenth Century Syria and Palestine in the Book of Jihannuma*. Istanbul: Bahcesehir University.

Beshara, Adel. 2011. *The Origins of Syrian Nationhood: Histories, Pioneers and Identity*. Abingdon, Oxfordshire, U.K.: Routledge.

Birzeit: Histoire d'une localite et de sa mission latine dans las Montagne d'Ephraim. 2008. Beit Jala, Jerusalem: Latin Patriarchate Press.

Bosworth, Edmund. 1986. "The Land of Palestine in the Late Ottoman Period as Mirrored in Western Guide Books." *British Journal of Middle Eastern Studies* 13, no. 1: 39.

Bracy, R. Michael. 2011. *Printing Class: 'Isa al-'Isa, Filastin, and the Textual Construction of National Identity, 1911–1931*. Lanham, MD: University Press of America.

Brummett, Palmira Johnson. 2000. *Image and Imperialism in the Ottoman Revolutionary Press, 1908–1911*. SUNY Series in the Social and Economic History of the Middle East. Albany: State University of New York Press.

Campos, Michelle. 2011. *Ottoman Brothers: Muslims, Christians, and Jews in Early Twentieth-Century Palestine*. Stanford, CA: Stanford University Press.

Cedid Atlas. 1803. Tab'hane-yi Hümayunda (Istanbul, Turkey).

Çelebi, Kâtip. 2008. *Tuhfetü'l-kibârfı esfâri'l-bihâr*. Edited by Idris Bostan. Ankara: TC Basbakanlik Denizcilik Mustesarligi.

Çelik, Zeynep. 2008. *Empire, Architecture, and the City: French-Ottoman Encounters, 1830–1914*. Seattle: University of Washington Press.

Cemal Pasha. (1922). 2000. *Memories of a Turkish Statesman, 1913–1919*. Whitefish, MT: Kessinger.

Cicek, Talha. 2013. *War and State Formation in Syria Cemal Pasha's Governorate during World War I, 1914–1917*. New York: Routledge.

Cleveland, William L. 1971. *The Making of an Arab Nationalist: Ottomanism and Arabism in the Life and Thought of Sati al-Husri*. Princeton, NJ: Princeton University Press.

Daraghmeh, Izzat. 1991. *The Women's Movement in Palestine (1903–1990)* [in Arabic]. Jerusalem: Maktab Dia.

Darwazeh, Muḥammad 'Izzat. 1993. *Mudhakkirāt Muḥammad 'Izzat Darwazah: Sijill ḥāfil bi-masīrat al-ḥarakh al-'Arabīyah wa-al-qaḍīyah al-Filasṭīnīyah khilāl qarn min al-zaman, 1305–1404 H., 1887–1984 M*. Beirut: Dār al-Gharb al-Islāmī.

Darwazeh, Muḥammad 'Izzat, and Muḥammad 'Izzat Darwazeh. 1971. *Nash'at al-ḥarakah al-'Arabīyah al-ḥadīthah: Inbi'āthuhā wa-mazāhiruhā wa-sayruhā fī zaman al-dawlah al-'Uthmānīyah ila awā'il al-Ḥarb al-'Ālamīyah al-Ūlá: Tārīkh wa-mudhakkirāt wa-dhikrayāt wa-ta'līqāt.* Saida, Lebanon: Al-Maktabah al-'Aṣrīyah.

Dolbee, Sam, and Shay Hazkani. 2015. "'Impossible Is Not Ottoman': Menashe Meirovitch, 'Isa al-'Isa, and Imperial Citizenship in Ottoman Palestine, 1911–1912 and After." *International Journal of Middle East Studies* 47, no. 2: 241–262.

Doumani, Beshara. 1995. *Rediscovering Palestine Merchants and Peasants in Jabal Nablus, 1700–1900.* Berkeley: University of California Press.

———. 1998. *I'ādat iktishāf Filasṭīn: Ahālī Jabal Nābulus 1700–1900.* Beirut: Mu'assasat al-Dirāsāt al-Filasṭīnīyah.

Dumper, Michael. *The Politics of Jerusalem since 1967.* New York: Columbia University Press, 1997.

Eldem, Edhem, Daniel Goffman, and Bruce Alan Masters. 1999. *The Ottoman City between East and West: Aleppo, Izmir, and Istanbul.* New York: Cambridge University Press.

Ergut, F. 2007. "Surveillance and the Transformation of Public Sphere in the Ottoman Empire." *METU Studies in Development* 34, no. 2: 173–194.

Fakher Eldin, Munir. 2008. "Communities of Owners: Land Law, Governance, and Politics in Palestine, 1858–1948." PhD diss., New York University.

Fakhri Ed-Din, Munir, and Salim Tamari. Forthcoming. *Landed Property and Public Endowments in Jerusalem.* Beirut: IPS.

Fischbach, Michael. 2006. "As'ad Shuqayri." In *Palestinian Personalities: A Biographic Dictionary,* edited by Mahdī 'Abd al-Hādī. Jerusalem: PASSIA.

Fleischmann, Ellen. 2000. "Nation, Tradition, and Rights: The Indigenous Feminism of the Palestinian Women's Movement (1920–1948)." In *Women's Suffrage in the British Empire: Citizenship, Nation, and Race,* edited by Ian Christopher Fletcher, Laura E. Nym Mayhall, and Philippa Levine. London: Routledge.

———. 2003. *The Nation and Its "New" Women: The Palestinian Women's Movement, 1920–1948.* Berkeley: University of California Press.

Ghazi, Ali Afifi al-. 2013. *Muhammad Kurd Ali, the Explorer.* Beirut: Dar al-Fikr.

Gradus, Y. 1977. *Beer-Sheva, Capital of the Negev Desert: Function and Internal Structure.* Beersheva: Ben-Gurion University of the Negev, David Tuviyahu Archives for the History of the Settlement of the Negev.

Greenberg, Ela. 2010. *Preparing the Mothers of Tomorrow: Education and Islam in Mandate Palestine.* Austin: University of Texas Press.

Hajj, Badr al-. 2001. "Khalil Raad, Jerusalem Photographer." *Jerusalem Quarterly* 11 (Winter).

Hakan, Anameriç. 2008. *History of Maps and Important Map Collections in Turkey.* www.melcominternational.org/wp-content/content/past_conf/2008/2008_papers/Anameric.pdf.

Ḥakīm, Yūsuf. 1964. *Bayrūt wa-Lubnān fī 'ahd Āl 'Uthmān.* Beirut: Al-Maṭba'ah al-Kāthūlīkīyah.

———. 1966. *Sūrīyah wa-al-'ahd al-'Uthmānī.* Beirut: Al-Maṭba'ah al-Kathulikiyah.

Hanania, Mary. 2007. "Al-Quds: 100th Anniversary of a Pioneering Press and Newspaper." *Jerusalem Quarterly*, no. 32 (Autumn).

A Handbook of Syria: Including Palestine. 1920. London: H.M. Stationery Office.

Hanioglu, M. Sükrü. 2008. *A Brief History of the Late Ottoman Empire*. Princeton, NJ: Princeton University Press.

Hanssen, Jens. 2002. "Public Morality and Fin de Siècle Beirut." In *Outside In: On the Margins of the Modern Middle East*, edited by Eugene Rogan. New York: I.B. Tauris.

———. 2011. "Malhamé—Malfamé: Levantine Elites and Trans-imperial Networks in the Late Ottoman Empire." *International Journal of Middle Eastern Studies* 43, no. 1: 25–48.

Hanssen, Jens, Thomas Philipp, and Stefan Weber. 2002. *The Empire in the City: Arab Provincial Capitals in the Late Ottoman Empire*. Würzburg, Ger.: Ergon in Kommission.

Husarī, Abū Khaldūn Sāti al-. 1966. *The Day of Maysalūn: A Page from the Modern History of the Arabs*. Translated from the Arabic by Sidney Glazer, with a new preface by the author. Washington, DC: Middle East Institute. Memoirs, with an introduction relating the struggle of the powers for the Arab lands and an appendix of documents.

Hysler-Rubin, Noah. 2011. *Patrick Geddes and Town Planning: A Critical View*. Abingdon, U.K.: Routledge.

Ibn Nāṣir, Mūsá. 1998. *Tārīkh qaryat Bīr Zayt mundhu khurūj al-rajul al-awwal*. San Francisco, Kālīfūrnīyā: Lajnat al-Nashr wa-al-Maṭbūʿāt, Jamʿīyat Bīr Zayt fī al-Wilāyāt al-Muttaḥidah.

Issa, Yusif Mustafa Rashad. 1997. *The Women's Movement in Palestine (1900–1950)*. Cairo: Arab Union Catalogue.

Jacobson, Abigail. 2011. *From Empire to Empire: Jerusalem between Ottoman and British Rule*. Syracuse, NY: Syracuse University Press.

Jad, Islah. 1990. "From Salons to the Popular Committees: Palestinian Women, 1919–1989." In *Intifada: Palestine at the Crossroads*, edited by Jamal R. Nassar and Roger Heacock. New York: Praeger.

Jaussen, Antonin. 1908. *Coutumes des Arabes au pays de Moab, par le P. Antonin Jaussen*. Paris: J. Gabalda.

Jawharīyah, Wāṣif, Salīm Tamārī, and Issam Nassar. 2003. *Al-Quds al-ʿUthmānīyah fī al-mudhakkirāt al-Jawharīyah: Al-kitāb al-awwal min mudhakkirāt al-mūsīqī Wāṣif Jawharīyah, 1904–1917*. Al-Quds: Muʾassasat al-Dirāsāt al-Maqdisīyah.

Jawharīyah, Wāṣif, Salīm Tamārī, Issam Nassar, and Nada Elzeer. 2014. *The Storyteller of Jerusalem: The Life and Times of Wasif Jawhariyyeh, 1904–1948*. Beirut: IPS; Northampton, MA: Olive Branch Press.

Kana'an, Ruba. 2001. "Waqf, Architecture, and Political Self-Fashioning: The Construction of the Great Mosque of Jaffa by Muhammad Aga Abu Nabbut." *Muqarnas* 18: 120–140.

Kayali, Hasan. 1997. *Arabs and Young Turks: Ottomanism, Arabism, and Islamism in the Ottoman Empire, 1908–1918*. Berkeley: University of California Press.

————. 1998. "Wartime Regional and Imperial Integration of Greater Syria during World War I." In *The Syrian Land: Processes of Integration and Fragmentation: Bilād al-Shām from the 18th to the 20th century*, edited by Thomas Philipp and Birgit Schäbler, 295–306. Stuttgart, Ger.: F. Steiner.

Kazziha, Walid. 1972. *The Social History of Southern Syria (Trans-Jordan) in the 19th and Early 20th Century*. [Beirut]: Beirut Arab University.

Keith-Roach, Edward, and Paul Eedle. 1994. *Pasha of Jerusalem: Memoirs of a District Commissioner under the British Mandate*. London: Radcliffe Press.

Kendall, Henry. 1948. *Jerusalem, the City Plan: Preservation and Development during the British Mandate, 1918–1948*. London: H. M. Stationery Office.

Khalidi, Rashid. 2006. *The Iron Cage: The Story of the Palestinian Struggle for Statehood*. Boston: MA: Beacon Press.

Khālidī, Rūḥī. 2010. *Al-Inqilāb al-ʿUthmānī wa-Turkiyā al-fatāh: Aṣdaq tārīkh al-aʿẓam inqilāb*. Cairo: Ruʾya lil-nashr wa-l- tawziʿ.

Khalidi, Walid. 1984. *Before Their Diaspora: A Photographic History of the Palestinians, 1876–1948*. Washington, DC: Institute for Palestine Studies.

Kharita Daʾiratsi Matbaasinda Tabaa Idilishder. 1328/1912. *Kudus Sherif Sinjaghink Haritah*. Kudus (Jerusalem): Kharita Daʾiratsi Matbaasinda Tabaa Idilishder.

Khater, Akram. 2010. "Introduction: How Does New Scholarship on Christians and Christianity in the Middle East Shape How We View the History of the Region and Its Current Issues?" *International Journal of Middle East Studies* 42, no. 3 (August): 471–479.

Khoury, Philip S. 1987. *Syria and the French Mandate: The Politics of Arab Nationalism, 1920–1945*. Princeton, NJ: Princeton University Press.

————. 1993. "Abu Ali al-Kilani: A Damascus Qabaday." In *Struggle and Survival in the Modern Middle East,* edited by Edmund Burke. Berkeley: University of California Press.

Khuri-Makdisi, Ilham. 2010. *The Eastern Mediterranean and the Making of Global Radicalism, 1860–1914*. Berkeley: University of California Press.

Koleksiyonu, Alexander, and Kemal Giray. 2004. *Ottoman Post in Palestine, 1840–1918: The Economic and Social History Foundation of Turkey*. Istanbul: Economic and Social History Foundation of Turkey.

Kolordu. 1915. *Filistin risalesi*. Jerusalem: Military Press.

Kudus and Nablus. 1328/1912. Harita dairesi matbaasında tab edilmiştir (Government Map Publishing Unit). Ottoman Map Collection, Cambridge University Library.

Kurd ʿAlī, M. 1916. *Al-riḥlah Al-anwarīyah ilā al-Asqāʿ al-hijāzīyah wa-al-shāmīyah: Wa-hiya safaḥāt dammat shaml mā tafarraqa min siyāḥat rajul al-ʿuthmānīyīn wa-baṭal al-islām wa-al-muslimīn, sāḥib sl-dawlah wa-al-ʿuṭūfah Anwar Bāshā*. Beirut: Al-Maṭbaʿah al-ʿIlmīyah Yūsuf Ṣādir.

Kushner, David. 1996. "Ali Ekrem Bey, Governor of Jerusalem, 1906–1908." *International Journal of Middle East Studies* 28, no. 3: 349–362.

————. 2005. *To Be Governor of Jerusalem: The City and District during the Time of Ali Ekrem Bey, 1906–1908*. Istanbul: Isis Press.

Kusti, Jamileh Costa. 1996. *Zahrat al-Ihsan: A Historical Study*. Beirut: Rum Orthodox Parish Publication.

Lemire, Vincent. 2000. "Water in Jerusalem at the End of the Ottoman Period (1850–1920)." *Bulletin du Centre de recherche français à Jérusalem* (July): 136–150. http://bcrfj.revues.org/index2572.html.

LeVine, Mark. 2007. "Globalization, Architecture, and Town Planning in a Colonial City: The Case of Jaffa and Tel Aviv." *Journal of World History* 18, no. 2: 180–182.

Lüdke, Tilman. 2005. *Jihad Made in Germany: Ottoman and German Propaganda and Intelligence Operations in the First World War*. Studien zur Zeitgeschichte des Nahen Ostens und Nordafrikas, bd. 12. Münster, Ger.: LIT.

Luke, Harry Charles, Edward Keith-Roach, Arthur Wauchope, and Herbert Samuel. 1922. *The Handbook of Palestine*. Jerusalem: Issued under the authority of the Government of Palestine.

Lutfi Beyk, Anton Yusif. 1891. *Kharitat al-Sikak al-Hadidiyyah Bil Mamlakah al-Uthmaniyyah*. Cairo: Khedival Society of Geography.

Luz, N. 2005. "The Re-making of Beersheba: Winds of Modernization in Late Ottoman Sultanate." In *Ottoman Reforms and Muslim Regeneration*, edited by I. Weissman, and F. Zachs. Studies in Honor of Prof. Butrus Abu-Manneh. London: I. B. Tauris.

Mahamid, Umar. 2004. *Brūfīsūr Kulthūm ʿAwdah Fāsīlīfā: Min al-Nāṣirah ilá Sānt Biṭirsbūrgh fī al-wathāʾiq al-maḥfūẓah fī Arshīf Akādīmīyat al-ʿUlūm al-Rūsīyah*. Kafr Qarʿ, Israel: Markaz Abḥāth Ḥiwār al-Ḥaḍārāt Maʿhad Iʿdād al-Muʿallimīn al-ʿArab, Bayt Bīrl.

Makdisi, Ussama Samir. 2000. *The Culture of Sectarianism Community, History, and Violence in Nineteenth-Century Ottoman Lebanon*. Berkeley: University of California Press.

———. 2002. "Rethinking Ottoman Imperialism: Modernity, Violence, and the Cultural Logic of Ottoman Reform." In *The Empire in the City: Arab Provincial Cities in the Ottoman Empire*, edited by Jens Hanssen, Thomas Philipp, and Stefan Weber, 300–330. Würzburg, Ger.: Ergon in Kommission.

Malak, Hanna Issa. 1996. *Al-Judhur al-Yafiyya*. Jerusalem: Matbaʾat al-sharq al-ʿArabiyya.

Manaa, Adel. 1990. *Aʾlam Filasteen fi Awakhir al-ʿAhd Uthmani*. Beirut: Institute for Palestine Studies.

Mandel, Neville. 1976. *The Arabs and Zionism before World War I*. Berkeley: University of California Press.

Mannāʿ, ʿĀdil. 1995. "Al Hajj Tawfiq Hammad." In *Aʿlām Filasṭīn fī awākhir al-ʿahd al-ʿUthmānī (1800–1918)*. Beirut: Muʾassasat al-Dirāsāt al-Filasṭīnīyah.

———. 1999. *Tārīkh Filasṭīn fī awākhir al-ʿahd al-ʿUthmānī, 1700–1918: Qirāʾah jadīdah*. Beirut: Muʾassasat al-Dirāsāt al-Filasṭīnīyah.

Masters, Bruce Alan. 2013. *The Arabs of the Ottoman Empire, 1516–1918: A Social and Cultural History*. Cambridge: Cambridge University Press.

Mazza, Roberto. 2009. *Jerusalem from the Ottomans to the British*. London: I.B. Tauris.

McCarthy, Justin. 1990. *The Population of Palestine: Population History and Statistics of the Late Ottoman Period and the Mandate*. New York: Columbia University Press.

Melhim, Adnan. 2002. "Samaritan Conditions in Nablus as Presented in Tamimi and Bahjat's Book, *Welayet Beirut*: A Systematic Historical Study" [in Arabic]. *An-Najah University Journal for Research—Humanities* 16, no. 1.

Miliji, Ali al-. 1949. "Yafa, Mashru' al-Takhtit al-'am" (Jaffa development project). *Majallat al-Imarah* 9, nos. 9–10: 29–40.

Misselwitz, Philipp, and Tim Rieniets. 2006. *City of Collision*. [New York]: Birkhüser Publishers for Architecture.

Moghanam, Matiel E.T. 1976. *The Arab Woman and the Palestine Problem*. Westport, CT: Hyperion Press.

Monterescu, Daniel, and Dan Rabinowitz. 2007. *Mixed Towns, Trapped Communities: Historical Narratives, Spatial Dynamics, Gender Relations and Cultural Encounters in Palestinian-Israeli Towns*. Aldershot, U.K.: Ashgate.

Moors, Annalies, and Steven Machlin. 1987. "Postcards of Palestine: Interpreting Images." *Critique of Anthropology* 7, no. 2: 61–77.

Musallam, Adnan. 2013. "Arab Press, Society and Politics at the End of the Ottoman Era." Accessed November 19. www.bethlehem-holyland.net/Adnan/publications/EndofTheOttomanEra.htm#_edn34.

Nashāshībī, Nāṣir al-Dīn. 1990. *Jerusalem's Other Voice: Ragheb Nashashibi and Moderation in Palestinian Politics, 1920–1948*. Exeter, U.K.: Ithaca Press.

Nimr, Iḥsān. 1938. *Tārīkh Jabal Nābulus wa-al-Balqā'*. Nablus: Maṭbaʻat Jami'at 'Ummāl al-Maṭābiʻ al-Taʻāwūnīyah.

———. 1961. *Tarikh ğabal Nābulus wa-al-Balqā'*. Nablus: Maṭbaʻat al-Naṣr al-tiğāriyya.

Obenzinger, Hilton. 1999. *American Palestine: Melville, Twain, and the Holy Land Mania*. Princeton, NJ: Princeton University Press.

Odat, Yaʻcoub al-. 1992a. "Rafiq al-Tamimi." In *A'lam al-Fikr wa-l-Adab fi Filastin*. Jerusalem: Dar al-Isra'.

———. 1992b. "Sheikh Ali al-Rimawi." In *Alam al-Fikr wa-l-Adab fi Filastin*, 221–222. Jerusalem: Dar al-Isra'.

Papastathis, Konstantinos, and Ruth Kark. 2014. "The Effect of the Young Turks Revolution on Religious Power Politics." *Jerusalem Quarterly* (Paris), 56–57: 118–139.

Philipp, T., and B. Schäbler. 1998. *The Syrian Land: Processes of Integration and Fragmentation: Bilād al-Shām from the 18th to the 20th Century*. Stuttgart, Ger.: F. Steiner.

Qadrī, Aḥmad. 1993. *Muḏakkirātī 'an aṭ-ṭaura al-'arabīya al-kubrā: 1375 H–1956*. Dimašq: Manšūrāt Wizārat aṭ-Ṭaqāfa.

Qafisheh, Mutaz M. 2010. "Genesis of Citizenship in Palestine and Israel." *Bulletin du Centre de recherche français à Jérusalem*, no. 21. http://bcrfj.revues.org/index6405.html.

Ra'ad, Ḥalil, and Rona Sela. 2010. *Ḥalil Ra'ad: Tatslumim 1891–1948: Photographs 1891–1948* [in Hebrew]. Tel Aviv: Gutman Museum.

Raymond, André. 2002. *Arab Cities in the Ottoman Period: Cairo, Syria, and the Maghreb.* Aldershot, U.K.: Ashgate/Variorum.

Robson, Laura. 2011a. *Colonialism and Christianity in Mandate Palestine.* Austin: University of Texas Press.

———. 2011b. "Communalism and Nationalism in the Mandate: The Greek Orthodox Controversy and the National Movement." *Journal of Palestine Studies* 41, no. 1 (Autumn).

Rogan, Eugene L. 1999. *Frontiers of the State in the Late Ottoman Empire: Transjordan, 1850–1921.* Cambridge: Cambridge University Press.

Sakakini, Khalil al-. 2004. *Yawmiyat Khalil al-Sakakini: Yawmiyat, rasa'il wa-ta'ammulat.* Edited by Akram Musallam. Vol. 2. Ramallah, Palestine: Markaz Khalil al-Sakakini al-Thaqafi.

Salhi, Muhannad. 2008. *Palestine in the Evolution of Syrian Nationalism (1918–1920).* Chicago Studies on the Middle East. Chicago: Middle East Documentation Center.

Ṣāliḥ, Jihād Aḥmad. 2011. *Asmā Ṭūbī (1905–1983): Rā'idat al-kitābah al-nisā'iyah fī Filasṭin.* Ramallah, Palestine: Ministry of Culture.

Salih, Muhsin Muhamad al-. 2005. "The Position of North Palestinians toward the Ottoman at the End of Their Rule and the Beginning of British Occupation" (Mawqif ahl shamal filistin min nihayat al-dawlah al-ʿuthmaniyyah wa-bidayat al-ihtilal al-baritani). *Majallat al-Dirasat al-filistiniyyah* (Beirut), no. 63 (Summer): 63–65.

Sanbar, Élias. 2004. *Les Palestiniens: La photographie d'une terre et de son peuple de 1839 à nos jours.* Paris: Hazan.

Sarınay, Yusuf. 2009. *Osmanli belgelerinde Filistin.* Istanbul: T.C. Basbakanlık Devlet Arsivleri Genel Müdürlügü.

Scholch, Alexander. 1993. "Palestine as an Historical-Geographical and Administrative Entity." In *Palestine in Transformation, 1856–1882: Studies in Social, Economic, and Political Development,* edited by Alexander Scholch. Washington, DC: Institute for Palestine Studies.

———, ed. 2006. *Palestine in Transformation, 1856–1882: Studies in Social, Economic, and Political Development.* Washington, DC: Institute for Palestine Studies.

Seikaly, Samir. 1981. "Damascene Intellectual Life in the Opening Years of the Twentieth Century." In *Intellectual Life in the Arab East, 1890–1939,* edited by Marwan R. Buheiry. [Beirut]: Center for Arab and Middle East Studies, American University of Beirut.

Sela, Rona. 2010. *Ḥalil Ra'ad, tatslumim 1891–1948.* Tel Aviv: Muze'on Naḥum Guṭman.

Semmerling, Tim Jon. 2004. *Israeli and Palestinian Postcards: Presentations of National Self.* Austin: University of Texas Press.

St. Laurent, B., and H. Taskomur. 2013. "The Imperial Museum of Antiquities in Jerusalem, 1890–1930: An Alternative Narrative." *Jerusalem Quarterly* 55: 6–45.

Strohmeier, Martin. 1991. *Al-Kullīya aṣ-Ṣalāḥīya in Jerusalem: Arabismus, Osmanismus und Panislamismus im ersten Weltkrieg.* Stuttgart, Ger.: F. Steiner.

———. 2001. "Al-Kulliyyah al-Salahiyya, a Late Ottoman University in Jerusalem." In *Ottoman Jerusalem: The Living City, 1517–1917*, edited by Sylvia Auld and Robert Hillenbrand Altajir, 57–62. London: World of Islam Trust.

Tamari, Salim. 2008. *'Am al-jarad: Al-Ḥarb al-'Uẓmá wa-maḥw al-maḍi al-'Uthmani min Filasṭin.* Beirut: Mu'assasat al-Dirasat al-Filasṭiniyah.

———. 2009. *Mountain against the Sea: Essays on Palestinian Society and Culture.* Berkeley: University of California Press.

———. 2011a. "Shifting Ottoman Conceptions of Palestine. Part 1: *Filistin Risalesi* and the Two Jamals." *Jerusalem Quarterly,* 47: 28–38.

———. 2011b. "Shifting Ottoman Conceptions of Palestine. Part 2: Ethnography and Cartography." *Jerusalem Quarterly* 48: 10–13.

Tamari, Salim, and Iḥsan Ḥasan Tarjuman. 2011. *Year of the Locust: A Soldier's Diary and the Erasure of Palestine's Ottoman Past.* Berkeley: University of California Press.

Tamimi, Muhammad Refiq, and M. Behçet Yazar. 1916. *Wilāyat Bayrūt.* Beirut: Maṭba'at al-Iqbāl.

Tamīmī, Samīr Shiḥādah. 1991. *Ḥisān Filasṭīn: Salīm Abū al-Iqbal al-Ya'qūbī, 1880–194: Ḥayātuhu wa-shi'ruh.* Al-Quds: Manshūrāt Ittiḥād al-Kuttāb al-Filasṭīnīyīn.

Tekin, R., and Y. Bas. 2001. "Ottoman Map of Palestine, 1917—the Boundaries of the Jerusalem Governorate." In *Osmanli Atlasi,* 12–13. Istanbul: Ekim.

von Sanders, Liman. 1928. *Five Years in Turkey.* London: Bailliere, Tindall and Cox.

Women of the East Congress, Cairo. 1938. *Proceedings of the Women of the East Congress for Palestine, Held in the Headquarters of the Egyptian Women's Union, 15–18 October 1938* [in Arabic]. Cairo: Modern Press.

Ya'coub, Aws Dawood. 2014. *Ruhi Yasin Khalidi, 1864–1913: Pioneer of Historical Research in Palestine.* Al-Quds: Institution for Culture and Heritage. Accessed August 29. http://alqudslana.com/index.php?action=article&id=2480.

Yehoshua, Jacob. 1981. *Tārīkh al-ṣiḥāfah al-'Arabīyah al-Filasṭīnīyah fī bidāyat 'ahd al-intidāb al-Barītānī 'alá Filasṭīn 1919–1929* (The Arabic press in Palestine during the British Mandate: 1919–1929). Haifa: Sharikat al-Abḥāth al-'Ilmīyah al-'Amalīyah.

Yehôshua', Y. 1974. *Tārīḫ aṣ-ṣiḥāfa al-'arabīya fī Filasṭīn fī 'l-'ahd al-'utmānī: 1908–1918* (The Arabic press in Palestine during the Ottoman regime: 1908–1918). Al-Quds: Maṭba'at al-Ma'ārif.

Ziad, Na'imeh. 2012. "Ihsan al Nimer, Da'irat al Ma'arif al Filastiniya." Najah University website, http://ency.najah.edu/node/23.

Zurcher, Erik Jan. 2016. "Ottoman Labour Battalions in World War I." Accessed March 17. www.arts.yorku.ca/hist/tgallant/documents/ zurcherottoman laborbattalions.pdf.

INDEX

Page numbers in italic refer to illustrations.

Amin, Qasim, 140, 150
Amin, Yuzbashi, 132
Amman, 40, 61
Amzalek, 114
Anabta, 23
Anatolia, 2, 9, 16, 20, 22, 24, 33, 35, 65, 89,
    102, 116, 117, 119, 125, 132, 143; mapping
    of, 27, 31–32; Osmenlilik in, 8, 10–11, 13;
    peasants in, 36, 69; "Scientific Expedi-
    tion" in, 7, 73, 75–79, 82, 84–86
Anglicans, 93
Ankara, 7
Anshas (Egypt), 153
Antioch, Orthodox Church of, 7, 92–96,
    100, 102, 105, 114–15
Antonious thesis, 91
Anwar. See Enver Pasha, Ismail
Anwarite Expedition to the Hijazi and
    Syrian Lands, The (Kurd Ali), 81, 82, 86
Anzac-British forces, 84
al-Aqsa (Jerusalem), 53
Arab Cities in the Ottoman Period (Ray-
    mond), 41
Arabic language, 1, 2, 4, 36, 59, 61, 68–75,
    83, 98, 11, 120, 131, 132, 163; Jewish
    speakers of, 22, 35; newspapers pub-
    lished in, 97, 1101, 107–8, 113–14, 126;
    Osmenlilik writings in, 10, 81; rise of
    bilingualism in Turkish and, 77–78,
    82–83; in school and college curricula,
    33, 35, 68–69, 71, 74–75, 93, 116, 147–48,
    153, 154
Arabism, 2, 19, 70, 74, 80, 88–89; Arab
    nationalism and, 95, 99, 138; Orthodox
    Church and, 92–93, 95, 99, 101, 105, 113,
    115
al-Arabiyya al-Fatat, 2–3, 18
Arabization, 7, 71, 77, 86, 88, 94, 97, 100,
    102–4, 115, 117, 155
Arab Ladies Association, 145
Arab nationalists, 10, 48, 50, 70, 80, 84,
    89–91, 113, 115, 135, 138, 159; Ahmad
    Cemal's repression of, 17–20, 26, 48, 72;
    in Arab rebellion of 1908, 35, 36; execu-
    tion of, 20, 67, 84, 85, 159; in Orthodox
    Church, 99, 100, 104, 117; Turkification
    and, 20, 77, 86
Arab Revolt, 35, 135, 138

Arabs, 5–27, 32–44, 60, 63–67, 88–92,
    113–18, 123, 124, 157; and Jews, 10, 22,
    35, 56, 59, 113, 114, 164; and Orthodox
    Christians, 6, 7, 10, 11, 88, 90–92,
    94–95, 97–106, 109, 113–15, 122, 140–
    42; Ottoman provinces populated by, 3,
    9, 11, 13, 120; rebellions of, 17–18, 23–24,
    33, 35, 135, 151; during revolution of
    1908, 120–21; "Scientific Expedition"
    involvement of, 12, 69–80, 82, 84–86;
    Turkish antagonism toward, 14–15,
    134–35, 165; in women's movement, 8,
    141, 145–55
Arab Women's Associations, 145
Arab Women's Congress, 153
Arab Women's Union, 141, 145, 151–53
Arafat, Yasir, 153
Ar'ara, 22
Ard Filistin, 27, 28
Aref, Aref-al, 3, 13
al-Arish, 28, 158
Armenians, 8, 11, 17, 36, 76, 86, 90, 94, 116,
    124, 161, 165
Arrabeh, 22, 122, 127
ArRihla al-Anwariyyeh, 67–68, 71–72
Arsalan, Prince Shakib, 18, 26, 80
Artz-i Filistin, 30
al-Asali, Shukri, 74
Ashbee, C. R., 40, 41
al-Ashi, Salim Musa (Dr. Dahesh), 105,
    177n67
Ashkenazi Jews, 56, 122
Ashour family, 23
Asitanah. See Istanbul
Al-Asma'i (newspaper), 97, 101, 104, 113
Ataturk, 17
Athens, 94
Austria, 5, 34
Austria-Hungary, 39
Avci, Yasemin, 61
Azar, Adele, 6, 8–9, 140, 141, 141, 143,
    145–48, 149, 151–56, 152, 181nn28,
    29
Azar, Afteem Ya'coub, 140
Azar, Ustaz Constantine, 140
al-Azhar, 71, 72
Azharites, 101
Azuri, Najib, 113

Baalbak, 15
Bab al-Sahira (Jerusalem), 54, 55
Bab al-Sbat. *See* Herod's Gate
Babylonians, 22
Baghdad, 17, 181n34
Bahar Lut. *See* Dead Sea
Bahjat, Muhammad, 1–4, 24
Al-Balagh, 67, 73
Balfour Declaration, 23–24
Balkans, 11–12, 90, 99, 102
Balkan Wars, 17, 42
Balqa and Jabal Nablus (Nimr), 133–35
Balqa region, 138
al-Bandak, Yousif, 98
Bani Haritha, 99
Baq'a (Jerusalem), 51, 158
Baqi, Halim Abdul, 132
al-Baqir, Muhammad, 67, 73, 85
Bar al-Sham, 29
al-Barghouti, Omar Salih, 60, 95, 115,
    172n70
Basra, 15
Bassa, 46–47
Ba'thists, 70
Batroun, 94
Battikha, Suriya, 148
Bat Yam, 48
Bauhaus, 40, 48
Bayrut Vilayeti, 24
Bedouins, 35, 42, 50, 61–63, 83
Beer al-Sabi'. *See* Beersheba
Beer Ayyub (Jerusalem), 59, 66
Beersheba, 47, 50, *61,* 70, 73, 82–83, 136, 158,
    162, *165;* planning of, 4–5, 38–39, 42, 52,
    61–65, *63*
Before the Diaspora (Khalidi), 157
Beidas, Khalil, 6, 7, 97, 115
Beirut, city of, 43, 73, 83, 91, 107, 129, 131,
    147–48; colleges and universities in,
    105, 116, 123, 161; executions of Arab
    nationalists in, 20, 67, 84, 85; urban
    development in, 40, 44, 48, 49, 60,
    66, 119
Beirut, province of, 1–3, 14, 16, 24, 31, 37,
    42, 60, 94, 105, 107, 116, 124; in *Filistin
    Risalesi,* 27, 31, 34, 42; Hamidian regime
    in, 132, 134. *See also specific municipali-
    ties and regions*

Beisan, 2
Beit al-Maqdis (newspaper, 71
Beit Dajan, 108
Beit Jala, 97
Beit Rima, 70, 72
Bey, Fathi, 132
Bey, Husni, 125
Bey, Jamal, 102
Bey, Nihad, 157
Bey, Sari, 14
Beyk, Abdi Tawfiq, 81
Beyk, Amin, 125
Beyk, Anton Lutfi, 29
Beyk, Asef, 110
Beyk, Aziz, 19, 25
Beyk, Azmi, 78
Beyk, Bashir, 83
Beyk, Dahesh, 105, 177n67
Beyk, Fawzi, 112
Beyk, Jamal, 83
Beyk, Midhat, 78
Beyk, Uthman, 134
Bible, Christian, 99
Bilad al-Sham. *See* Syria
Bir Hassana, 83
Bir-I Sebi. *See* Beersheba
Birzeit, 98
al-Bitar, Omar Effendi, 110, 111, 114
Bolshevik revolution, 99
Bosnia, 33, 90
Britain, 3, 18, 33–36, 62, 80, 92, 97, 104, 112,
    138
British Mandate, 3, 13, 21, 40–42, 51–52, 57,
    65, 66, 99, 118, 123, 164–66; urban
    development during, 39–41, 48, 54–55;
    women's movement during, 8, 144, 146,
    151–52, 155
British military forces, 6, 21, 23–24, 26, 35,
    40, 70, 79–80, 82–84, 73, 85, 147, 159,
    161, 164; Ottoman territories occupied
    by, 72, 134, 148, 162, 165
Brotherhood of the Holy Sepulcher, 101,
    104
Brummett, Palmira, 33
al-Budeiri, Sheikh Musa, 125
Bulgaria, 33, 43, 86, 89, 99, 135
Bursa (Turkey), 76
al-Bustani, Butrus, 10, 87, 89, 90

al-Halabi, Sami Bey, 125

Hamat, 32

Hamid, Sultan Abdul, 6, 11, 38, 44, 49, 66, 71, 72, 74, 90, 100, 116, 128–34, 138–39; depiction of counselors of as monkeys, 14, *15*, 33; despotism of, 10, 65, 80, 88, 106; overthrow of, 105–6, 118–19, 138–39; support for restoration of, 17, 50, 75, 81, 87, 120–21, 125–26, 136

Hammad, Hajj Tawfiq, 125, 129, 132, 139

Hammad family, 126

Hammadi Society, 129–30

Hanania, Issa Habib, 101

Hanania, Jurgi Habib, 71, 97, 101–2, 104

Handbook of Palestine (Luke and Keith-Roach), 21

Handbook of Syria: Including Palestine, A (British Naval Intelligence), 21

Hanioglu, Sukru, 36, 89–90

Hannsen, Jens, 11, 38–39

Haram al-Sharif, 70

Hasanat al-Yara (Ya'coubi), 72

Hashemites, 8, 79, 80, 85, 86, 107

Haski Sultan, 148

Hawran, 35

Haydar, Rustum, 3

Heart Club (Nadi al-Qalb), 125, 126, 131

Hebron, 12, 28, 40, 53, 62

Helleno-Orthodoxia. *See* Greek Orthodox Church

Herod's Gate (Jerusalem), 54, 55, 58

High Porte, 12, 31, 42, 63, 94, 102, 103, 105–7, 113, 128, 172–73n88

Hijaz, 5, 7–8, 33, 35–36, 42, 44, 48, 56, 67–68, 79, 81–86, 89, 90, 173n1

Hijjawi family, 23

Histoire d'une localite et de sa mission Latine dans la Montagne d'Ephraim (Medabeel), 98

Hizb al-Hirriyah wal I'tilaf. *See* Entente (Liberal Union) Party

Hohenlocke, Prince, 163

Holy Land, 4, 5, 8–9, 12, 21–22, 27, 30–31, 34, 42, 69, 79, 114, 157

Holy Sepulcher (Jerusalem), 53–54, 101, 104, 109

Homs, 32

al-Hout, Shafiq, 153

Hurriet, 119

Hurriyat wa I'tilaf (Freedom and Reconciliation Party), 20, 110, 111, 114

Hürriyet ve İtilâf Fırkası. See Entente (Liberal Union) Party

al-Husary, Sati, 99, 115

Hussein, Sherif, 18, 21, 33, 36, 72, 79, 80, 84, 85, 135, 175n83

al-Husseini, Haj Amin, 88, 147, 151–52

al-Husseini, Kamel Effendi, 83

al-Husseini, Kazim Beyk, 52, 53, 161, 162

Iben military airport, 62

Ibn al-Athir, 123

Ibn Khaldun, 123

Ibn Nasir, Musa, 98

Ibn Qayyim al-Jawziyya, 123

Ibn Samhan al-Najdi, Suleiman, 123

Ibn Taymiyyeh, 123

Ibn Thanbit, Hassan, 72

Ibrahim Pasha, 12, 30–31, 42, 46, 69, 118, 124, 127

Al-Ikhlas (newspaper), 106

al-Imam, Raghib, 110

Imarat al-Haj, 18

Imperial Citadel (Jerusalem), 54

Imperial College, 1, 2

Imperial Museum of Antiquities (Jerusalem), 5

In'as al-Usra Society, 42

India, 5, 31, 41, 80, 84, 164

Indonesia, 5, 80

Inqilab Uthmani (constitutional revolution of 1908), 81

Al-Insaf (newspaper), 97, 104

al-Insi, Abdul Basit, 77

Institute for Elevating Childhood, 153

"Iqlim Jazirat al-Arab" (map), 27

Iraq, 18, 35, 69, 73, 74, 89, 119

Iron Cage, The (Khalidi), 107

Irshad al-Albab (newspaper), 81

Isdud, 22

Iskandarun, 31

Islam, 40, 22, 27–28, 81, 120, 123–24, 128, 137, 139; in campaign for wartime mobilization, 18–19, 36, 80, 84; cultural traditions of, 5–8, 10–12, 92; legal system in, 64, 126–27, 131, 132; Orthodox

Maktab Sultani, 1, 2
Malhamé clan, 11
Malhas, Abdul Fattah, 125, 128, 132
Malik, Hafiz Abdul, 105
Mallul, Nessim, 107, 113, 114
al-Ma'louf, Issa Iskandar, 116
Manaa, Adel, 121–22
Al-Manar (newspaper), 120
Mandate period. *See* British Mandate
al-Manfaluti, Mustafa Lufti, 123
Manshiyyeh Mosque, 72, 73
Manshiyyeh Quarter (Jaffa), 47–48
al-Maqdisi, Muhammad ibn Ahmad Shams
    al-din, 118, 138
Mardah, 137
Maronites, 16, 32
Marseille, 48
Marxism, 130
Mar Ya'coub Church (Jaffa), 109
Masabni, Bad'ia, 153
Masih, Ibrahim Abdul, 106
Masri family, 129, 139
Matawleh, 22
McLean, William, 40–41, 48
Mecca, 28, 56, 78, 79, 84, 175n83
Medabeel, Butrus, 98
Medina, 5, 12, 42, 56, 73, 83–84, 175n83
Meirovitz, Menashe (Abu Ibrahim), 108
Metwalis, 16, 32
Midhat Pasha, 2, 4, 120, 137, 186
Mikhael, Father, 93
al-Miliji, Ali, 48
Miss Arnot's Mission School, 140, 147–48,
    149
Moghanam, Matiel, 145
Mohammadan Ladies Society, 145
Mohammadan Sharia Society, 125, 126,
    179n15
Moors, Annalies, 157, 182n1
Morgenthau, Henry, 107
Morocco, 35, 84
Mount Lebanon, 8, 32, 78, 87, 89, 91, 94,
    116, 123, 147, 155
Mount Nablus, 137
Mount of Olives, 17, 41, 58
Moyal, Shim'on, 107, 110–11, 113–14
Al-Mu'ayyad (newspaper), 107
Mubarak, Ali, 74

al-Mudhafar, Sheikh Abdul Qadir, 26, 73
al-Mughrabi, Muhammad, 101
Muhammad, Baqer, 12
Munadhamat Hizb al-Shabab (Youth
    Party), 123
Al-Munadi (newspaper), 101
Al-Muqattam (newspaper), 107
Al-Muqtabas (newspaper), 67–68, 71, 74
Murad, Muhammad Affendi, 70
Murjan College, 2
Musa, Najla, 148
al-Musaghar, Sheikh Abdul Qadir, 25
Mushahwar, Bandali Elias, 97, 104
Muslims, 10, 13, 31, 36, 39, 54, 80, 79, 93, 97,
    113, 164–65; Orthodox Christians and,
    96–99, 102, 115; urban festivals cel-
    ebrated by, 50, 55, 57–59; in women's
    movement, 145–46, 148, 151, 154–55. *See
    also* Islam
Musrara (Jerusalem), 59
Muwasha'hat, 59

Nabi Musa, 53
Nabi Samuel (Jerusalem), 158
Nablus, 1–3, 14, 16, 22–24, 27, 30, 31, 40, 43,
    47, 60, 70, 92, 118–39, 167; agriculture
    in, 5–6, 51; credibility of local historians
    of, 126–39; Hamidian restoration
    support in, 87, 118, 125–26, 130, 132, 136;
    Jerusalem province designation of, 42,
    45–46; peasant rebellions in, 118, 124;
    politics in, 6, 70, 118–26; women's
    organizations in, 145, 146, 152
Nablus Maktab Rashid school, 137
Nablus Road, 54–55, 59
Nabrawi, Ceza, 143, 150, 155
Nadi al-Qalb (Heart Club), 125, 126, 131
Al-Nafa'is (newspaper), 97
Al-Nafeer al-Uthmani (newspaper), 101
Nafir Suriyya group, 10, 89, 90
Nahda, 9–10, 68, 90–91
al-Nahda al-Urthuduxiyyah al-Arabiyya.
    See Orthodox Renaissance movement
Al-Najah (newspaper), 71, 101
Najah College, 123
Napoleon, Emperor, 46
al-Nashashibi, Is'af, 113
Nashashibi, Nasser Eddin, 52